Investiga

Investigating Me‍‍‍‍ ‍‍‍urse ‍‍‍‍‍‍‍‍‍‍‍‍ ‍g
chat shows, int‍ ‍ wi‍ ‍ vs
with leaders such as ‍ny ‍‍‍ ‍nd
television extracts from around the Eng‍‍‍sh-s‍‍ ‍‍ ‍‍ ‍‍vo

The main theoretical framework used in this work is influenced by Erving
Goffman, where the media encounter is viewed as a three-way participation framework involving the broadcaster, interviewee and audience, all of whom shape the
interaction. From this viewpoint the interactions are analysed to illustrate how
they are managed, how pseudo-relationships are established and maintained, and
how 'others' are created.

The book brings together methodologies of discourse analysis, conversation
analysis and corpus linguistics so that the media extracts presented are explored
from different perspectives in a practical way and numerous insights are provided
that could not have been achieved using one method alone.

Anne O'Keeffe is Lecturer in Applied Linguistics at the Department of English
Language and Literature, Mary Immaculate College, University of Limerick,
Ireland.

The Routledge *Domains of Discourse* series features cutting edge research on specific areas and contexts of spoken language, bringing together the framework and tools for analysis of a discourse.

As our understanding of spoken communication develops, corpus linguistics promises to provide the unifying link between previously compartmentalized areas of spoken language such as media discourse and language pedagogy.

Designed to present research in a clear and accessible form for students and researchers or practitioners, each title in the series is developed around three strands:

- **Content** each title focuses on the subject matter of a particular discourse, e.g. media or business
- **Corpus** each title is based on a collection of relevant spoken texts in its domain of discourse
- **Methodology** each title engages with a number of approaches in language and discourse analysis

Titles in the series

Investigating Media Discourse
Anne O'Keeffe

Investigating Classroom Discourse
Steve Walsh

Investigating Workplace Discourse
Almut Koester

The series editor

Michael McCarthy is Emeritus Professor of Applied Linguistics at the University of Nottingham (UK), Adjunct Professor of Applied Linguistics at the Pennsylvania State University, USA, and Adjunct Professor of Applied Linguistics at the University of Limerick, Ireland. He is co-director of the five-million-word CANCODE spoken English corpus project, sponsored by Cambridge University Press, at the University of Nottingham.

Investigating Media Discourse

Anne O'Keeffe

Routledge
Taylor & Francis Group

LONDON AND NEW YORK

First published 2006
by Routledge
2 Park Square, Milton Park, Abingdon, Oxon OX14 4RN

Simultaneously published in the USA and Canada
by Routledge
270 Madison Ave, New York, NY 10016

Routledge is an imprint of the Taylor & Francis Group, an informa business

© 2006 Anne O'Keeffe

1004959174

Typeset in Perpetua by
The Running Head Limited, Cambridge
Printed and bound in Great Britain by
The Cromwell Press, Trowbridge, Wiltshire

British Library Cataloguing in Publication Data
A catalogue record for this book is available from the British Library

Library of Congress Cataloging in Publication Data
O'Keeffe, Anne Maria, 1968–
Investigating media discourse / Anne O'Keeffe.
    p. cm. — (Domains of discourse)
    Includes bibliographical references.
1. Mass media and language—Research—Methodology. 2. Discourse
analysis—Research—Methodology. I. Title. II. Series.
P96.L34O39 2006
302.2301'4—dc22

2006002956

ISBN10: 0–415–36466–3 (hbk)
ISBN10: 0–415–36467–1 (pbk)
ISBN10: 0–203–01570–3 (ebk)

ISBN13: 978–0–415–36466–9 (hbk)
ISBN13: 978–0–415–36467–6 (pbk)
ISBN13: 978–0–203–01570–4 (ebk)

For Ger, a great media man

Contents

Acknowledgements

Writing this book has been an interesting challenge for me. Much of it stems from my existing work on radio phone-ins, but most of it involved applying my work to the broader context of media discourse. This book is part of the *Domains of Discourse* series and I am very indebted to the series editor Michael McCarthy, first of all, for inviting me to write this book, and secondly, for his encouragement, advice and support throughout. I also owe much to Steve Walsh and Almut Koester for their comments on certain chapters. Thanks are also due to the people at Routledge, especially Elizabeth Walker and Louisa Semlyen, who were always eager to assist. To Carole Drummond, The Running Head, thank you for such a thorough and professional job.

There are many extracts in this book that have been taken from broadcast sources around the English-speaking world. Most of the transcripts from which the extracts are taken are available in full on the internet, where this is the case, the URL has been provided. The availability of such material online makes the possibility for further research endless. The author and publisher would like to thank the following for permission to reproduce material in this book: The Australian Broadcasting Corporation for the transcripts from *Sunday Nights with John Cleary*, and *The Media Report*; KTTV Fox11 for the transcript from *The Donny and Marie Show*; NBC for the transcripts from *The Tonight Show* with Jay Leno and the Laura Bush interviews; Virgin 1215 and LBC (a subsidiary of the Chrysalis Group plc) for the transcripts of *The Nick Abbot Show*; ITV for the transcripts from *Parkinson*; ABC (America), WABC and WNDB 1150 for the transcripts of the Donald Rumsfeld interviews; the BBC for the transcripts of *Breakfast with Frost*, *Newsnight*, *Today* and *Panorama*; the Radio Telefís Éireann for transcripts of the *Prime Time* interview with President George W. Bush, and extracts from *Liveline*, *Morning Ireland* and *The Gerry Ryan Show*.

Every effort has been made to trace and acknowledge ownership of copyright. The publishers will be glad to make suitable arrangements with any copyright holders whom they have not been able to contact.

I would also like to thank my fellow IVACS researchers Ronald Carter, Svenja

Adolphs, James Binchy, Brian Clancy, Fiona Farr, Bárbara Malveira Orfanó, Bróna Murphy, Róisín Ní Mhocháin, Aisling O'Boyle, María Palma Fahey, Elaine Vaughan, and also Geraldine Brosnan in the Learner Support Unit, as well as my colleague Margaret Childs, who passed away while I was writing this book, but who was never far from my thoughts.

On a personal level, writing a book is a selfish pursuit and would not have been possible without the understanding of those closest to me who provided love and encouragement, so thanks most of all to Ger Downes, and also to my parents in Ballynoe, John D. and Eileen O'Keeffe, and to my brother John T. O'Keeffe and his wife Nuala in whose house the best of this book was written.

Note on transcription conventions

Most of the media transcripts used in this book are from internet sources and so they have been transcribed in a very broad manner and are not marked for interruptions, truncations, hesitations, etc. Where data has been taken from existing corpora, the following transcription conventions may be used:

+	interrupted utterance
=	truncated utterance
⌊	overlapping utterance
< X >	extralinguistic information, for example, *<laughing>*

1   Introduction

1.0 Introduction: media discourse

> As individuals we are all influenced, our opinions shaped, reinforced and altered
> by our exposure to the media.
>
> Sánchez Macarro (2002: 13)

Media discourse is a broad term which can refer to a totality of how reality is represented in broadcast and printed media from television to newspaper. Here we are interested in media discourse in its narrowest sense. This book focuses on the discourse of interactions in broadcast settings and so in this context, media discourse refers to political interviews, chat shows, radio phone-ins, and so on, where two people are interacting and an audience is listening. In this sense, media discourse will be viewed within an interactional rather than a representational or critical framework. Essentially, we are interested in spoken language in the context of the media. Everyday spoken discourse has been looked at by a number of researchers (Chafe 1982, 1985, 1992; Biber 1988; Carter and McCarthy 1995, 1997a, 1997b; Hughes 1996; Eggins and Slade 1997; McCarthy 1998) and building on this work, we look at how interactions differ when they are transmitted through a different medium.

In some ways everyday conversation and media interactions have much in common, but in other respects they are very different. Throughout this book we will attempt to place media interactions in the context of the genre of casual conversation from which they have a certain lineage. Our primary experience of talk is through everyday conversational interactions and despite the imposition of institutional conditions, we can still draw on our knowledge of its norms to mix and blend new genres such as media discourse. Throughout the book we stress that media discourse, in the narrow sense that we have confined ourselves to, is not an homogeneous type. Interactions vary from those involving celebrities being interviewed on chat shows, politicians being questioned on the evening news, to an ordinary person calling a radio phone-in show seeking advice about some personal issue. By taking a narrow focus on spoken media discourse, we hope to bring to light the different types of interactions found in the media and the features that differentiate them.

Casual conversation has evolved over the millennia and in contrast media discourse is only starting out as a genre. Interviews have moved from being prescribed where interviewees prepared their answers in advance to questions provided by the interviewer/broadcast company, to being more and more 'naturalistic'. Corner (1991) provides an insight into the evolution of the media interview, particularly within documentaries. He attributes the change and development in the mid- to late-1950s, where interviews became more immediate and natural, to the move towards on-location reality settings for the actual interviews. This development, he suggests, freed the programme makers from the limitations of studio treatments and, along with 'a newly democratic/populist sense of appropriate topics and framing', helped to construct 'naturalisms of behaviour and speech to exploit fully the possibilities for heightened immediacy and dynamism' (ibid.: 40). Whale (1977) tells us that, until the 1950s, the broadcast interview was of little importance lvargely because until then broadcasting the spoken word was traditionally regarded as a matter of reading the printed word aloud. Moreover, statutory requirement for impartiality was strictly interpreted. This adherence prevented the use of the interview as a real means of investigation. As Dimbleby (1975: 214) noted, the interview was not yet

> a means of extracting painful or revealing information; it did not test or challenge ideas, beliefs, attitudes and assumptions. The interviewer had not yet become an official tribune of the people, or prosecuting counsel, or chat show host. His job was to discover some very simple facts: if he did more than that, it was chance not design. It was not thought proper to enquire (even gently) into private lives, or social problems.

As Wedell (1968) puts it, interviewers were little more than respectful prompters who fed the interviewees with soft-soap questions in interviews that were often prearranged and lacking spontaneity (Day 1961). The broadcast interview was a set-piece interaction in which the function of the interviewer was simply to provide a series of topic headings 'for the carefully prepared views of famous men and women designed to impart to their viewers or listeners' (Wedell 1968: 205). The monopoly of deferential interviewing style prompted by the BBC and copied by many national broadcasting stations was undermined with the advent of independent television (ITV) in the mid-1950s in the UK. ITV producers took a looser interpretation of statutory obligations and brought more inquiry and investigation into news stories. This facilitated a more direct, searching and penetrating style of interviewing (Day 1961). Interviewers began to challenge and probe where previously they would have moved politely onto the next prearranged question. As a result, the news interview became a more flexible, lively and influential instrument of journalistic inquiry.

1.1 Media interactions and casual conversation

Media interactions as essentially conversations that are heard by others, and the notion of having a conversation that is overheard is not a new phenomenon in a descriptive sense. Many of our everyday conversations in public places such as in cafés or on public transport are regularly overheard. However this 'overhearing' model is too narrow for media discourse. When a presenter and an interviewee or guest interact on television or radio, they do so with the knowledge not only that they are being overheard, but also that they are having a conversation in front of an audience. In this way, they are having a different kind of conversation than two people talking on a train beside others who cannot avoid hearing their conversation. The former requires inclusion and involvement of the audience, the latter very often requires exclusion (e.g. through guarded or coded references) and detachment (e.g. lack of eye contact and lack of inclusive reference). A media interaction, because it knowingly takes place *in front of* rather than *beside* an audience must therefore draw on a broad cache of shared knowledge, whereas a casual conversation usually draws on a narrow and local store of shared knowledge. Let us summarize the differences between an overheard conversation and a media interaction in front of an audience (see table 1.1).

Table 1.1 Comparison between contextual conditions of a conversation in public and an interaction in the media

	Everyday interaction overheard in a public place	*Media interaction on television or radio*
communicative context	takes place beside overhearing public	takes place in front of hearing audience
	participants and non-participants co-present	participants and audience not normally co-present
	private sphere	public sphere, institutional
status of audience	unratified	ratified
relationship to audience	detached	inclusive and involved
durability	ephemeral	recorded and archived

The conditions of a media interaction differ from an overheard public conversation to the extent that we need to have a separate communicative model to account for it and to arrive at this model is one of the aims of this book. We propose the notion of media interactions taking place in a *participation framework* (after Goffman 1981) which is constructed between the presenter/host/interviewer, the interviewee/guest/caller and the audience. This is a three-fold construct inclusive of the audience as a participant in the interaction since the talk that unfolds from moment to moment in a media interaction is aimed not just at the interviewer who has asked the question or the interviewee who is being asked the question, it is shaped for and by the audience who watch or listen to that show in that social context. An Australian news interview will take cognisance of its Australian audience, just as an Irish interviewee will reply to a question within a range that is suited to an Irish audience, and so on.

Media interactions also differ from casual conversations in general because they take place in an institutional setting and with this comes institutionalized roles and in turn institutionalized turn-taking rights (see Drew and Heritage 1992; Koester 2006). Institutional power is bestowed upon the presenter/host/interviewer. It is within the gift of this power-role holder to decide when and how to open the interaction, and how to frame it, and with this comes the right to be the questioner following up on each answer with a new question, and so on. Having this power in the interaction means that the presenter/host/interviewer places the interviewee/guest/caller in the role of answerer. Other manifestations of the discoursal asymmetry that result from this include the power-role holder being able to decide when to raise a topic, when to change it and when and how, if at all, to close the conversation (media conversations can just be terminated rather than closed). This exogenous or institutionalized apportioning of speaker roles, power and turns-taking rights is what distinguishes media interactions most from everyday conversations. Let us summarize these differing interactional conditions (see table 1.2).

Table 1.2 Comparison between conditions of a causal conversation and an interaction in the media

	Casual conversation	*Media interaction*
Power relationship	symmetrical	asymmetrical
Turns	not pre-allocated	pre-allocated
	usually short and often overlapping	can be long and usually not overlapping
Roles	non-institutionalized; tied into socio-relational identities (e.g. mother, best friend, lover)	institutionalized and exogenous

Goals	emergent within conversation, mostly relational in nature	institutionalized, mostly transactional (e.g. to find out more about someone or someone's political position)
Ritual brackets[1]	collaboratively negotiated and orchestrated	planned and orchestrated by the power-role holder (and production team)
Topics	collaboratively negotiated	pre-planned
	opened, changed and closed collaboratively	opened, changed and closed/ terminated by power-role holder

While the communication context and conditions of casual conversations and media interactions differ considerably, the internal features have much common ground, that is, in terms of spoken language itself. While many of the same features exist in casual conversation and media interactions, their form, function and distribution may differ and this is what proves very revealing when comparing the two types of interactions. Let us look at these points of commonality.

Exchange structures

Both casual conversation and media interactions comprise speaker turns and these make up exchange structures (after Sinclair and Coulthard 1975). Two-part *initiation → response* (IR) and three-part *initiation → response → feedback* (IRF) exchange structures exist in both casual conversation and media interactions but the former is more characteristic of media discourse. In extract 1.1 we see an example of the typical IR pattern in an interview on the BBC Sunday morning television programme *Breakfast with Frost*. Presenter David Frost interviews a newly appointed British government minister, Ruth Kelly, the youngest woman ever to have a seat at the British Cabinet table.

Extract 1.1 Two-part exchange: initiation → response

David Frost:	Has this promotion meant that you had to give up your proud aim, was always, you said, you would never take any of those red boxes home, and work at home, because you had a family waiting at home. Have you had to relax that a bit since becoming Secretary of State for Education?	Initiation

Ruth Kelly:	Well inevitably when you get a new job there are huge demands and in education just as anything else. It's been really important for me to get to grips with the portfolio, to get out and talk to people, to go and visit schools and to really read myself in. I mean I've spent a lot of time doing that now and we've got a lot of policy announcements coming up. But I do try and maintain a work life balance and that is very important to me. Sometimes it's easier than others.	Response
David Frost:	Because you have four children, seven and younger now don't you?	Initiation
Ruth Kelly:	That's absolutely right.	Response

23 January 2005. Full transcript and video available at http://news.bbc. co.uk/1/hi/programmes/breakfast_with_frost/4199507.stm

Extract 1.2 is an example of a three-part exchange taken from the Irish afternoon radio phone-in *Liveline*, broadcast on Radio 1 by Radio Telefís Éireann (RTÉ). Here a caller is telling the story of her struggle with facial hair.

Extract 1.2 Three-part exchange: initiation → response → feedback

Presenter:	And do you wax under your eye?	Initiation
Caller:	Yeah under both eyes I get waxed.	Response
Presenter:	Holy mother of the Lord.	Feedback

3 March 1998. Full transcript not available online. *Liveline* website www.rte.ie/radio1/liveline/

Extract 1.3 is an example from *The Donny and Marie Show*, an American talk show hosted by Donny and Marie Osmond (KTTV, Channel 11). Here they are interviewing ice-skater Kristi Yamaguchi.

Extract 1.3

Marie:	What does that '3' mean on your necklace?	Initiation
Kristi:	Ah it's a lucky number.	Response
Marie:	Really?	Feedback

4 January 1999. Full transcript available at http://www.geocities.com/ amyc521/article/dmtranscript.html

While two-part and three-part exchanges exist in media discourse, two-part exchanges are considerably more common. The feedback move is less likely to happen in media discourse as this slot is usually taken up with another question (i.e. another initiation). Comparing exchange structure types is one means of contrasting different types of media interactions. Chapter 5 will look further at the effect of feedback moves as illustrated above. Beyond the structural level, we also find many common spoken discourse features in both casual conversation and media discourse. Again the forms they take, the functions they fulfil and the degree to which they occur may differ both between everyday conversation and media discourse and within media interaction types.

Pragmatic markers

Pragmatic markers are a pervasive feature of spoken interaction. According to Carter and McCarthy (2006), they are a functional class of items which operate outside the structural limits of the clause and which encode speakers' intentions and interpersonal meanings. They include, for example, hedges, discourse markers and interjections (see chapter 5).

Hedging

Hedging is a strategy frequently used in spoken (and written) language. It involves choosing words or phrases that lessen the directness of one's message and in so doing lessen its potential threat to the face, that is the dignity/self-esteem of the receiver. Hedges include the use of a wide range of language, including *vague language*. They are commonly used when someone is expressing an opinion about something (see Carter and McCarthy 1997b: 16). Words like *just*, *kind of*, *sort of* and *like* often have this function. Farr and O'Keeffe (2002) provide a number of examples of how hedging is used in the context of media discourse. Here are some examples from media interactions.

Extract 1.4 is from an interview with the US First Lady Laura Bush being interviewed on NBC news. Notice how the interviewer downtones her question by choosing to use hedges (marked in italics).

Extract 1.4

| Interviewer: | *A couple of real quick things.* Your husband [President George W. Bush] says he wants to be a uniter, not a divider. Are you *at all* worried that this *particular* issue, Social Security, will further divide Washington? |

Mrs Bush: Well, I hope it won't. I hope that people will . . .

> 1 February 2005. Full transcript available at http://www.whitehouse.gov/
> news/releases/2005/02/20050201-12.html

Extract 1.5 is another example where British Labour MP Tony Benn is being interviewed on the Australian television programme *Sunday Nights with John Cleary* (Australian Broadcasting Corporation) and he is being asked about his meeting and televised interview with the former Iraqi leader Saddam Hussein in the lead up to the 2004 US-led invasion. Notice how the interviewer hedges his face-threatening question by attributing the negative portrayal of his interviewee to others.

Extract 1.5

John Cleary: . . . your trip to Iraq has been portrayed *by those who wanted to caricature you as* as foolish as Chamberlain's to see Hitler.
Tony Benn: Yes but that's a load of rubbish, because in the case of Chamberlain and Hitler, Chamberlain supported Hitler . . .

> 23 February 2003. Full transcript available at
> http://www.abc.net.au/sundaynights/stories/s794833.htm

Removing potential face-threat by attributing utterances to others is referred to as 'other-attribution' (see Halliday and Hasan 1976; McCarthy 1994). In so doing the interviewer above avoids any face threat. His more direct alternative would have been something like '*Don't you think that your trip to Iraq was as foolish as Chamberlain's to see Hitler?*' This is a very common strategy in media discourse. Hedging in questions is examined in detail in chapter 4.

Discourse markers

Discourse markers are another pragmatic feature common in everyday conversational language and in media interactions. These tokens indicate the speaker's intentions with regard to organizing, structuring and monitoring the discourse (Carter and McCarthy 2006). These words or phrases normally mark boundaries in a conversation such as the start of a story, getting back to the point, initiating, changing or ending a topic or even an interaction (see Schiffrin 1987, 2001; Fraser 1999; for more on the local versus global functions of discourse markers, see Lenk 1998). Typical examples include: *okay, right, so, well, now, oh, anyway,* but they can also include phrasal items such as *as I was saying, getting back to* . . . Extracts 1.6 and 1.7 are some examples from media interactions.

Extract 1.6 Australian television show *Sunday Nights with John Cleary* (Australian Broadcasting Corporation) interview with South African Muslim academic, author and activist Farid Esack

John Cleary:	*Again, going back to the example of Jesus.* Jesus saw God in the Samaritan.
Farid Esack:	Absolutely. How do you find the presence of God in the despised? And you know there is a saying of the Prophet Mahomet that we have an equivalent for in the Gospels . . .

11 July 2004. Full transcript available at http://www.abc.net.au/
sundaynights/stories/s1151

Extract 1.7 American news interview between Norah O'Donnell and US First Lady Laura Bush, *NBC News*

Presenter:	*Let's talk about the G8 summit here today.* You are hosting the spouses.
Mrs Bush:	That's right.
Presenter:	What's your goal?
Mrs Bush:	*Well,* I'm hosting the spouses of the G8. And if people don't know, the G8 is made up of the largest economies, the countries with the largest economies in the world. And because we are the most developed countries with the largest economies, I think we have a special responsibility to other countries around the world.

9 June 2004. Full transcript available at http://www.whitehouse.gov/
news/releases/2004/06/20040609-3.html

Chapter 5 focuses on the differing use of discourse markers across media discourse and compares their use and distribution with casual conversation.

Response tokens

Response tokens are interjections that an addressee makes in response to the speaker's utterance, typical examples are *mm, umhmm, yeah* (minimal response tokens) or *really?, wow, that's right, absolutely* (non-minimal response tokens). Much research has been done into the forms and use of these tokens in casual conversation (see, for example, Yngve 1970; Tottie 1991; Gardner 1998; McCarthy 2002). These tokens often fill the feedback slot within a three-part initiation→ response→feedback exchange structure as discussed above and so they are not as common in media discourse. However, they do occur and they can be an indicator of a more intimate type of media interaction, as chapter 5 will illustrate. Extract 1.8 is an example from an interview from the UK-based BBC *Newsnight* television programme. Jeremy Paxman, the interviewer, is talking to the Harry Potter author, J.K. Rowling. Here they are talking about the secrecy that surrounds the lead-up to the release of a new book in the series.

Extract 1.8

Jeremy Paxman:	But do you find the whole secrecy issue, the need for secrecy, a bit ridiculous?
J.K. Rowling:	No.
Jeremy Paxman:	Why not?
J.K. Rowling:	No not at all. Well, a lot of it comes from me.
Jeremy Paxman:	*Really?*
J.K. Rowling:	Yeah definitely. I mean, of course one could be cynical, and I'm sure you would be disposed to be so and say it was a marketing ploy, but I don't want the kids to know what's coming . . .

19 June 2003. Full transcript available at http://news.bbc.co.uk/
1/hi/programmes/newsnight/3004594.stm

Vague language

Vague language is another common feature of everyday spoken language and it is very much related to hedging (see above). When we interact, we often avoid explicitness. For example facts are often hedged through the use of vague quantifiers, for example, 'there were *around* 40 people at the party' (see Powell 1985; Channell 1994; Overstreet and Yule 1997a; Zhang 1998). Another aspect of vague language is the use of vague categorization. That is when we create categories such as 'unhappy homes *all that kind of thing*'. The speaker creates the category on an ad hoc basis at the time of speaking and as such does so relative to what is perceived to be within the addressee's range of shared knowledge (Barsalou 1983; Overstreet and Yule 1997b). That is, if the speaker chooses to create a category, he or she expects that the addressee will understand it and so, as chapter 6 explores in detail, the examination of these categories in the context of media discourse can be very revealing socio-culturally as it provides an indicator of the range of shared socio-cultural knowledge within any media participation framework.

1.2 Overview of the book

The reasons for writing this book stem from the central part that the media play in our everyday lives. The broadcast media are an all-pervasive source of information and entertainment for billions of people. Their discourse is relatively new; for the first time in human history, the 20th century brought into people's homes and their most intimate environments, the voices and images of others, especially their leaders, celebrities and other figures of public attention and recognition. These media have brought in their wake emergent forms of talk that scarcely existed a century ago, and for this reason alone, media discourse is of great interest to linguists and applied linguists alike.

The book moves from theoretical to empirical. In chapter 2 we explore a communicative model that accounts for media interaction at a schematic level. This leads to the notion of a participation framework (after Goffman 1981), a model which accounts for all the participants in the interaction, the presenter, the interview and the audience. This model forms the basis for the rest of the book and all empirical analyses that are done subsequently are examined within this framework. It proves very applicable to the context of media interactions, where research hitherto has largely ignored the impact of the audience. We continuously draw on comparisons with everyday conversation and chapter 2 also explores the link or chain of communication (after Bakhtin 1986) that links spoken genres. This leads to a reflection on the nature of media interactions as spoken genres. We discuss whether they are hybrids, or generic blends (McCarthy and Carter 1994) as well as factors such as intertextuality and interdiscursivity (see Candlin and Maley 1997). This chapter is the heart of the book and provides a crucial theoretical centre through which analyses are conducted and findings are interpreted.

Chapter 3 introduces the empirical phase of the book by overviewing the main methodological approaches that have been employed in the study of spoken language in the media. Here we see the major contribution that conversation analysis has made to the area. We examine the powerful methodological tool that it provides in terms of comparing media talk with the baseline of casual conversation. This has allowed researchers to study how talk is structured differently in institutional settings and how those settings structure talk compared to everyday casual conversation. Other methods of analysis are also surveyed, such as pragmatic interpretations of media interactions where power relations, asymmetries and face are key concerns, as well as discourse analysis (DA) which we have referred to above in terms of comparing exchange structure types. Here also we look at an emerging method of analysing media discourse, namely corpus linguistics (CL). The key analytical functions of this method are explained and exemplified and it is argued that an eclectic approach to examining media interactions has most to offer the analyst. By way of illustration, we take a combined approach to the analysis of call openings to the Irish radio phone-in *Liveline* using conversation analysis, interactional pragmatics and corpus linguistics. Chapter 3 also introduces the corpus of transcribed media interactions that has been assembled for the purpose of analyses in the remaining chapters of the book. This data has been divided into three types of interactions. The categorization is based on social roles or participant persona variables:

1   interactions involving a known persona (a media presenter) and an unknown persona (someone from the private sphere, e.g. a caller to a radio phone-in show)
2   interviews between two known personae from the public sphere, e.g. a chat show presenter and a celebrity
3   political interviews which also involve personae from the public sphere, an interviewer and a politician, but here the interviewee fulfils a social role in the political sphere.

The afore-mentioned eclectic approach to analysing media interactions is operationalized in chapters 4, 5 and 6 where three themes are explored: *managing the discourse, creating and sustaining pseudo-intimate relationships* and *creating identities*.

Chapter 4 looks at how media interactions are managed by the presenter in different interactions within the participation framework of presenter, interviewee and audience. It also addresses the responsibilities that go with the role of presenter, for example, responsibility for maintaining common ground. In casual conversation this is something that is shared between participants but in media interactions it is the responsibility of the presenter and this has an impact on the structure of media interactions. This will be explored especially in terms of the role of *footing* (as used by Goffman 1981). The most institutionalized aspect of the presenter's management role is as questioner and this will be explored in the context of existing research and using the corpus of data that has been assembled. Having divided the data into the three interactional types, as described above, we are able to compare how the interactions vary. For example, the distribution of question types in political interviews differs considerably from those found in interactions in chat shows between a presenter and a celebrity and even more so from interactions on a phone-in show.

While chapter 4 focuses on how interactions are managed and controlled, chapter 5 looks at the other end of the relational cline, namely how *pseudo*-intimate relationships are created and sustained in media interactions. The term 'pseudo' is used here because the participants in a media interaction do not normally know each other and if they do, it is typically only at the level of public persona. In this chapter lexico-grammatical features more commonly associated with everyday conversation between friends, such as vocative use, response tokens and other pragmatic markers, will be examined in the media corpus to explore their role in the simulation and maintenance of pseudo-familiarity within the participation framework between the presenter, the interviewee and the audience. We will look at how a sense of co-presence is simulated, the role of footing in ratifying the audience members and making them feel part of the participation framework. Other markers of pseudo-intimacy such as pronoun and vocative use will also be examined as well as pragmatic markers such as response tokens and discourse markers. In the process of the analysis we will also explore how these features vary across the different types of media interactions.

Chapter 6 is concerned with the shared space of the participation framework of a media interaction between a presenter, an interviewee and an audience where there is a collective understanding of (1) the range of shared space: participants know the boundaries or 'territory', (2) the cache of shared knowledge that is held between participants; this awareness manifests, for example in the implicitness of culturally-specific references and (3) the sense of common identity that the participants share. All of these features are marked through language use. Linguistic markers of shared space, knowledge and identity can provide indices of commonality. These indices also point to where the participants locate themselves in space, how much knowledge they assume as shared and how they position themselves relative to what they are not. In this chapter we focus on linguistic indices such as ad hoc vague categories (*the rugby season and the Cup and everything*), pronoun use, deictic referencing (*those people*) and self-reference tokens (*here in Britain, on this island*). All of these features also occur in casual conversation between friends but in the case of media interactions, they operate on a much larger scale and so points of shared reference will normally be broader so as to be inclusive within the participation framework. For the analyst, they offer an interesting insight into the identity of the collective of participants since they are markers of membership.

2 A framework for analysing media discourse

. . . speakers and audience are equals not simply because their roles are inter-
changeable – in fact they may not be in some situations – but rather because every
act of speaking is directed to and must be ratified by an audience.

Duranti (1986: 243)

2.0 Introduction

The main aim of this chapter is to show how the traditional dyadic speaker–hearer
model of communication cannot fully accommodate media interactions. The main
reason for its inadequacy is its inability to account for the different types of hearers in
a media encounter. On television or on radio, some participants (including the audience) can be hearers and addressees while others can only be hearers.[1] As we have
discussed in chapter 1, seeing media interactions as akin to overheard conversations
does not fully describe the situation either since media audiences, unlike overhearing
audiences, are ratified by the other participants in the interaction and their talk takes
cognisance of this audience. The aim in this chapter is to arrive at an alternative
model, one which is sensitive to the interactive complexity of a media interaction.
This model will form the basis for the analysis of actual media interactions that we
will undertake in chapters 4, 5 and 6. Here we will propose a participation framework model based on the work of Erving Goffman. In this model the various and
varying participation statuses of a media interaction can be accommodated.

As we have discussed in chapter 1, there are many differences between the contextual conditions of casual conversation between friends and families and those
that take place in media interactions, however, we noted also that in terms of
actual spoken language features, there is much in common, for example, hedging,
discourse marking, response tokens, and so on. Spoken language in everyday
contexts is where we gain our interactive experience and build our norms of communication and in this respect there is a certain lineage to the relatively new form
of interaction that is found in the media. Some media encounters, for example
radio phone-ins, as we shall illustrate in chapter 5 in particular, simulate and draw
on the intimacy that exists between real friends and families. In this chapter we

will reflect at a theoretical level on the notion of spoken genres and how they can be invoked, mixed and blended, and how language users have it within their resources to simulate genres relative to their socio-historic reality. We look at the notion of spoken genre as it, too, is core to the establishment of an analytical model for media discourse within any participation framework. Though this chapter is mostly a discussion of theoretical concepts such as genre and participation, it is not a futile endeavour, as the 'new' territory of mediated interpersonal spoken discourse demands a reworking and synthesis of received models of communication. This chapter will draw heavily on the work of Bakhtin and also Goffman, Foucault, Fairclough, Swales and Hall.

2.1 Towards a model for dyadic communication

The most basic and relatively unquestioned model of communication involves the notion of a two-way flow between a speaker and a hearer. The speaker encodes a message and the hearer decodes it, and so on. While, at a schematic level, this dyadic model abstracts the core process of communication, many have commented on its inadequacies and the need for its refinement so as to accommodate the actual conditions of spoken encounters (Clark and Carlson 1982; Bakhtin 1986; Duranti 1986; Schiffrin 1987; Harness Goodwin 1997; Antaki, Díaz and Collins 1996; Matoesian 1999, among others). In fact Goffman (1981) argues that the traditional speaker–hearer model of interaction is insufficient for all forms of talk. Media discourse, on the surface, appears to fit the dyadic model of speaker and listener, for example a newscaster (speaker) and an audience (listener). Even more straightforward might be mediated interactions such as radio phone-ins or television chat shows where the speaker and hearer roles alternate, for example a caller or chat show guest who has an issue, grievance or problem is sometimes the speaker and sometimes the listener, and the same can be said of the presenter. Even after a brief analysis it becomes clear, however, that there is an inherent inadequacy in the traditional dyadic speaker–hearer model. Media discourse is an institutionalized form of talk. While it has much in common with casual conversation, as discussed in detail in chapter 1, it takes place under very different conditions. Casual conversation is not normally open to the public through a broadcast medium, it is not usually recorded and archived, it does not normally require a facilitator such as a presenter to open and close conversations and establish topics, and so on. Hutchby's analysis of the London-based LBC talk radio programme, *The Brian Hayes Show*, concurs with this duality between everyday conversation and pseudo-casual talk simulated in radio phone-ins:

> The talk produced on talk radio exhibits a variety of features which formally liken it to everyday conversation or 'mundane' conversation, on the

one hand, and more 'institutional' forms of verbal interaction (e.g. broadcast news interviews, courtroom or classroom exchanges), on the other.

Hutchby (1991: 119)

Let us consider the communicative parameters of spoken media discourse encounters:

- Conversation takes place between at least two people in either a voice-only medium (radio) or full audio-visual medium (television).
- The participants very often do not know each other.
- At least one participant (a media persona) may be 'known' to the audience and may have a relatively constant 'presence' in the encounter and so he or she (as a persona) is familiar to the audience, but the audience as individuals are not familiar to him or her.
- Unlike in casual conversation, one of the participants (the media persona) usually has more power than the non-media participant and so has extra discourse rights, for example to open/close calls and topics, and control turn-taking.
- The mediated encounter normally has an audience which can interject and react verbally to what it hears but it is not normally co-present so an audience member's utterance usually has no bearing on the ongoing interaction.
- With the advent of internet access, any media audience is potentially global.

Already, we can see that the basic dyadic conversational paradigm of speaker–hearer is not broad enough to account for mediated encounters between participants and an audience.

Clark and Carlson (1982) examine how the reception of speech acts needs to be accounted for beyond the level of the hearer, in that utterances in conversations involving more than two people are intended not only to be understood by the person being addressed, but also by the other hearers present at the time of speaking. The distinction between *addressee* and *hearer* is therefore essential to speech act theory. Speakers project illocutionary acts not only towards addressees, but also towards certain other hearers (Clark and Carlson 1982: 333). Clark and Carlson define a type of hearer they call 'participant' who has a role distinct from the roles of 'addressee' or 'overhearer'. Bakhtin (1986: 95) says 'an essential (constitutive) marker of the utterance is its quality of being directed at someone, its *addressivity*' (italics from original source). Goffman argues that the traditional paradigm takes 'global folk categories (like speaker and hearer) for granted instead of decomposing them into smaller, analytically coherent elements' (Goffman 1981: 129). The term 'hearer' fails to discriminate between different reception formats, for example hearers who are addressed, hearers who are not addressed, hearers who overhear, hearers who 'eavesdrop', hearers whose setting defines their role as passive, for example a public gallery in a court or parliament (Goffman 1981; Schiffrin 1987; see also Jefferson 1972 on side sequences). Essentially, the traditional model cannot account for how utterances are received differently depending on participants' hearing status.

In accepting the traditional paradigm, the question of the hearing status of the audience in broadcast genres (such as radio phone-ins, chat shows, news interviews, and so on) is for the most part ignored by analysts. In the literature, the audience is often described as 'overhearers' or 'eavesdroppers'. For example Montgomery (1986: 428) says that it is common for the audience to be the 'overhearing recipient of a discourse' (see also Heritage 1985). Moss and Higgins (1979: 291) acknowledge that there are clear signals of a wider audience that seem almost to be 'eavesdroppers on a cozy chat'. Other researchers into broadcast genres such as news interviews (Heritage and Roth 1995) and television talk shows (Illie 1999) also use the term 'overhearer' to refer to the listening status of the audience (see also Cameron and Hills 1990). Within the traditional speaker–hearer model, this is an accurate statement but its descriptive potential is very limiting. Hutchby (1991), for example, in setting up a framework for the analysis of radio phone-in talk, makes the following generalization:

> . . . we can say that mundane talk is designed, interactively, *explicitly for co-participants* and is differentiated from institutionalized talk by the fact that the latter is designed, and displays itself as being designed, *explicitly for overhearers*.
> Hutchby (1991: 119) [Hutchby's italics]

Cameron and Hills (1990: 53), also describing radio phone-ins, note that above all the interaction is a conversation 'designed to be overheard'. They note that in radio phone-ins, we have two different levels of listener: 'the individual who is actually calling, and the collectivity of listeners "out there"' (ibid.), which obviously fails to include the 'in there' listeners, namely the presenter and the studio personnel.

Limiting one's analysis to talk as a product of an institution for a public audience of *overhearers* will not be helpful. An unquestioning acceptance that the audience falls somewhere between involvement and exclusion is tantamount to saying that the audience has an unofficial status. Let us now look at a *participation framework* model that will help to account for the participation dynamics between mediated discourse and audience.

A participation framework

Goffman (1981: 137ff) stresses that the participants in any exchange guide, orient and modify their talk within their *participation framework* in pursuit of their goals.

Participation framework refers to the instantaneous view of any social gathering relative to the act of speaking at any one moment. It offers an alternative for media discourse to the dyadic model of communication which, as we have discussed above, fails to accommodate the audience. For the purposes of media discourse there are two key insights to be gained from Goffman's argument:

> The traditional speaker–hearer model takes no account of the unratified hearers, that is, anyone intentionally or unintentionally within earshot of the conversation.
>   The traditional model does not accommodate the ambiguity of the listener. In multi-party talk a listener as a hearer and a listener as an addressee are not always synonymous.
>
> (Goffman 1981: 132)

On the first point, Goffman's views underpin the analysis of media discourse as a participative event. Goffman's notion of *ratified* and *unratified* hearers can be applied to say that everyone who watches/listens to a television or radio programme, is a *ratified hearer*. They are part of the discourse event and may join in if they choose (albeit under certain conditions as will be discussed below). We can say, therefore, that in media discourse events, there are no unratified hearers. There are no eavesdroppers. Some of the audience may be 'half listening', with televisions or radios turned on in the background as they attend to local matters, but parallels for this are easily found in everyday conversational frameworks also. This model allows us to promote the audience to official hearer status within the event. The audience is no longer an overhearer of talk on television or radio; they have a place within the *participation framework*. This provides the analyst with a mandate to examine how talk is modified and guided by the studio participants (e.g. host and guest) to meet the demands of fully-ratified hearers who are not physically present but who are *out there* within the participation framework. To summarize at this stage, within this more dynamic paradigm, we can say that:

- Television and radio audiences are never overhearers (the nature and function of television and radio in any case is to *broad*cast).
- Members of the audience are official or ratified hearers even if they are not fully watching/listening.
- As in casual conversation, the roles of speaker, hearer and addressee can, where conditions allow, interchange. As we will discuss in chapter 5, the audience can be directly addressed by the presenter of a show, and a hearer in a radio interaction can, in the case of a phone-in show, contact the studio and become a speaker/addressee in a dyadic interaction.

Having established a participation framework for the communicative dynamic of media interactions, let us now look at the more schematic level of generic structure and consider how we can best describe this type of talk that has emerged in relatively recent times.

2.2 Media interactions, institutionalized generic structure and genre

Many media interactions have socially recognizable formats within which a certain type of communicative activity takes place. For example, we understand what is meant by communicative formats such as a news report, a chat show, a fly-on-the-wall documentary, and so on, just as we understand what is meant by a university lecture or a sales presentation, etc. The many generic labels for media formats broadly signal the kind of communication to expect. All of these communicative events have a widely recognizable structure because they are institutionalized events. Benwell (1996), in her discussion of the university tutorial as a genre, argues that genres presuppose a certain degree of institutionalization, if only because their existence depends on repetition within a defined setting. When communicative events are mediated for public reception, replication is both predictable and expected. Referring to talk radio Hutchby (1996a: 7) calls it a form of institutionalized interaction, where talk takes place within an organization, the broadcasting company, which has its own structure and stability. Across spoken media discourse in general, mediated formats can be said to have varying degrees of structure and stability, which, according to analysts such as Boden (1994) and Drew and Heritage (1992), propagate themselves through talk and interaction. However, even though institutionalized interactions may be structured and stable, and in their turn, structure and stabilize talk, this is not necessarily the same as saying that they constitute discrete genres of spoken discourse. In other words, mediated formats may be generic in nature (in so far as each programme is replicable in its compositional structure) without necessarily comprising unique genres of talk.

Schematic structure: static versus dynamic

Schematic structures can be abstracted from most recurring human interactions; it is in our interest as social beings to have precedents for interaction rather than having to face each new encounter, in writing or in speaking, as novel, unfolding and without recognizable structure to orient towards. Since these schematic structures are both socially generated and socially grounded, they may vary from culture to culture (see, for example, Sifianou 1989 who looks at differing interactional strategies in telephone behaviour in England and in Greece). A mediated interaction may have a generic, identifiable and stable structure imposed by the broadcasting institution within a society, while internally it may emulate or reproduce existing everyday spoken genres within its formal 'contrived' generic structure. A programme's generic structure, in this instance, is something imposed from outside. At this point, therefore, an important distinction is being made between *institutional generic structure* (the structure imposed on radio or television programmes by the broadcasting institution) and the, yet to be defined, notion of internal speech genre(s) which evolve from within. On one hand, we are dealing with an institutionalized, external generic format, that is the programme structure itself. Just as the 'traditional' parameters of a sonnet, for example, define its structural features, the institutionalized generic features of a programme dictate its structural character in terms of the lengths of interactions, the time at which these interactions take place, the duration of the show, the sequence and the range of topics, the number of commercial breaks, the sequencing of events, and so on. Such a framework is essential for perpetuation and replication. On the other hand, within the bounds of this generic shell of radio and television programmes, participants interact, and the talk that results may or may not constitute generic activity in response to the specific conditions at any moment of interaction. Therefore, a fundamental distinction is drawn between the institutional generic *structure* of the programme and the nature of the real-time *activity* of talk contained in and constrained by this programme structure.

Candlin and Maley (1997: 202) make a distinction between text as *product* and discourse as *process* (they stress that the process is 'socially situated'). This distinction is very useful here. The *static* programme structure and the *dynamic* of the ongoing interaction allow us to discern between *text* and *discourse*. The programme as a product of the aggregation of talk within the institutional structure can be seen as the text, while the interaction contained within the structure of the text, at any point in time, can be looked at dynamically, in its collaborative real-time construction, as a process of discourse. In asserting that there is a distinction between the programme as a text and the talk as discourse, respectively the product and the process (representing the static structure and the dynamic activity), we are released from the pursuit of finding obligatory stages within media encounters (as in the work of Ventola 1987). Stable repeated stages may emerge as patterns within the accumulated product, but this would be a retrospective observation rather than an imposed framework to be proven. In this book, we will take the view that, at any point in the process of media discourse, interactants have options to draw on. These options are based on existing discourse *resources* to use Hall's term. Hall (1995: 208) defines resources as varying arrangements of expected linguistic and paralinguistic instantiations. Discourse resources may become patterned in their use and sequential in their order, but they may also be changed, deconstructed, recreated and modified by the 'resourceful' user as long as the other participants share the same access to the resources. Referring to institutionalized resources, Hall says 'what makes the meaning of a resource institutionalized . . . is not where or by whom it is used, but rather by its unquestioned, authoritative use over time' (Hall 1995: 212). We also note that in line with the Candlin and Maley (1997) distinction between text as a product and discourse as a process is Duranti's (1986: 239) assertion that verbal communication is an achievement, the culmination of the collective activity of individual social actors whose final product (the resulting 'text') is qualitatively different to the sum of its parts (the individual utterances of the individual speakers).[2]

To summarize at this point, we can say that media discourse formats (i.e. programmes on radio or television) have a generic prototype or template which is socially recognizable to listeners or viewers. New types of formats may evolve, such as fly-on-the-wall documentaries, but through institutionalized replication of their structure, they gain a certain amount of stability in so far as it can be labelled as distinct from other types of broadcast talk such as news interviews or political discussion programmes, and so on. We can say then that there are many prototypes for the talk that takes place on radio and television.

2.3 Utterance, genres and generic blends

Bakhtin, in discussing *genres* in the context of great literary works, says that they are prepared by centuries, they break through boundaries of their time and they live in centuries (Bakhtin 1986: 5, originally written circa 1935). Even more fundamentally, talk, as the primary carrier of meaning, must have the same transcendental quality if meaning is to be transmitted. How we have chosen to frame talk into units such as narratives, expositions, arguments, and so on, finds meaning in human relations. As a more technologically advanced society, we now have substantial means of mediating communication and this may have a far-reaching impact not only on how we 'package meaning', but also on how we relate as humans. It is interesting to read what Bakhtin wrote in the 1930s about the work of Shakespeare in his discussion of genres and epochs:

> The semantic treasures Shakespeare embedded in his works were created and collected through the centuries and even millennia: they lay hidden in the language, but also in those strata of the popular language that before Shakespeare's time had not entered literature.
>
> Bakhtin (1986: 5)

It can be said that within the generic structure of media discourse, one finds 'strata of the popular language' carrying themes that reflect what is meaningful and contemporary in society. The linguistic means of communicating this meaning may modify and adapt to obligatory aspects of this 'new' structure, but traditional 'units' such as narrative, exposition, argumentation, and so on, are flexible enough to sustain and evolve in the process of mediation. For the analyst, media discourse offers an interesting research ground for spoken discourse especially in terms of auditing the agility and resourcefulness of interactants within a mediated institutional structure. Participants, who very often have not met before, have the ability to enact sometimes with pseudo-intimacy, while at the same time, create their own public identities.

Genre, therefore, for the purposes of investigating media discourse, requires a flexible definition that will accommodate both the orthodoxy of a stable *structure* and the instantaneous and spontaneous *activity* of those who participate within it. McCarthy and Carter (1994: 32–3), in their discussion of genre, suggest such a flexible notion of genres, as opposed to the relatively monolithic or fixed notion as advanced in particular by Ventola (1987). In their view:

> There may . . . be an endless continuum of genres mixing with one another to form generic blends. It may be that there are too many exceptions to the rules to be proved with the result that the notion of genre becomes as slippery as the notion of register. (In fact, how might one differentiate between a genre and a register, if it is necessary to distinguish between genre and register at all?)
>
> McCarthy and Carter (1994: 33)

For Bakhtin, speech genres are relatively stable types of *utterances*, where an *utterance* is a structural unit, which can vary in length from a single word turn to a (written) novel or longer, as long as it contains the turn of an individual (Bakhtin 1986: 61). Under these terms, an *utterance*[3] ends when the speaker/writer changes. Bakhtin sees language as being realized by individual concrete *utterances* (oral and written) by participants in various areas of human activity, and these *utterances* reflect the specific conditions and goals of each sphere of communication through:

> thematic content
> linguistic style (the lexical, phraseological and grammatical resources of the language)
> compositional structure
>
> Bakhtin (1986: 60)

Each separate *utterance* is seen as individual, but each sphere in which language is used develops its own relatively stable types of *utterances* – or speech genres (Bakhtin 1986: 60). McCarthy's comments, on the importance of Bakhtin's work on genre, reinforce this idea: 'it breaks down the distinction between language as the product of the individual psyche and language as a social construct' (Mc-Carthy 1998: 30). Another interesting perspective on genres is found in the work of genre analysts who study genres in professional settings. Such research allows for the abstraction of models for (particularly) written and spoken professional interaction (see Dudley-Evans 1987; Jordan 1989; Bhatia 1993). This research is instructionally motivated in that native speaker patterns can be isolated and used in language teaching, or indeed as models of 'best practice'.

For many, genres are seen as linguistic vehicles, or means to an end. As Martin (1985) puts it, genres are how things get done when language is used to accomplish them. This practical, utilitarian definition of genres is attractive, not least of all because it is functional, straightforward and succinct. However, Hall (1995: 206) identifies theoretical shortcomings to functional approaches to examining language use. Referring in particular to the work of Halliday and Hasan (Halliday 1978; Halliday and Hasan 1989) and Hymes' *Ethnography of Speaking* (1972), she points out that, while they have offered useful paradigms for building generic models of practice as well as descriptions of contextually based uses of language (my italics and paraphrase of Hall 1995: 206):

- they do not consider the *differentially weighted potential* which the meanings of the resources themselves have in being open to possible *modification* or *transformation* by an individual at any particular *moment of use*.
- they fall short of considering that *individuals are differently weighted* in their *potential to use*, *modify* or *transform* the resources.

As such, Hall is advocating a dynamic model for the analysis of language in use which accounts for language as potential accomplishment at a point in time, where our talk comprises *interactive practices*, differently enacted and differently valued, whereby individuals come together to create, articulate and manage their collective histories via the use of socio-historically defined and valued resources (Hall 1995: 207). She explains that our interactive practices involve the interplay of (at a minimum) three mutually shaping spheres (based on Hall, 1995: 208):

- the concomitant expectation of their uses (e.g. the practices and goals they invoke)
- our social identities and those of the participants
- the spatio-temporal conditions of the moment.

Hall draws heavily on the work of Bakhtin and she operationalizes his concept of *utterance*, giving it two simultaneously enacted functions. Firstly, we (re)create the contexts of utterances by invoking the genres to which the *utterances* typically or socio-historically belong, and secondly, we create our own voices in relation to the expectations of their uses and in relation to the other participants with whom we are interacting (Hall 1995: 208). This ties in with the previously quoted ideas on genre(s) from McCarthy and Carter (1994: 33), who suggested the possibility of 'an endless continuum of genres mixing with one another to form generic blends'. Generic blends are suggestive then of participants spontaneously invoking genres within their collaborative, shared, socio-history as well as their socio-cultural *range* of expectations of uses.

2.4 Towards a working definition of genre for investigating media discourse

So far, at the core of our evolving definition of speech genres, we find the following premises:

*   They are instantaneously invoked and (re)created.
*   They are in flux.
*   They are collaboratively achieved.
*   Their realization is relative to the parameters of shared expectations about how language can be used. The more culturally and historically diverse the interactants, therefore, the less scope there is for mixing, deconstructing, recreating and/or modifying speech genres.

By way of practical application of this perspective, let us look at an extract from an Irish radio phone-in show *Liveline* broadcast on Ireland's public broadcasting station Radio Telefís Éireann (extract 2.1).

Extract 2.1

1	Presenter:	Welcome back to the programme. Noel, what's the weather like in Cork today?
2	Caller:	It's absolutely lovely, Marian.
3	Presenter:	And what are you doing?
4	Caller:	Me unfortunately I have to work for a living <*presenter laughs*> I have a pub in Cork city+
5	Presenter:	Don't we all?
6	Caller:	+so.
7	Presenter:	It's just you're not the wisest of men are you when it comes to the sun? <*mock scolding tone*>
8	Caller:	It would appear as though I'm not. Having had many years of experience of travelling abroad and sun-worshipping and being

sallow-skinned. Again this weekend I was sunbathing at home
and fell into the trap and am quite swollen in parts.

20 May 1998. Full transcript not available online. *Liveline* website
www.rte.ie/radio1/liveline/

In extract 2.1, we see an example of the unfolding accomplishment of meaning,
where, in the conditions of the moment, we find the ritual brackets (Goffman
1981) of opening including greeting, phatic exchanges about the weather (the presenter is in a studio in Dublin on the east coast of Ireland and the caller is based in
Cork in the south of the country). In this opening, we see also an acknowledgement of the audience as hearer in the opening move with the greeting *Welcome back
to the programme.* This fulfils institutional requirements within the external generic
structure. A (first name) vocative *Noel* and phatic language are used strategically
to invoke a pseudo-intimate relationship. The presenter and caller joke with one
another about who really works for a living (turns 3–5). Then in turn 7, the presenter introduces the caller's reason for calling. At this point in the call opening,
the presenter has many options or *resources* available to her to introduce the call
justification. She chooses to invoke a genre of mock-chastising for wrong-doing
(using linguistic and paralinguistic resources): *It's just you're not the wisest of men
are you when it comes to the sun?* <*mock scolding tone*>. This instantiates the voice and
expectation of mother (or teacher)–child scolding, the caller recognizes the genre
and responds to the expectation of the moment by casting himself as deserving of
chastisement for his errant ways (going in the sun without sunscreen).

Important points to abstract from this are the following: the presenter chose
to invoke this genre and mix it into what was ostensibly a trouble-telling genre;
she did so instantaneously by means of an aggregation of linguistic (a formulation)
and paralinguistic resources (mock scolding tone). She did so because she could
as presenter and she did so with the expectation that the caller would know the
genre because of his shared socio-historic and socio-cultural background (which
he did) and so it was collaboratively achieved. This is an example of what Bakhtin
(paraphrased by Hall 1995: 209) refers to as the conventionality of the resources
and the specific ways in which interactants use these resources to respond to and
to create specific locally situated conditions. As an aside, it could be said also that
in invoking this genre, the presenter was taking a risk. If the caller were not to
orient towards or co-operate with the invocation, then a face-threatening situation would have resulted. Genres can be 'called up', instantiated and blended
by participants who share a certain resource range or generic commonage. The
ability to genre-switch and mix in this way could be seen as part of a competent
language user's resource.

Examples such as this, of how participants orient in collaborative generic activity, exemplify what McCarthy (1998: 33) refers to as a 'socio-psychological reality

for language users'. Examining how language users draw on generic resources tells us a great deal about the nature of the real time collaborative orchestration of speech activity. In an interview from an American television news programme broadcast on NBC News (extract 2.2), we see the NBC interviewer using a directive *Talk to me a little bit about* . . . with her interviewee who is the US First Lady at the time, Laura Bush. In certain contexts, a directive would be a face-threatening act, especially with such a high-status addressee, however in a news interview it is pragmatically specialized. Interviewees expect directives in these speech events, such as *tell me*, *explain*, *talk about*, and so on, and they play their role as interviewees by collaboratively enacting the event by taking the directive as a prompt rather than a face-threatening act.

Extract 2.2

Presenter:	One in every three women will die from heart disease. *Talk to me a little bit about* risk factors.
Mrs Bush:	Well, one of the major risks is that women don't know heart disease is a number one killer of women, and so if they start to suffer any symptoms of a heart attack, they don't think they're having a heart attack.

1 February 2005. Full transcript available online at
http://www.whitehouse.gov/news/releases/2005/02/20050201-12.html

In another example from a British radio phone-in on the Virgin 1215 station from the 1990s (extract 2.3), presented by Nick Abbot, we find the presenter and caller orienting in a highly transactional manner to the call, where the presenter's reference to the location of the caller suffices as a greeting and the caller seems so familiar with the genre that she even provides a metadiscourse marker, *well something really exciting just happened to me*, before launching directly into her reason for calling without need for a directive or prompt on the part of the presenter. The presenter calls up the genre of casual conversation and provides a response token *ooooh!* to show mock-surprise (see chapters 3 and 4 for more on openings).

Extract 2.3

Presenter:	Northampton.
Caller:	Hello.
Presenter:	Yes.
Caller:	Um, well something really exciting just happened to me.
Presenter:	Oooooh!
Caller:	I know. Um, I'm a student and I rang a friend's house but he

wasn't in and one of his housemates answered. And we just like had this hour long conversation. I mean, I don't know who he is, what he looks like or anything. But erm . . . and it's just really exciting. [*laughter*]

Date unknown, 1994, Virgin 1215, http://www.w2s.co.uk/
nick-abbot/transcripts/phone.html

If we accept language as a social construct, we must also accept the existence of such generic activity as indicative of some type of social cohesiveness or collectivity. If, in the extracts above, the presenters' utterances: *It's just you're not the wisest of men are you when it comes to the sun?* [mock scolding tone], *Talk to me a little bit about* or *ooooh!* [mock surprise] are generically coherent to the respective addressees, we can say that this indicates that they have socio-cultural common ground, in other words, participants can intuit the genre from the linguistic and pragmatically specific primers employed by the speaker. The generic dexterity of a participant is relative to his or her access to and mastery of linguistic resources and these resources are accrued through familiarity and exposed over time in a socio-cultural context.

2.5 Generic activity, intertextuality and interdiscursivity

As society changes, so do the means and formats of interaction. Text messaging and email are obvious examples of such changes. As new means and formats of communication evolve, they often draw on and invoke existing genres. For example email formats make use of existing letter formats, usually with formulaic openings and closings that are already familiar to us while at the same time new electronic formats add new features such as subject line headers, time stamping, and so on. Such activity leads to what McCarthy and Carter (1994) termed generic blending or mixing. Each *utterance*, according to Bakhtin (1986: 94), is a 'link in a chain of speech communication' and contains echoes and reverberations of other *utterances*. This notion is also found in the work of Foucault (1972) who says that there can be no statement that in one way or another does not reactualize others. The term 'intertextuality' (after Kristeva 1986) is often used to describe this interweaving of old and new formats. Fairclough (1992: 84) defines intertextuality as 'the property texts have of being full of snatches of other texts, which may be explicitly demarcated or merged in, and which the text may assimilate, contradict, ironically echo, and so forth'. Fairclough goes on to say that in terms of production, an intertextual perspective stresses 'the historicity of texts . . .' (ibid.) (after Bakhtin's 'chain of communication'). Fairclough also raises the notion of 'interdiscursivity' (after Pecheux, cited in Fairclough 1992: 47) which reflects the same concept in relation to different types of discourse – or by extension, different types of generic activity. Intertextuality and interdiscursivity are linked by Candlin and Maley (1997: 203) in their research into *alternative dispute resolution*, where they explore the emerging nature of this 'new' way of helping parties resolve disputes. Principally, they are interested in the extent to which it is possible to speak of this type of mediation as a discrete social and linguistic phenomenon, as well as the degree to which it draws creatively on other related and more established professional genres. What they say has particular relevance to the investigation of media discourse, in that it too is a relatively new phenomenon within our society:

> evolving discourses[4] are . . . intertextual in that they manifest plurality of text sources. However, in so far as any text evokes a particular discourse value in that it is associated with some institutional and social meaning, such evolving discourses are at the same time interdiscursive.
>
> Candlin and Maley (1997: 203)

Internal variability is made possible, Candlin and Maley say, by means of intertextuality and interdiscursivity. So we can say that when we are faced with uncharted situations of generic activity, that is, generic structures we have not previously encountered, we can draw on and adapt the 'historicity' of our resources. This malleability allows for the emergence of new applications for old schemas and most of all allows for change. By 'recycling' genres we can come up with new 'products' and this process is contingent on participants' access to the 'chain' of resources. To return to Bakhtin's metaphor – if one is not within the chain, one cannot be part of the process of change. In the context of media discourse, this means that to participate in the evolving generic activity, one must have appropriate 'historicity' – a cache of suitable generic discourse behaviour which will allow one to participate in genre blending and mixing or chain-making so as to exchange meaning in a 'new' format. By extension, we can say that the interplay and exchange of meaning in this way is one of the principal constituents of a culture.

2.6 Media discourse as a generic structure with a socially binding forum

Media discourse is shaped both by itself and by what becomes a norm of practice in a given social context just as Candlin and Maley (1997: 202) tell us that any discourse is a way of talking about and acting upon the world which both constructs and is constructed by a set of social practices. This brings us to the question of media discourse as a collective practice within some kind of *discourse community* (to draw on the work of Swales). According to Swales (1988: 212), speech communities are centripetal (they pull people in), while discourse communities are centrifugal (they set people, or parts of people, apart). A discourse community, apart from comprising components such as commonality of interest, public goals, purposeful interchange of information and feedback, also has a *forum* (a term which Swales attributes to Herrington 1985). This concept of forum has a lot to offer to the study of media discourse. For Swales, fora can consist of bulletins, meetings, conferences, telephone calls, emails and websites, and so on. Via these fora, discourse communities develop and continue to develop *discourse expectations*: 'these may involve the appropriacy of topics, the form, function and positioning of discoursal elements' (Swales 1988: 212). These discoursal expectations, according to Swales, create the genres that articulate the operations of the discourse community. Essentially, he sees the resultant genres as properties of discourse communities and, as such, they serve as social binding agents to hold together a critical mass of members, via a forum or fora, even if members are physically distant and/or without any intimate level of interpersonal relationship – and so his definition can attribute the status of discourse community to diverse groupings such as 'the Book of the Month Club, members of political parties . . . patrons of Harry's Bar, and so on' (Swales 1988: 213). This is not far removed from the previously cited ideas of Candlin and Maley, Hall, Bakhtin, and so on, in that forms of talk are seen as evolving and perpetuated by participants, out of previous contexts and at the same time creating expectations and constructing future meaningful interactions.

If we modify the ideas of Swales, we can apply the notion of forum to the mediated programme format (the institutionalized generic structure) and say that these are fora for the socially binding generic activity where participants (including the audience) interact. In this model, a forum, that is a programme, is itself a means through which the participants can engage. Obviously, the level and degree of engagement differs depending on the type of media interaction. Presenters and interviewees usually interact face-to-face while the audience is limited to interacting in asides with fellow viewers, by email, by way of solicited ballots (e.g. news programme opinion polls) or through comments to the television or radio that will not be heard in the studio. Nonetheless, the programme provides the forum and the generic speech activity could be seen as the binding agent for the discourse community. Of relevance here also is the work of critical discourse analyst, Fairclough (1995a) who provides the notion of *conversationalization*, a process where linguistic devices are used to make representational public language resemble more the language of ordinary conversation (see Fairclough 1995a). Conversationalization is the process by which 'public language' is made more like 'private language' by means of drawing on linguistic features from ordinary conversation. Fairclough (1995a: 8), for example, illustrates a case of conversationalization of

the public language of science and technology in a BBC science education programme through the use of words such as 'booze', 'massive' and idiomatic
language such as 'it's a miracle . . .' in the description of 'liquid' as well as the paralinguistic feature of the reporter's non-standard regional accent. Forms of media
discourse which engage the audience directly such as radio phone-ins or television
chat shows are a good example of conversationalization of the media forum itself
where ordinary talk, everyday themes and conventional speech genres bind a particular audience. Private worlds are brought to the public sphere via the forum of
the programme's institutional generic structure, in the form of private language.
New fora such as internet chat rooms are part of this process, and similarly, they
provide fora that bind, through generic activity, participants who do not have a
prior interpersonal relationship.

2.7 Conclusion

This theoretical chapter set out to explore how a traditional model of communication could be expanded so as to adequately account for media discourse. We
see this as a necessary prerequisite before looking at empirical data in this book.
This model is needed to account for core features and structures of media discourse. The notion of a participation framework was put forward to accommodate
the communicative event of media interactions. We will apply this model in the
coming chapters and it will help us in chapter 4 to explain how media interactions
are managed within this framework. We will explore different alignments that
can be taken up within it and how these manifest in terms of language use. The
institutional role and responsibilities that come with the power-holder, the presenter or host, in the participation framework will also be discussed such as the
presenter's responsibility to keep the ratified hearers within the common ground
of shared knowledge and the effect this has on speaker–hearer alignments and
on how the interactions are structured (for example, presenters usually align
with the audience as opposed to the interviewee at the start and end of an interview). We will also look at the institutional role-relatedness of questions and how
question types and interactional types are linked. In chapter 5 the participation
framework model will allow us to look at how pseudo-intimacy is constructed
between participants who are actually strangers, how co-presence is simulated
between the presenter and the audience when the presenter routinely aligns with
the audience of ratified hearers so as to reinforce their place within the framework. The participation framework, as we have noted, has a range or territory
created and defined by its audience and chapter 6 will look at indices of identity, at
how participants centre themselves and in so doing create 'others' who are outside
the framework.

Here we also looked at the notion of genre in relation to mediated interactions.

We established that a distinction was needed between the structure and the activity that happens within a programme format. Those who take part in the activity of a media interaction are said to have options and these options are contingent on their collective socio-historic and socio-cultural reality. Participants behave collaboratively and they can avail of new communication fora by recycling 'generic packages' from related fora. These instantaneously enacted blends are sometimes unique and one off, but if they recur over time they may become institutionalized. Within the orthodoxy of this structure, we have choices and options relative to our socio-historic and socio-cultural selves and these choices are mutually shaped by the socio-historic and socio-cultural selves of our co-participants. The crucial point, however, is that in television and radio interactions, we normally do not know our co-participants, other than at the level of general cultural presupposition. The language and knowledge resources employed and the choices made at any moment in the generic activity are indicative of some socio-historic and socio-cultural commonage assumed by those who participate. Throughout chapters 4, 5 and 6 we will draw comparisons between casual conversation and also institutional discourse such as academic interactions to show the generic links and blends that exist between these types of talk and media discourse.

Before we set about looking empirically at media interactions within the participation frameworks model, we will in the next chapter survey the prevailing research models that have been used in the study of media discourse such as conversation analysis, discourse analysis and pragmatics and suggest that corpus linguistics also has a role to play. We will overview the instruments of corpus-based analysis such as concordancing and cluster analysis and employ these along with other methods in a sample analysis. However, before any empirical work can be done, we need to find adequate categories for the different types of media interactions that exist from radio phone-ins to televised political interview. In the early part of chapter 3, we will propose a participant-based categorization system which differentiates between media interactions where (1) one participant is from the private sphere and one is from the public sphere, (2) both are known personae from the public sphere and (3, a sub-category of 2) political interviews where both participants in the interaction are from the public sphere but where one has been elected or appointed as a public representative in a political role.

3 Review of methodologies for analysing media discourse

... even serious linguistics . . . have failed to understand the nature of utterances because they adopt a passive model of meaning and understanding

Bakhtin (1986: 80)

3.0 Introduction

The aim of this chapter is to overview analytical approaches that have been employed in the study of media interactions such as conversation analysis, discourse analysis, pragmatics and emerging approaches such as corpus linguistics. We will also look at how methods can complement each other. For example, conversation analysis offers a powerful means of looking at the significance of turn sequentiality and placement while corpus linguistics can show systematic patterns of language use quantitatively as well as qualitatively, while pragmatics can shed light on power relations and face issues.

First we will look at how media interactions can be categorized across a wide range of users and situations. We are familiar with labels such as chat show, phone-in, political interview, and so on, but in order to look at these interactions systematically and draw conclusions about linguistic patterns, we need to have a basis for comparing them. By looking at how the participation framework (as discussed in chapter 2) of the various interactions is structured and composed we can identify interaction types and use these categories to create a corpus of data for analyses in chapters 4, 5 and 6 where we look at how the discourse is managed, how pseudo-intimacy is created, how identity is indexed and how these features vary depending on the type of interaction and participation framework.

3.1 Categorizing media interactions

The book focuses mostly on dyadic spoken interactions in the media and so it is concerned with a range of different types of spoken contexts from radio phone-ins, chat shows, to political interviews on television. If we consider the participation framework at a generic level, that is the interactional structure that all of these have in common, we can say that:

- there is a presenter/interviewer/host who represents the broadcasting institution and he or she is a known public person.
- there is an interviewee/caller/guest who can be a celebrity/publicly known individual or can be someone from the private sphere. This person may be co-present with the presenter/interviewer/host at the time of the interaction or they may be at a distance on a radio or phone line or linked by video.
- there is an audience either present in the studio at the time of recording and/ or listening to or watching the interaction.

For the purposes of looking at the language of media interactions, we will use the following three-way classification which is based on the interviewee's persona:

1 *Unknown* – these interactions involve an interviewee/caller/guest who is from the private sphere. This person from the private sphere interacts with a presenter/interviewer/host who is known in the public sphere. In this category we mostly find radio phone-ins. Television talk shows broadly fall into this category but, because they are more open fora than dyadic interactions, they have not been included in the corpus of data for analysis as they lack direct comparability with the other types of data. This is not to say that they do not merit examination as media interactions in their own right (see section 3.3 below).

2 *Known* – these interactions involve an interviewee/caller/guest who is from the public sphere, such as a celebrity. In these interactions both the interviewer and the interviewee are known public personae. In this category we include mostly television chat shows and radio interviews. We do not include political interviews in this category.

3 *Political* – these interactions involve an interviewee/caller/guest who is from the political sphere. Both the presenter/interviewer/host and the interviewee/ caller/guest are known in the public sphere. Though these interactions also involve two known personae, they are treated separately as they involve publicly elected/appointed figures as opposed to celebrities and are focused on political issues.

When we look at actual interviews in the next three chapters we will keep this distinction between *unknown, known* and *political* types of interactions. For the purposes of these chapters, we have assembled a corpus of media interactions comprising 271,553 words, almost all of which is available in transcribed format on the internet (and often in sound and video files also). Data is drawn from international English-speaking media sources including material from the UK, USA, Canada,

Australia and Ireland. Using the categories that have been outlined above, table 3.1 gives a breakdown of the corpus.

Table 3.1 Breakdown of the media corpus and its *unknown, known* and *political* sub-corpora

Sub-corpus	Description	Total number of words
Unknown	17 interviews from radio phone-ins	89,148
Known	46 interviews from radio and television chat show interviews	89,225
Political	29 political interviews from television and radio	93,180

Before we survey the prevailing methodologies that have been used under these three media interaction types, it is worth examining the background to the most influential methodology in the study of media interactions, that is conversation analysis, especially to show its lineage from the study of casual conversation.

3.2 Conversation analysis

Conversation analysis (CA) is a research tradition that has grown out of ethno-methodology, an area within sociology rather than linguistics. One of the main influences was sociologist Harold Garfinkel, who sought to understand how social members made sense of everyday life (Eggins and Slade 1997). Most notable in the area of CA are the American researchers Sacks, Schegloff and Jefferson whose work, since the 1970s, has contributed to and strongly influenced research into conversation (for example Schegloff 1968; Sacks, Schegloff and Jefferson 1974; Schegloff, Jefferson and Sacks 1977; Sacks 1992). CA takes a 'bottom-up' approach to the study of the social organization of conversation, or 'talk-in-interaction', by means of a detailed inspection of tape recordings and transcriptions (ten Have 1986). That is, it focuses in on how conversations are structured and organized locally turn-by-turn and from this makes inductive comments about social organization. As Scannell (1998) notes, the object of study for CA is social interaction rather than language. McCarthy (1998) points out that it offers the possibility of fine-grain descriptions of how participants orient themselves towards mutual goals and negotiate their way forward in highly specific situations. These highly specific situations are usually socially-defined, such as the beauty salon (LeBaron and Jones 2002) or institutional settings such as courtroom interaction (Atkinson 1979; Atkinson and Drew 1979), doctor–patient interactions (Maynard 1997, 2003; Maynard and Heritage 2005) or emergency phone calls (Whalen and Zimmerman 1987; Tracy 1997; Tracy and Anderson 1999). In the area of media discourse quite a substantial amount of CA research has amassed around news interviews, talk shows and radio phone-ins, which we will examine below.

The norms of the turn-taking structure of casual conversation were delineated in the influential Sacks, Schegloff and Jefferson (1974) study and this forms the basis of much CA research. When we talk about the norms of turn-taking we are concerned with what is systematic about the way speakers decide when to speak during a conversation, how speaker turns can be related to each other in sequence and may go together as adjacency pairs, for example a greeting + reciprocation pair:

A: How are you?
B: Fine. How are you?

Other typical adjacency pairs include question + answer, summons + acknowledgement, request + compliance, and so on. Not all second pair parts have the same significance; therefore, there is said to be *preference organization*, that is some second pair parts are preferred and some are dispreferred (see Pomerantz 1984). Here is an example of a dispreferred sequence (an invitation anticipates acceptance rather than rejection or hesitation):

A: Would you like a cup of tea?
B: [*pause*] Well. I just don't know.

Another focus of turn-taking analysis in CA is how turns are organized in their local *sequential* context at any given point in an interaction and the systematicity of these sequences of utterances (see Schegloff 1982). For example, one can talk about the sequentiality of greeting or leave-taking routines in different situations. Seemingly minor or mundane changes in turn placement within utterances and across turns are also seen as very significant in CA turn-by-turn analysis, for example the difference between the placement of a vocative at the beginning, mid- or end-point of an utterance (see Jefferson 1973).

Moving above the level of individual turns or adjacency pairs, conversation analysts are also interested in identifying the 'canonical' structure of interactions, that is the sequential norms of interaction in particular settings. Telephone call openings have received particular attention (Schegloff 1968; Godard 1977; Schegloff 1986; Whalen and Zimmerman 1987; Hopper 1989; Cameron and Hills 1990; Hopper *et al.* 1991; Hutchby 1991, 1996a, 1996b and 1999; Halmari 1993; 1992; Drew and Chilton 2000, among others). This has proved a very powerful comparative tool in the analysis of institutional interactions, including media discourse, because baseline sequences of interaction from mundane conversation can be compared with interactions in institutional or other settings.

Using casual conversation sequences as a comparative baseline has been the basis for many CA studies that look at telephone openings in institutional settings. Schegloff (1986) characterized the canonical structure for a phone call opening between 'unmarked forms of relationships' (that is those who are not particularly intimate, but who are not strangers) as having the structural organization shown in figure 3.1.

Figure 3.1 Schegloff (1986) Canonical call opening between 'unmarked forms of relationships' (Drew and Chilton 2000)

Summons-answer:	0	Phone rings	
	1	Answerer:	**Hello**
Identification-recognition:	2	Caller:	**Hello Jim?**
	3	Answerer:	**Yeah**
	4	Caller:	**'s Bonnie**
Greetings:	5	Answerer:	**Hi**
	6	Caller:	**Hi**
'How are you?' sequences:	7	Caller:	**How are yuh?**
	8	Answerer:	**Fine, how're you?**
	9	Caller:	**Oh, okay I guess**
	10	Answerer:	**Oh okay**
First topic:	11	Caller:	**What are you doing New Year's eve?**

Using this sequence as the norm or baseline, other telephone openings where the setting and speaker relationship differ can be compared and conclusions about the influence of these variables on the sequence of the interaction can then be drawn. For example, Whalen and Zimmerman (1987) present a typical sequence of call openings between strangers on an emergency phone line (figure 3.2). We see by comparing this institutional interaction with the baseline from Schegloff (1986) that there is an attenuation or cutting short of the stages because the relationship and setting are different.

Figure 3.2 Call openings between strangers – Whalen and Zimmerman 1987 (after Hopper and Drummond 1992: 191)

Summons-answer:	0	Phone rings	
	1	Answerer:	**Mid-city emergency**
Business of call:	2	Caller:	**Um yeah. Somebody jus' vandalized my car.**

There is no identification–recognition phase, nor do caller and answerer engage in 'how are you?' sequences. This reflects the institutional organization of talk in this context of interaction. Drew and Chilton (2000) look at call openings between intimates, drawing on a corpus of calls made between a mother and daughter during three two-month periods spread over three years. Most of these calls are for the purpose of 'keeping in touch', in other words there is normally no express purpose for calling other than to maintain contact. They call each other once a week around the same time every week and the role of *caller* alternates each week. In line with Schegloff's correlation between call type and caller relationship, Drew and Chilton find these 'keeping in touch' call openings follow a stable pattern, as illustrated in figure 3.3,[1] and as we see, this pattern is again different to the canonical structure for openings as detailed in Schegloff (1986).

Figure 3.3 Call openings between intimates after Drew and Chilton (2000)

Summons:	0	Phone rings	
Answer + identification–	1	Answerer:	**Hello**
recognition +:			
Greetings ('How are you?'	2	Caller:	**Hello**
also possible):			
	3	Answerer:	**Oh hello**
First topic:	4	Answerer:	**I've been waiting for you**

Again here we see attenuation of call stages, similar to the institutional calls from the emergency call setting between strangers, though for different reasons. As Drew and Chilton point out, the relationship of the callers allows for the attenuation of the canonical stages because the callers are intimates, and because they are expecting the call. The voice sample provided by *hello* achieves all Schegloff's stages of answering, identification–recognition and greeting in this interaction.

3.3 Interactions with unknown personae

The most common media forum where ordinary members of the public can interact with relative immediacy is through phone-in programmes on the radio. These may take the form of programmes dedicated solely to radio phone calls, music shows with occasional call-in segments, or those which are talk shows led by a presenter who sometimes takes calls from the public and sometimes has expert guests on the show to discuss specific topics. The former are caller-led (in that the content of the show is driven by the nature of the concerns of those who call the show) and the latter are led by the production team who decide in advance what topics will be covered on the show, and callers may phone in reaction to these issues. The predominant research methodology used in the study of radio phone-ins and talk radio is conversation analysis. Television also provides a forum for 'ordinary' people in the form of television talk shows. However, these are not as immediately accessible to the public insofar as one can pick up the phone and within a matter of minutes be on live radio, whereas television requires co-presence, pre-production stages, and so on. Here we look at how radio and television interactions with unknown personae have been researched.

Radio interactions

Using CA turn sequentiality as an analytical tool has proved very successful in the study of radio discourse. Again here Schegloff's canonical call opening sequence provides a baseline with which media call openings can be compared. For example, a number of authors have dealt with radio call openings. Cameron and Hills (1990) looked at 50 calls from the London-based talk radio station LBC. Fifty per cent of calls involved discussions of current affairs between a caller and host, while 50 per cent were drawn from a selection of expert advice phone-ins on topics ranging from medical problems to gardening. When they compared the radio call openings with the Schegloff (1986) canonical structure, they found that unlike a normal telephone call, the roles of *summoner* and *summoned* are initially reversed. In a normal phone call, the person who answers the phone (the summoned) does not know who is calling and awaits the summoner's identification, whereas in radio phone-ins the summoned (the presenter) knows the summoner's name (i.e. the caller), as well as his or her location and reason for calling (Cameron and Hills 1990: 55).[2] This overturns the canonical order where the caller always proffers the reason for calling (figure 3.4).

Figure 3.4 Typical LBC radio call opening (adapted from Cameron and Hills 1990: 55)

Summons	1	Presenter:	Maria on the line now in Sudbury
Answer	2	Caller:	Hello
Greeting	3	Presenter:	Hello Maria
Greeting	4	Caller:	Good evening Mike

Cameron and Hills (1990) note the following features in the canonical sequentiality of LBC call openings:

• The presenter normally mentions the caller's name and call location, for example: 'Let's try Marie in Edgware' or 'Beatrice is on the line now in Mitcham'.
• This places the caller (the original summoner) in the position of 'answerer', so the [name] + [location] serves as a summons on the part of the presenter,

constraining the next turn of the caller, who is expected to answer rather than identify themselves.

- The calls often follow the pattern of summons (i.e. [*name*] + [*location*]) – answer – greeting – greeting, as illustrated in figure 3.4.
- The callers *always* identify the call topic (i.e. their reason for calling).

Cameron and Hills (1990) also note that the following even more attenuated opening is frequently found. In figure 3.5 we see the answer and greeting turns are collapsed into the caller's first turn.

Figure 3.5 'Collapsed opening' commonly found on LBC radio call opening (adapted from Cameron and Hills 1990: 55)

Summons	1	Presenter:	John in Holloway
Answer/greeting	2	Caller:	Yes morning Ed
Greeting	3	Presenter:	Morning

In contrast with Drew and Chilton (2000) who saw turn attenuation as a by-product of the intimate relationship between the mother and daughter in their data, Cameron and Hills attribute attenuation in radio phone-in openings to orientation to the institutional genre on the part of the caller, which is in line with Whalen and Zimmerman's (1987) findings in relation to emergency calls. Both standpoints are not incompatible; the extremes of intimacy (in the case of the mother and daughter), and anonymity (in the case of the emergency calls), each allow for attenuation of the canonical stages for different reasons as the call emerges and callers orient themselves according to their interactional goals. The mother and daughter attenuate their turns because they recognize and expect each other's voices and orient themselves towards their weekly call and this marks their close relationship, whereas 'strangers' calling an emergency helpline orient towards expediting an urgent call for help, a transactional goal as compared with a relational one which pertains in the mother–daughter calls. This is in line with Hutchby and Wooffitt (1998) who point out that as far as CA is concerned, what characterizes interaction as institutional is not to do with theories of social struc-ture, as in most sociology, but with the special character of speech exchange systems that participants orient to.

The work of Hutchby on the LBC talk radio show *The Brian Hayes Show* has con-tributed greatly to the study of media discourse (see Hutchby 1991, 1996a, 1996b and 1999). His focus on the turn sequentiality of openings in *The Brian Hayes Show*, in line with Cameron and Hills (1990), reveals that callers always initiate the topic,[3] which he says exhibits and sustains 'their identity as "lay" contribu-tors entering into the institutional frame of the broadcast' (Hutchby 1999: 60).

Hutchby (1991) asserts that callers' second turn is restrained by the hosts' first turn (typified by those quoted in extracts 3.1 and 3.2), being 'received as *invitations to produce news*' (ibid.: 121 – Hutchby's italics).

Extract 3.1

| 1 | Presenter: | John is calling from Ilford good morning |
| 2 | Caller: | .h good morning Brian [*pause: 0.4*] .hh what I'm phoning up is about the cricket |

Hutchby (1991: 120–1)

Extract 3.2

| 1 | Presenter: | Mill Hill is where Gloria calls from good morning |
| 2 | Caller: | Good morning Brian hh erm re the Sunday opening I'm just phoning from the point of view hh as an assistant who actually does do this . . . |

Hutchby (1991: 120–1)

As we can see these patterns conform to Cameron and Hills' characterization of call openings across a range of radio calls within the same station, LBC. Also in line with their analysis is Hutchby's (1991) observation that openings are achieved minimally, usually within two turns, where the host offers a vocal signature (purportedly recognizable lexical-intonational sample) which he says is in keeping with Schegloff (1986) in that it serves as a 'projected "recognition source" to which the "recognition solution" is provided by the caller in a minimized . . . greeting' in the second turn (Hutchby 1991: 120). Thus, notes Hutchby, the canonical opening as detailed in Schegloff (1972, 1979, 1986) (see figure 3.1) is compacted into two turns and this, he maintains, is typical of institutionalized openings.

Relative to openings, call closings get far less attention in existing literature. Nevertheless, Schegloff and Sacks (1973: 289) observe that a conversation does not simply end 'but is brought to a close'. Closings, they say, are not randomly brought about, they are negotiated and interactively-produced activities. LeBaron and Jones (2002) look at 'a departure sequence' of a single interaction that took place between two clients in a beauty salon. They claim that by examining in detail a single encounter, much longer in duration than the segments of interaction employed in related studies, they can show that the function of behaviours in a departure sequence may best be understood by analysing their relationship to the social and physical situation in which they are embedded. Button (1987) points out that while conversational openings regularly employ a common starting point, for example, greetings, and then diverge, closings do the opposite moving from divergence to convergence to a goodbye form. Hutchby (1991) notes that while the same circumstances hold for radio phone-in closings, 'the technical problematics of the accomplishment of a call's "closing" exhibit a radical dissimilarity from those observable in mundane talk' (ibid.: 131). He associates this radical dissimilarity with 'the talk's institutional colouring' (ibid.) dominated by one pervasive characteristic: namely that 'conversational closings in talk radio are not required to be, and overwhelmingly are not in practice negotiated in any overt respect between the host and the caller'. He adds that given the host's siting as 'organisational hub' (ibid.: 132) of the broadcast and 'as processing agent', both allowing callers on the air and removing them from the air, 'it is in a very basic sense the host's task not only to "open" calls . . . but also to "close" them' (ibid.). From his data he observes that while the norm for the presenter is to give a *bid for closing* there is no compulsion to pay regard to the norms of routine conversation where there is usually reciprocation of closing bids. Extracts 3.3 and 3.4 are two examples of closings from *The Brian Hayes Show* (LBC).

Extract 3.3

Caller:	. . . I mean (0.3) .h it – it is it's really it is the poo. The poorer pensions that've had it taken away from them (0.4) because of this er money that's been er the means uh th- the needs allowance money
Presenter:	so you don't think the government's being all that marvellous and generous about this
Caller:	⌊I think they're disgusting. I really do.
Presenter:	⌊Thank thank you Margaret

Hutchby (1991: 132)

Extract 3.4

Caller:	but all we saw was a woman's grief and an ordinary young man who=
Presenter:	⌊ok well erm ⌊y-y-eh
Caller:	=was in the boy scouts and who was whatever
Presenter:	⌊right I understand. I understand Eva and er understand m- the point you're making particularly from the your starting point which was that you will see controversial programmes from a particular point of view and we've had two of those particular points of views er yours and earlier Richard's thank you very much indeed for calling us.

Hutchby (1991: 132)

Television interactions

Apart from radio phone-ins where the general public has the opportunity to access the airwaves, television tabloid talk shows also fall into the category of interviews where one of the participants is from the private sphere and these have received considerable coverage in recent years by a relatively small number of researchers, most notably Carbaugh (1988); Livingston and Lunt (1994); Gregori-Signes (1998a, 1998b, 1999, 2000a, 2000b, 2000c, 2001, 2002); Ilie (1998, 1999, 2001); García Gómez (2000, 2002a, 2002b, 2005); Thornborrow (2001a, 2001b, 2001c); Lorenzo-Dus (2001, 2003, 2005); Timberg (2002); Rama Martínez (2003a, 2003b). Most of these shows are based in the US and almost all research in this area takes a CA perspective. Though they have evolved their own distinct genre of broadcast interaction, Thornborrow (2001a, 2001b) notes that they come from a lineage of several decades of television and radio talk tradition. The wide variety of talk show genres that combine talk with entertainment, particularly on US television, sometimes makes it difficult to clearly define it (Carbaugh 1988; Rama Martínez 2003a). Gregori-Signes (2000a) argues that the talk show genre is a social speech event whose rules of interaction become recognizable to a community that shares or has knowledge of those rules. She sees the tabloid talk show as a quasi-conversational or non-formal (Drew and Heritage 1992) television genre that can be identified by a series of generic features, which combine characteristics of both conversational and institutional genres. The talk show hybridness is constructed progressively during the interaction, and it establishes a role relationship between the participants that is local in nature and can be transformed at any moment. Livingstone and Lunt (1994) also note the hybrid nature of tabloid talk shows and suggest adopting a comparative perspective to show how interaction takes place in such contexts. While Gregori-Signes' work is largely based on the five major dimensions of CA as identified in Drew and Heritage (1992: 36) – lexical choice; turn design; sequence organization; overall structure; social epistemology and social relations – she also places her work within corpus-based genre analysis after McCarthy (1998). She sees a combined approach to the analysis of talk shows as allowing for the quantitative and qualitative description of talk shows as a genre. Timberg (2002) refers to these shows as a microcosm of society, a forum in which society tests out and comes to terms with social and cultural issues.

A richly eclectic approach to the study of talk shows is found in the work of García Gomez who draws on conversation analysis, discourse analysis, pragmatics (politeness theory), systemic functional linguistics (appraisal theory after Eggins 1994; Eggins and Slade 1997; and Martin 1996, 2000) and cognitive psychology (schema theory, social identity theory and auto-categorization theory) (see García Gómez 2000, 2002a, 2002b, 2004, 2005). His work looks at conflict talk in British, American and Spanish talk shows. He argues that by looking at the talk show turn-taking system the different mechanisms that operate in turn-taking distribution in the interaction make it possible to identify institutional, conversational and confrontational sequences. He proposed that the adjacency pair can be considered as the organizational unit in the institutional sequences; however, the three-part exchange is a better description of both conversational and confrontational sequences in television talk shows. Looking at conflict talk in these shows within a discourse analysis framework, he notes that the 'equilibrium' in the exchange in a conflictive episode occurs at 'three-turn-length', where the follow up move is a very important element of the exchange. Using a pragmatic framework he asserts that guests' pragmatic motivations in a conflictual episode not only cause the presence of specific speech acts in the initiating move but also the existence of a third move. In other words, there is a clear connection between the discursive level (pragmatic motivations) and the pragmatic level (speech acts), and between these two levels and the basic organizational unit of conflict talk. For example, García Gómez (2004) carries out a detailed analysis of the uses, functions and pragmatic motivations of the three main initiating moves; that is, elicitations, directives and informatives in the context of talk shows. From the perspective of systemic functional linguistics, García Gómez looks at the semantics of conflict talk using appraisal theory. He takes his definition of appraisal from Eggins and Slade (1997: 125) who define it as analysis which 'examines the attitudinal meanings of words and the expression of attitude used in conversation'. García Gómez (2005), using a sample of data from 20 programmes of a popular American late-night show hosted by Bill Maher, *Politically Incorrect*, attempts to sketch the relations between this attitudinal meaning and what he terms the consequent construction of the social identity of the American guests and the host. He argues that the appraisal system of interpersonal semantics gives us an insight into how people share their perception and feelings about the world and each other in talk show interactions. Using this framework, he argues, is a useful device for constructing guests' speaker identity and that the distinct attitudinal meanings of words used by British, American and Spanish speakers are due to cultural-relativistic ways of reasoning (see also García Gómez 2004). He is also led to conclude that the semantics of involvement is a sensitive index of social relationships which can reflect different degrees of social closeness and of relative power between interactants.

Using a cognitive approach, García Gómez applies schema theory to conflictual episodes (see García Gómez 2002b, 2004). As Cook (1989) explains, for discourse analysis, the most important idea to come out of artificial intelligence research is the notion of knowledge schemata, which he defines as mental representations of typical situations, and they are used in discourse processing to predict the contents of the particular situation which the discourse describes. Knowledge schemata are also very important to the field of educational psychology (see Driscoll 1994; Kaplan 1966; Armbruster 1996; Schwartz *et al.* 1998). García Gómez

(2002a, 2004), applying this theory to topic management in conflict episodes in talk shows, asserts for example that it provides a set of social and psychological characteristics of topic and a possible interpretational framework for the understanding of a talk show conflictual episode. He also notes that cognitive interpretation of topic management is an effective analytical tool for structuring talk show interactions and identifying guests' discourse agendas. Approaching his data from the perspective of politeness theory, García Gómez conducts a contrastive analysis of the British talk show *Kilroy* and the American show *Jerry Springer* and examines how participants exploit different politeness strategies in talk show conflict talk and discursively build public identities for themselves and their opponents (2004). He concludes that (1) the study of face management in British and American confrontational episodes makes it possible not only to prove a cultural-relativistic stance of the expression of politeness, but also to characterize and define a different conception of the notion of face in this specific anger-evoking context and (2) that the cultural dimension of politeness strategies refers to two culturally patterned social systems: the British and the American psyches. This cultural-relativistic stance is clearly reflected in differences in the way in which the self is construed and how social relationships are understood. By combining some concepts from social psychology and politeness theory, García Gómez argues that talk show guests exploit a number of politeness strategies to categorize themselves, compared with the opponent, and invoke a precise social identity. In other words, guests negotiate their opposing realities by activating a specific positioning in discourse (see chapter 6 where we look at positioning in detail). Focusing on guests' positioning in talk shows, he notes, one can shed light on the functionality and dysfunctionality of conflictual episodes and establish a connection between the different levels of self-presentation and the exploitation of specific politeness strategies.

3.4 Interactions with known personae

Media interactions with people from the public sphere, for example celebrities from entertainment or sport, usually take place on television or radio *chat shows*. Carbaugh (1988) makes a useful distinction between chat shows and talk shows. Chat show interviews differ from talk shows in that they are *personality focused* whereas talk shows are *issue focused*. Rama Martínez (2003a: 9) defines chat shows as comprising 'a series of short interviews with (and occasionally performances of) personalities, mainly of the entertainment industry'. She also notes that in a conversation analysis model, its characteristics are loosely based on the rules defining the political interview (see below). Within the parameters of our persona-based categorization, chat shows differ from talk shows in that they involve interviews with personae from the known world, usually celebrities whereas television tabloid talk shows as discussed above involve interviewees or participants who come from the private sphere. Chat shows differ from political interviews because the known personae from the public sphere are not political actors elected to the public sphere. Politicians sometimes appear as guests on chat shows but these interviews, to use Carbaugh's terms, are usually personality focused rather than issue focused. In chapters 4, 5 and 6, this distinction will prove important in the analysis of the different types of talk in media interactions. Relative to tabloid talk shows, surprisingly little research has been done into chat show interviews with known personae. However, some studies have been done into specific interviews or talk show hosts.

Carbaugh (1988) looks at the American talk show *Donahue*. Carbaugh seeks to 'unveil cultural discourses that are used in an American scene' (ibid.: 187). Within a broadly CA framework, he looks at how joint, social, institutionalized constructions can be accounted for by looking at the structure of the interaction between Phil Donahue, his guests and his audience. Talk is seen as organized performance, centring around various symbols such as the individual, the self, choice and social roles, and these symbols are themselves seen as mutually organized. As part of a broader study of the cross-cultural reception of American programmes, Carbaugh (1996) noted that a Russian audience found the *Donahue* show not to their taste. McCarthy and Carter (1994), using a discourse analysis model, focused on the structure of exchanges and the internal structure of moves in recording of the highly successful British chat show *Wogan*, hosted by Irishman Terry Wogan, which was broadcast in the 1980 to 1990s. With a pedagogical goal in mind, they identify a number of discourse strategies used by the presenter such as using 'a conventional expression' to take the interviewee back to an earlier question so as to expand on a topic (for example '*going back* to your family how important are they to you in your work?') or linking your question to your last answer (ibid.: 193).

Tolson (1991: 179) takes a very broad definition of *chat* and uses the term to include forms of 'studio talk, which can be found in all types of interviews, panel discussions, game shows and human interest shows . . . wherever in fact there is a studio'. He notes that though the chat show is loosely based on the 'protocols for the television interview' (see Heritage 1985 for example), the talk frequently transgresses these and 'presumes an increasing sophistication on the part of the television audience' (ibid.: 178). Broadcast chat, he maintains, does not simply follow norms and conventions, it opens up the possibility of transgression, for example interviewees putting questions to interviewers. As a result, he points out, there is a certain ambivalence between the forms of talk which are designed both 'to inform and entertain; to appear serious and sincere, but also sometimes playful and flippant' (ibid.). Within a mass communication model, he looks at a number of British chat shows in the mid-1980s, particularly *Wogan* and *The Dame Edna Experience* (see also Tolson 1985), and suggests that the 'playful' tendency had at that time become the 'assumed position of dominance, giving rise to certain effects across the public sphere of broadcasting discourse' (ibid.: 170). On *Wogan*, he says that it developed chat to the point where it was 'virtually an art form' (ibid.: 181). Focusing on an interview from *Wogan* broadcast on 10 March 1984, he observes that the participants seem very aware of their interaction as a public performance. The interviewee stretches her position to the limit; she asks most of the questions and introduces most of the topics. The interview that he analyses, he claims, provides a rich illustration of the three defining features of 'chat' as a speech genre:

1   In terms of content, there is a focus on the personal sometimes in the form of gossip and/or sexual innuendo, also at this level he points to a common cultural knowledge that is invoked (see chapter 6 for more on this topic). He notes that 'this is the kind of mass-mediated cultural knowledge which is classified in many contexts today as "trivia"' (ibid.: 183).
2   Building on this characteristic, there is a sustained and highly self-reflexive metadiscourse about television as a cultural institution, where participants not only invoke the cultural knowledge of the viewer, they also draw attention to the construction of their own performances.
3   He likens the dialogic improvisation in television chat to a jazz performance, not only because it is apparently unrehearsed, but also because it involves a play of thematic repetition and variation in front of a live audience.

3.5 Political interviews

Heritage (1985) noted that news interviews, despite their influential and immediate interactional generation of on-air news and opinion, had not received systematic analytical attention over the years. This neglect he attributes to the lack of a coherent analytical framework with which to handle such material. Since then considerable work has been done on the discourse of interviews with political personae, particularly within the CA model, but also using discourse analysis, pragmatics and latterly corpus linguistics. As we noted above, Rama Martínez (2003a) finds that political interviews are information focused while chat shows and talk shows can fluctuate between being information focused and entertainment focused. Carter and McCarthy (2002) tell us that conversation analysts, discourse analysts and pragmaticians have revealed much about the political interview and other broadcast interviews as genres, and have done so largely by comparing interviews with the social, pragmatic or structural norms of everyday conversation. In this way, phenomena such as sequential organization, preference organization, turn-taking, topic management, opening and closure, etc. have been accurately described as indices of the unique generic configuration of the broadcast interview. From a CA perspective, Greatbatch (1988) profiles the turn-taking norms of political interviews using the baseline canonical framework provided by Sacks, Schegloff and Jefferson (1974) as a comparison. He notes that interviewers and interviewees generally confine themselves, respectively, to turn-types recognizable as questions and answers. The interviewer does not normally engage in a wide range of responses that questioners normally engage in during casual conversation when they provide follow up response tokens such as *that's right, really, absolutely, and so on* (see Schegloff 1982; Jefferson 1984a; Greatbatch 1986; Tottie 1991; McCarthy and Carter 2000; Gardner 2002; McCarthy 2002). Heritage (1985) compares question and answer sequences in news interviews with casual conversation and courtroom interactions and finds that unlike casual conversation, it is possible to search through hours of courtroom and news interview interactions without encountering a single *mm hm, oh* newsmarker (see Jefferson 1984a) or affiliative assessment (see chapter 5 where we look at the use of response tokens in media interactions). Instead, Heritage (1985) tells us, the interviews are conducted almost exclusively through chains of questions and answers, and in so doing, he claims, narratives are elicited step-by-step or opinions are developed and elaborated component-by-component. He points out that the news interview is a functionally specialized form of social interaction restricted by institutionalized conventions. In many countries, their enormous potential influence in political affairs has been controlled by charters and licenses obliging them to maintain impartiality and balance in their coverage and to refrain from editorial comment. These obligations, Heritage notes, have played a major role in shaping the ground rules informing interviewer conduct. Questioning will be examined in detail in chapter 4 drawing on data from the media corpus as detailed above.

Clayman (1991) looks at news interview openings and concludes that they are highly organized so as to achieve institutional ends: a) they mark the encounter from the outset as having been pre-assembled on behalf of the viewing audience and b) they set the agenda for the interview which is linked to newsworthy events in the world at large. Harris (1991) looks at political interviews and how politicians in particular respond evasively to questions in interviews. She finds that there is empirical evidence that politicians are evasive in political interviews especially when compared to responses with other non-politician respondents. She also notes that politicians are to a certain degree constrained by the syntax of the question and they are not free to ignore it with impunity. Jucker (1986), in his study of news interviews, maintains that it is difficult to determine on syntactic grounds whether a politician has given a direct answer to a question. Clayman (1993) looks at how reformulations of interviewers' questions by the interviewee, as a preface to a response, can be used both to answer questions and to manipulate them and evade answering them in various ways, for example shifting the topic agenda, ignoring the second part of a two-part question, agreeing with some embedded proposition in the question without engaging with the main proposition, and so on.

Within a discourse analysis model, Blum-Kulka (1983) looks at 20 hours of transcribed political interviews from Israeli television between 1980 and 1982. Her focus is on the initial exchanges at transaction boundaries. She holds that political interviews are highly structured speech events, governed by genre-specific discourse rules and that interviewer and politician are complicit in orienting towards these norms. Interviewers, she finds, constantly negoti-ate with politicians on the level of co-operation required in adhering to these norms. Opening moves are one example where negotiation about levels of co-operation can be found. She attempts to define the relationship between questions and answers in political interviews within the confines of different types of cohe-sion, which is often driven by the level of co-operation. For instance, politicians' responses are constantly being evaluated by the interviewers as to whether they are 'supportive' or 'non-supportive'. The former case, she notes, leads to a topic shift or clarification questions and the latter can result in a challenging formula-tion. Carter and McCarthy (2002) look specifically at one BBC radio interview with the British Prime Minister, Tony Blair, using a dual approach to its analysis. Firstly, they apply the framework of CA and subsequently they conduct a corpus-based analysis on the same data. They conclude that the CA analysis shows that the interviewer and interviewee both adhere to and exploit the generic conventions of the interview in terms of turn-taking, topic management and participant relation-ships. The interviewer presses an agenda of getting the interviewee to commit to action; the interviewee, in turn, responds cohesively and coherently and yet avoids direct commitment to action and maintains his topical agenda without losing face (and with useful soundbites delivered along the way, which are likely to be extracted and quoted in subsequent national news bulletins). The application of corpus techniques to the transcript reveals much about the lexical environment, especially of the high-frequency key words. Carter and McCarthy show how CA and corpus linguistics can complement each other and offer a more integrated way of understanding how conversational agendas are achieved when the two methods are used in combination.

In a substantial study of political interviews, Clayman and Heritage (2002: 7) set as their goal to 'examine the inner workings of the news interview in Anglo-American society'. Their focus was on news interviews between journalists and 'newsworthy public figures engaged in discussion of recent news events' (ibid.: 24). Their data comprised 250 interviews of roughly equal portions from British and American sources. The American data mainly came from *The News Hour* (PBS), *Newsline* (ABC), *Meet the Press* (NBC), *Face the Nation* (CBS) and *This Week* (ABC). While the British data came mostly from *Newsnight* (BCC2), *The Today Programme* (BBC Radio 4) and *The World at One* (BBC Radio 4). The data is spread across a 21-year period which they believe offers a stable era in the history of the broadcast news interview. In terms of longitudinal conclusions, they note that most changes took place in this genre in the early decades and they concur with Heritage and Roth (1995) that there is a striking level of similarity between these British and American contexts so much so that they consider the British-American database of interviews as an essentially cohesive subject of study. In line with CA methodology, they contrast the rules of conversation with what happens during news interviews. In comparing British and American news interviews, they conclude that in spite of different developments due in part to differing laws about broadcasting in these two countries, the development of news interviews and their current state is remarkably similar. They also explain that the practices that they describe are 'shaped by the basic institutional conditions of broadcast journalism in Western democracies' (ibid.: 337).

3.6 A corpus-based approach

As we have seen, conversation analysis is very much the prevailing approach to the study of interactions in the media and it is very suited to this purpose. Recently corpus linguistics has also been used in this area and we propose that it has a lot to offer the study of media discourse especially when used in tandem with existing models such as CA, DA and pragmatics. Aijmer and Altenberg (1991: 1) describe corpus linguistics as 'the study of language on the basis of text corpora'. CL has developed rapidly since the 1960s largely due to the advent of computers and especially their capacity to store and process masses of data. This has facilitated the systematic analysis of large amounts of language and in turn this has meant that descriptions (and prescriptions) about the English language have frequently been contradicted by corpus linguists who work with representative samples of naturally-occurring language (Holmes 1988; Baynham 1991; Boxer and Pickering 1995; Kettermann 1995; Baynham 1996; Carter 1998; Hughes and McCarthy 1998; McCarthy 1998). Essentially a corpus is 'a large and principled collection of [computerized] texts' in spoken or written form (after Biber, Conrad and Reppen 1998: 4) which is available for analysis using corpus software packages (for further definitions see Renouf 1997; Sinclair 1997; Tognini-Bonelli 2001). Some debate exists as to whether CL is a theory or a method (see Tognini-Bonelli 2001) or indeed whether it is a new or separate branch of linguistics. As Kennedy (1998) notes, corpus-based research derives evidence from texts and so it differs from other approaches to language that depend on introspection for evidence. Increasingly, CL is being applied to contexts and domains outside the study of language itself where the use of language is the focus of empirical study in a given context. Among the many fields where CL is being adopted to complement other methodological tools, such as discourse analysis and conversation analysis, are contexts such as courtrooms (including forensic linguistics, Cotterill 2003), the workplace (Koester 2000, 2006; McCarthy and Handford 2004), pedagogic and academic contexts (see Farr 2002, 2003; Walsh 2002; Swales 2002; O'Keeffe and Farr 2003; Walsh 2006), political discourse, advertising and the media (Carter and McCarthy 2002; Chang 2002; O'Keeffe 2002, 2003, 2005; Charteris-Black 2004).

In all of these cases CL offers a useful approach to the study of language, allowing for the quantification of recurring linguistic features to substantiate qualitative insights as well as the qualification of quantified findings. In the area of language and the media there has been a growing number of studies which draw on this approach. Coperías Aguilar and Besó (1999) conducted a corpus-based lexical study of Northern Ireland Republican and Unionist party websites (i.e. Sinn Féin and the Ulster Unionist Party) and they show systematic politicization of language in the data. O'Keeffe and Breen (2001) undertook an in-depth comparison of lexico-grammatical markers of stance in newspaper coverage of religious and non-religious child sexual abuse cases in a corpus of almost 700 Irish newspaper articles. Chang (2002) analyses pronoun use in a corpus of *Cartalk*, a US weekly phone-in on National Public Radio, involving two brothers, Ray and Tom Magliozzi, who answer questions about cars and car repair posed by listeners. She finds that the use of pronouns in the radio show closely parallels their distribution in a comparable corpus of casual conversation (see chapter 6 where we look at pronouns in detail). O'Keeffe looks at the discourse of an Irish radio phone-in programme using CL in tandem with CA, DA and pragmatics (O'Keeffe 2002, 2003, 2005). O'Keeffe (2002) focuses on socio-cultural indices of identity encoded in the language of radio phone-ins (see chapter 6). O'Keeffe (2003) uses a corpus-based methodology to examine vague language as a marker of shared knowledge (see chapter 6) in radio phone-in discourse while O'Keeffe (2005) focuses on questioning in the same data (see chapter 4). McCarthy and O'Keeffe (2003) compare the use of vocatives in radio interactions and casual conversation (see chapter 5).

Using corpus linguistics with other approaches

As we have suggested, corpus linguistics offers a useful approach to the analysis of language in the media, allowing for the quantification of recurring linguistic features to substantiate qualitative insights and vice versa. As in the case of CA, the notion of using casual conversation as a comparative baseline works very well in corpus linguistics also. A number of corpora are available which can be used for comparative purposes. In chapters 4, 5 and 6 we will draw on a number of these as comparative reference points against which we can compare results from our media corpus. Corpus software facilitates analytical functions such as word frequency list generation, concordancing, and cluster analysis that are useful when looking at media interactions. Each of these is illustrated below.

Word frequency lists

Corpus software can calculate the word frequency list of a corpus of texts extremely quickly. By doing this, one can obtain a list of all the words in the entire collection of data in order of frequency. This function facilitates enquiry across language varieties and contexts of use. In table 3.2, for example, we compare the first ten words from three different corpora:

1   Friends chatting: a sub-corpus of the Limerick Corpus of Irish English (LCIE) comprising female friends chatting (40,000 words).[4]
2   The *Liveline* corpus, a corpus of 44 radio phone-in calls to the Irish radio phone-in show *Liveline*, broadcast on the Irish public broadcasting station Radio Telefís Éireann, comprising 55,000 words.
3   The Australian Corpus of English (ACE), one million words of written Australian English including newspapers, fiction, reports, etc. (see Peters 2001; Hofland, Lindebjerg and Thunestvedt 1999).

Table 3.2 Comparison of word frequencies for the ten most frequent words across three datasets

	1	2	3
	Friends (LCIE)	Radio Liveline	ACE
	Spoken	Spoken	Written
Rank order			
1	I	the	the
2	and	I	of
3	the	and	and
4	to	to	to
5	was	you	a
6	you	that	in
7	it	it	is
8	like	a	for
9	that	of	that
10	he	in	was

Even from just the first ten most frequent words of these three corpora, we can see that the friends chatting column (1) and the *Liveline* radio data column (2) have many items in common, most notably that tendencies emerge in terms of genres and contexts of use. The friends chatting column (1) shows a high frequency of the markers of interactivity typical of spoken English *I* and *you* (see Carter and

McCarthy 2006). In the list of ten most frequent words from the ACE column (3), we find a high frequency of articles *a* and *the*, indicating a high instance of lexical noun phrases, the preposition *of*, suggesting post-modified noun phrases and prepositions *to*, *for*, *in* suggesting prepositional phrases. We will use the word frequency list function for comparative purposes in the context of media inter-actions in chapters 5 and 6.

Concordancing

Concordancing is a core tool in corpus linguistics which allows for the qualitative examination of data. It involves using corpus software to find every occurrence of a particular word or phrase. With the aid of a computer, corpora of millions of words can be searched in seconds. The search word or phrase is often referred to as the *node* and concordance lines are usually presented with the node word/phrase in the centre of the line with seven or eight words presented at either side. Concordance lines are usually scanned vertically at first glance, i.e. the analyst looks up or down the central pattern along the line of node word or phrase. Figure 3.6 is from a concordance of the word *now* from the *Liveline* corpus of Irish radio phone-ins mentioned above.

Figure 3.6 Concordance lines of *now* using the *Liveline* corpus

```
          the best bye bye.          NEW CALL Now yesterday ah one of our callers re
          Welcome back to the programme. Now recently am at the opening of the
               s so I've it was experience so. Now ah before I go to am the next pers
u Marian.          And likewise indeed. Now Jim.          Bye bye.          Good
          Thank you          NEW CALL Now we go on from weighty matters of s
o us.          IMMEDIATE NEW CALL Now Noel good afternoon to you.
          Okay bye bye.          NEW CALL Now Ciaran good afternoon to you. Hel
          you. Go=go=goodbye Josephine. Now Jim.          Good afternoon Marian
               (run on into) NEW CALL Now Matt. Good afternoon to you.
                         NEW CALL Now Mary good afternoon to you.
     NEW CALL immediate follow on Now Brian good afternoon to you.
That was Nathalie Imbruglia and Torn. Now Emmet good afternoon to you.
          That's REM Losing my Religion. Now Geraldine good afternoon to you.
     Welcome back to the programme. Now Richard good afternoon to you.
  oster and Allan and a Bunch of Thyme. Now Geraldine good afternoon.
n this village.          NEW CALLER Now Tess hello there.          Hello Ma
          n to you.          Hello Marian. Now we were talking yesterday ah about
d be the the solution to her problem''. Now Catherine you didn't like that did
bye bye bye bye.          NEW CALLER Now Josephine you want to reassure Bre
```

Here one can see quite readily that *now* frequently occurs at the start of a call and that the pattern *now* + vocative is very common. We also see that in this way *now* is functioning as a discourse marker and there is also evidence that the *now* + *time reference* is also systematic in call openings. We use concordance lines throughout chapters 5 and 6 to examine how lexical and lexico-grammatical items pattern within media interactions.

Cluster analysis

As a corpus technique the process of generating cluster lists is similar to making single word lists. Instead of ranking all of the single words in the corpus in order of frequency, the most frequent combinations of words can be calculated, for example two-word (*I mean*), three-word (*I don't know*), four-word (*I don't believe it*), five-word (*you know what I mean*), or six-word (*at the end of the day*) combinations. Using *Wordsmith Tools* (Scott 1998), table 3.3 gives us the first 20 most frequent four-word combinations from the media corpus that we have assembled.

Table 3.3 Four-word chunks from media corpus

 1 thank you very much
 2 a lot of people
 3 the end of the
 4 at the end of
 5 at the same time
 6 and I think that
 7 good afternoon to you
 8 good morning to you
 9 weapons of mass destruction
10 one of the things
11 I was going to
12 you very much indeed
13 a lot of the
14 in the United States
15 are you going to
16 do you want to
17 I don't want to
18 it seems to me
19 I have to say
20 no no no no

Multi-word list searches generate all statistically frequent combinations of words but many of these are syntactic fragments and so do not constitute complete syntactic units such as phrases or clauses in a conventional sense, for example from the above list *I was going to* and *a lot of the*. As noted by McCarthy and Carter (2002) these items should not be totally dismissed as their high frequency is an indicator of grammatical patterning which is linked to ways of interacting in speech and in writing. Hopper (1998) notes that these fragments give important clues as to how interaction unfolds and how grammar is emergent rather than being pre-existent in interaction. For example, 36 per cent of the concordance lines of the fragment *I was going to* in the media corpus that we have assembled are used as metadiscoursal items relating to the interview situation such as *I was going to ask/say*.

Figure 3.7 Concordance lines of *I was going to* from media corpus

Kristi Yamaguchi, limbering up. **I was going to ask** you how long do you like to limber up?
rush and flurry.   SM: Well, **I was going to ask** you what or who you blame for what's
            what, he's got a good point. **I was going to come on and say** that was live singing by
                just absolutely went boom. **I was going to say** all born, and then I said no, that
have a good job.' Darren: 'OK, **I was going to say** how much would the ring be worth?
                ll be in Saudi Arabia. **I was going to say** as good as Saudi
                        Well that's what **I was going to say** those people you spoke to who went to
.this is my .this is my. **I was going to say** this is my life, it's not my life, but

Here we see that the key phrase can serve two discourse functions: (1) as a discourse marker and (2) as a downtoner or hedging device. McCarthy and Carter (2002) note in the context of casual conversation that these grammatically incomplete strings can be seen as 'frames' to which new, unpredictable content can be added and that they are best understood as pragmatic markers (that is the different ways of creating speaker meanings in context, such as hedging), rather than syntactic or semantic ones. They argue that we are likely to find the reasons why many of the strings of words are so recurrent by seeing them as *frames* for pragmatic categories such as discourse marking, the preservation of face and the expression of politeness, acts of hedging and purposive vagueness.

3.7 Integrating approaches

Let us now examine how media discourse can benefit from integrating methodologies. Here we will return to the earlier theme of call openings. We will use the openings from the *Liveline* corpus and compare findings with those from Cameron and Hills (1990) and Hutchby (1991) who looked at call openings in the LBC radio programmes. The *Liveline* data comprises five radio phone-in pro-grammes collected in 1998 from the daily Irish radio phone-in *Liveline*. The five programmes were recorded randomly over a five-month period and transcribed to form a corpus of 55,000 words.

Let us compare some of the findings from the Irish data with the CA-based research above and where possible draw on CA, DA and pragmatics, as well as corpus linguistics. Firstly, as noted in Figure 3.4, Cameron and Hills (1990), within a CA framework, identified a typical radio call opening on LBC radio. They noted that the canonical sequentiality of LBC call openings featured the fol-lowing characteristics:

- The presenter normally mentions the caller's name and call location, for example: 'Let's try Marie in Edgware' or 'Beatrice is on the line now in Mitcham' (also noted by Hutchby 1991).
- This turn places the caller (the original summoner) in the position of 'answerer'. So the [*name*] + [*location*] serves as a summons on the part of the called (the presenter), constraining the next turn of the caller, who is expected to answer rather than identify themselves.
- The calls often follow the pattern of summons (i.e., [*name*] + [*location*]) – answer–greeting–greeting, as illustrated in figure 3.4.
- The callers *always* identify the call topic (or their reason for calling).

However, looking at the 44 openings in the corpus of *Liveline* phone-in calls, we find the following: in 100 per cent of calls the presenter uses the caller's name but caller location is mentioned in just four calls by the presenter, that is 9 per cent in all. These location references are less formulaic in nature compared to the LBC data (name + location):

Extract 3.5

. . . and now we head west.

Extract 3.6

David, where are you?

Extract 3.7

. . . and next to Galway.

Extract 3.8

What's the weather like in Cork today?

Compare these with the LBC examples from Cameron and Hills (1990) and Hutchby (1991):

Extract 3.9

Let's try Marie in Edgware.

Extract 3.10

Beatrice is on the line now in Mitcham.

Extract 3.11

John in Holloway.

The lack of formulaic location reference by the *Liveline* presenter creates a more intimate and less institutional effect at the opening of the interaction and avoids forcing the caller into the position of 'answerer', that is when the [*name*] + [*location*] serves as a summons on the part of the called (the presenter), constraining the next turn of the caller, who is expected to answer rather than identify themselves as is the case in Schegloff's canonical opening format (1986).

Unlike the findings of Cameron and Hills, and Hutchby, in the *Liveline* data, no single routine sequence was found to typify call openings and this is attributed to the less institutionalized nature of the Irish data. One of the features that becomes obvious is that many of the openings are either elaborated or attenuated. Those which are elaborated involve a collaborative setting up of the *reason for calling* (which both the presenter and the caller know in advance). For example in extract 3.12 the reason for calling (to give an opinion on a topic under discussion, namely whether boarding schools are a good idea) finally emerges in turn 8 with the metadiscourse marker *I just think that*.

Extract 3.12

1	Presenter:	Welcome back to the programme Aidan good afternoon to you. Hello there.
2	Caller:	Hello.

3	Presenter:	Hi how are you?
4	Caller:	Fine thanks.
5	Presenter:	You are attending boarding school at the moment?
6	Caller:	Yeah I'm in first year at the moment I'm just on a break at I've just gotten I'm feeling I've got a chest infection so I'm at home at the moment.
7	Presenter:	And ah how how long have you been at the boarding school?
8	Caller:	I've just started in September and **I just think that** eh it depends very much on the individual how well they get on or not and I think up to Christmas it was very hard . . .

3 March 1998. Transcript not available online. www.rte.ie

This assimilates more closely to Schegloff's (1986) canonical sequence with identifications, greetings, *how are yous*, and so on. It also contains some features which are very typical of *Liveline* openings, namely:

- the use of display questions (where the presenter asks a question to which she already knows the answer because based on the norms of broadcasting she will have the essence of the caller's reason for calling before her on a computer screen), for example, turn 5 in extract 3.12: *You are attending boarding school at the moment?*
- the use of *formulations*, that is summaries or evaluations (see below) by the presenter to formulate a summary of the caller's reason for calling.

These features are crucial to the establishing of a presenter–caller relationship which is more intimate and less institutional than in the openings illustrated in Cameron and Hills (1990) and Hutchby (1991). In the case of formulations, this assertion is at odds with Hutchby (1991: 129) who says that they are typical of institutionalized discourse where 'one . . . radically observable locus of organization is the bureaucratic requirement for "successful" processing of lay members passing through the institutional machinery'. He sees radio phone-ins as no different in this regard in that callers must be processed.

When we look at formulations in the *Liveline* data, we find that they do not function as part of the 'institutional machinery' but in a pragmatic way as *endearment agents* aiding the reduction in institutional power differential between the presenter and caller. Extract 3.13 is a typical example, where the presenter provides a formulation of the caller's reason for calling in turn 3, which the caller then verifies:

Extract 3.13

1	Presenter:	Now we go on from weighty matters of state to weighty matters of sport and ah sport on television in particular. John good afternoon to you.
2	Caller:	Hello Marian. How are you?
3	Presenter:	**You won't be seeing the match this weekend?**
4	Caller:	Yeah Yeah I believe that's the case I won't be seeing it live anyway on the television . . .

2 April 1998. Transcript not available online. www.rte.ie

Formulations are broadly defined as attempts by the speaker to summarize or paraphrase what he or she has heard or is saying (see Garfinkel and Sacks 1970: 350; Heritage and Watson 1979: 124; Heritage 1985; Iacobucci 1990: 93). Heritage (1985) has identified some specific types of formulations that occur with marked frequency in the institutional context of news interviews. McCarthy (1998: 32) states that formulations can be used by the analyst as direct evidence of the way the discourse is progressing, since they come from the mouths of the participants themselves, rather than from inferences by the analyst. Iacobucci (1990) examines formulations in the context of service encounters (specifically a corpus of telephone calls to a telephone company relating to billing troubles). In line with assertions made above that they have an *endearing agency*, she finds that they can serve in a relational manner to help expedite the call more successfully, and that they can also be used strategically to redirect the talk and so attain a task goal. It could be suggested that the role of the presenter's widespread use of formulations and the callers' expectation that this will be the case is an institutional norm for *Liveline* and that it leads to the setting up of a more symmetrical power semantic between the presenter and the caller. Figures 3.8 and 3.9 compare a typical LBC call opening containing a *caller account* with one from *Liveline* typically containing a *caller formulation*.

Figure 3.8   The Brian Hayes Show caller account (data from Hutchby 1991)

Presenter:	John is calling from Ilford good morning.
Caller:	**h good morning Brian hh what I'm phoning up is about the cricket.**

Figure 3.9   Liveline *presenter formulation*

Presenter:	Anne good afternoon to you.
Caller:	Good afternoon Marian.

Presenter:	**You hated every minute of it?**
Caller:	Every second cried my eyes out every single night.

As we see in figure 3.9, the *Liveline* presenter formulates the reason for calling based on prior knowledge of the caller's opinion, experience or problem whereas in the data from *The Brian Hayes Show* (figure 3.8), callers must provide an account or justification for calling even though it can be assumed, according to normal broadcasting practice, that the LBC presenter also knows the 'business of the call' in advance. The LBC caller is put in a more deficit position, and in terms of the power semantic, this consolidates the exogenous asymmetry between caller and presenter. In contrast, callers to *Liveline* are given an endearing formulation, and are immediately placed in a more symmetrical alignment than the callers in the LBC examples who have to account for themselves in the second turn.

Iacobucci (1990), as mentioned earlier, finds that formulations can serve to attain a task goal in a relational manner and it is proposed here that in *Liveline*, where the overall task goal is disclosure, questions based on formulations in opening sequences have a high endearing agency. To ask a question using a formulation is suggestive of an attempt to listen and to understand rather than to interrogate or to exploit, and so formulations help to establish and maintain the symmetry of the presenter–caller alignment (relational goal) and in so doing facilitate 'honest disclosure' (task goal). Questions and formulations in the openings, based on the presenter's prior knowledge, simulate an intimacy close to that of a normal telephone conversation between friends. That is where the friend who receives the call initiates by formulating the 'problem' or issue which he or she knows to be troubling his or her friend.

Let us look at some quantitative data from the *Liveline* corpus to back up these assertions: 64 per cent of all calls have presenter-initiated formulations of the caller's reason for calling. Table 3.4 profiles the placement of formulations in *Liveline* openings. Note that turn 1 is always the presenter (and subsequently turns 3, 5, 7, etc.):

Table 3.4 Profile of turn placement and occurrences of formulations in *Liveline* call openings

Turn placement		Frequency of formulation
Turn 1	Presenter	9
Turn 2	Caller	0
Turn 3	Presenter	17
Turn 4	Caller	0
Turn 5	Presenter	2
Turn 6	Caller	0
Turn 7	Presenter	1

Also of note is that 68 per cent of formulations are immediately followed by the caller consolidating or validating the reason for calling. We also find that 92 per cent of all formulations by the presenter result in the caller providing a call justification within three subsequent turns. The norm seems to be that calls are successfully established in a collaborative manner, see table 3.5.

Table 3.5 Formulations leading to call justification in *Liveline* call openings

	Total number	Percentage
Number of formulations immediately followed by call justification	19	68
Number of formulations followed by call justification within three turns (inclusive of above result)	26	92

If we concordance the word *you* in the *Liveline* corpus, we can find many examples of its use by the presenter in formulations where it refers to the caller. Figure 3.10 shows a sample.

Figure 3.10 Examples of concordance lines of *you* referring to the caller containing formulations in *Liveline* call openings

Hello Marian. Now as a teenager **you'd** a lot of facial hair? I did. I had facial hair
How are you Marian? **You** don't share Breda's view on tattoos?
Let me go to Vincent. Vincent **you** am graduated more recently now not from Newbridge
You are concerned about the detail about how we're going
Good afternoon. **You** are making history today.   Yes.   What
Hello Ciaran. Hello yeah. **You** also contacted us about what Michael McDowell had to
+so.   It's just **you're** not the wisest of men are you when it comes to
Good afternoon. Now . . . **you** say that when you were younger nobody would even

3.8 Conclusion

This chapter has covered a considerable amount of research in its overview of the types of approaches that have been used in the study of media interactions. We have seen throughout the large influence of conversation analysis as a methodology on the study of media interactions and how insightful its turn-by-turn comparative procedures can be. We have also seen the contribution of discourse analysis to understanding turns within the structure of the exchange. The expectation in institutional discourse settings such as media discourse is for two-part exchanges but this can be contravened and the effect of this change is interesting to examine, as we shall see in chapter 5. On a number of occasions, the pragmatics of the interaction were also noted. The work of Brown and Levinson (1987) has had a particular impact on the study of interaction in asymmetric contexts such as media settings where power is allotted exogenously. As we shall see in chapter 5, presenters in media interactions can try to downplay this power and they do so by careful use of language. Here also we have attempted to introduce the merits of using corpus linguistics as a complementary tool in the study of large amounts of transcribed media data. In our illustration of its application we looked at call openings in an Irish corpus of radio phone-in calls using comparative findings. Quantitative analysis allowed us to show features and tendencies, such as the use of vocatives, the tendency not to mention the location of the caller and, most notably, the tendency of the presenter to formulate the reason for calling. Using a pragmatic interpretation, we were able to look at the interactional effect of the presenter's use of formulations in opening sequences and argue within that framework that they are crucial to redressing the exogenous asymmetry of the interaction. When we compared *Liveline* openings with those from the LBC radio station, we found that the callers to *The Brian Hayes Show* are placed in a deficit position by having to account for their reason for calling. In this eclectic approach, we have been able to look systematically at a large amount of data and we hope to illustrate, using this combined methodological approach in chapters 4, 5 and 6, that it results in a more in-depth framework for the study of media interactions. In the coming chapters we will address how the discourse is managed, how pseudo-intimacy is created and sustained between strangers and how identities are created using the corpus that we have gathered from international television and radio sources so as to audit the three main participation frameworks that prevail in the context of media interactions: (1) between a presenter and someone who is from the private sphere, (2) between a presenter and someone from the public sphere (not including politicians) and (3) political interviews.

4   Managing the discourse

Over the years broadcasting has, on occasion, mischievously indulged in its own . . . experiments with audiences who have apparently preferred to believe that the Martians have landed or that spaghetti grows on trees than disbelieve networks or Richard Dimbleby on BBC's *Panorama* programme.

Scannell (1991: 4)

4.0 Introduction

One of the defining features of dyadic interactions in media discourse is that one participant, usually the presenter or host, has more institutional power than other(s). With this power comes the responsibility for managing the discourse within the interaction. Sometimes, as we shall discuss in chapter 5, the 'manager' can play down this role so as to make an interaction seem more symmetrical or pseudo-intimate, but normally in the reality of the broadcasting context, power is pre-allocated to the presenter or host. This is especially apparent when we look at how interactions are managed. The aim of this chapter is to identify the linguistic features of management, power and control which are used, to varying degrees, in media interactions. In particular, the participation frameworks of radio talk shows, news/political interviews and chat shows will be looked at and compared mainly using instruments of analysis from conversation analysis, discourse analysis and corpus linguistics as outlined in chapter 3.

4.1 The discoursal roles and personae of the media presenter

Before we consider issues of management and control, it is worth considering the role and persona of the media presenter to whom institutional power is allocated. In the context of academic writing, Tang and John (1999) distinguish between three roles that a writer moves between: *societal role*, *discourse role* and *genre role*.

These distinctions can be adapted to the context of media discourse to help us better understand its dynamics. The three roles can be summarized as follows:

- *societal roles:* those which are inherent to a person, for example, mother, father, daughter, American, Singaporean.
- *discourse roles:* the identities that a person acquires through participation in a discourse community, for example, a lawyer, a doctor, a patient, and so on. These roles only hold within the confines of the discourse community. Though Tang and John concede that a discourse role can permeate a societal role when a person becomes defined by his or her job, for example, 'when a prominent medical doctor is identified as such even when he or she is picking up a head of lettuce in the supermarket' (Tang and John 1999: 25).
- *genre roles:* these are identities that are created within a given genre. In the context of undergraduate essay writing, Tang and John (1999) give the example of identities such as: 'architect of the essay'; 'guide through the essay'. In the context of media discourse, we could talk about *manager of the discourse, discourse conduit, confidante,* etc.

Each of us, as Joseph (2004) puts it, is engaged in a lifelong project of constructing who we are, and who everyone is that we meet, or whose utterances we hear or read. For media personae, there are a number of levels at which identity and role interplay in the private and public sphere. Tang and John's distinctions above provide an interesting challenge to the media context. A media presenter is normally a public persona known and familiar in the public sphere. Usually, she would be identified by her discourse role if spotted in the supermarket. She obviously has a private sphere societal identity as a partner, a daughter or a mother, and so on, but in the public sphere, she is identified by her discourse role: a radio or television presenter, for example. In contrast to Tang and John's *three* distinctions, it might be more accurate to say that in the case of media personae, there are two parallel identities at work:

1   the *public sphere persona* (with societal, discoursal and genre identities)
2   the *private sphere persona* (with lesser known societal, discoursal and genre identities).

Crucially in media discourse the genre and discourse identities very often define the societal identity of the presenter. For example, if a news presenter is known for being very tough and dogged in her questioning style (an identity stemming from her genre role), this will interplay with her discourse identity as a presenter and this in turn can have an impact on the types of media interactions that she has as a presenter. For example, a chat show host with a publicly defined persona of being non-judgemental and kind will generate a certain type of pseudo-intimate relationship with her guests and so may achieve a greater level of disclosure (how pseudo-intimacy can be created and sustained linguistically will be explored in detail in chapter 5). By the same token, a presenter can build up a 'hard' public persona. Because talk is the tool of the media persona, his or her discourse traits and style are often open to public comment and a presenter's genre and discourse roles become bound up with their societal role. Here are three examples of public comments about presenters.

Firstly, the well known British television presenter, Jeremy Paxman, is referred to in the following way on the website of The British Film Institute:

> . . . In 1985 he became anchor of the BBC's new 6 *O'Clock News*, and the following year moved to *Breakfast News*. But it was as anchor of *Newsnight* [BBC, 1980–] from 1989 that he has become best known, attracting acclaim – and several awards – for his tough, even savage, approach to interviews . . . Some, however, liken him to a swaggering playground bully, and worry that the result of such an aggressive approach to politicians is a national cynicism which has debased Britain's political life . . .
>
> http://www.screenonline.org.uk/people/id/571500/
> (accessed 18 January 2005)

Another example, taken from *The Irish Times*, refers to a well known Irish radio presenter Marian Finucane. Note again here how the presenter's genre and discourse roles are bound up with her societal role:

> Finucane is justifiably regarded as a uniquely appealing presenter. Her occasional lapses in verbal fluency are more than compensated for by her extraordinary warmth of tone, intelligence and sense of sympathy with the concerns of her listeners. What she isn't is that rarest of breeds, a really accomplished interviewer. This was demonstrated both Tuesday and Wednesday in two contrasting formats . . .
>
> Brown (2000: 11)

Here is another example of comments about British chat show host Michael Parkinson:

> Michael Parkinson has a reputation that is positively Bradmanesque,[1] arguably the greatest the game has ever seen, he plays with style, grace and an unfailing sense of decency. His surname is his passport, he's just about everyone's point of comparison.
>
> http://www.abc.net.au/enoughrope/stories/s1153923.htm
> (accessed 21 January 2005)

These examples of how Paxman, Finucane and Parkinson have been characterized in the public domain are contrasting and it is argued that these publicly created perceptions of media personae can influence the interactions that they have at an interpersonal level in media interactions. We will look closely in this chapter, and in chapter 5, at the linguistic markers that create and sustain such identities as 'swaggering playground bully', 'extraordinary warmth of tone, intelligence and sense of sympathy' and 'style, grace and an unfailing sense of decency'.

4.2 The media presenter within the participation framework

It is worth returning to the theoretical notion of participation framework as defined and discussed in chapter 2. We need to understand the complexity of the presenter/ host position within the participation framework so as to appreciate the management role she has. As a preamble, it is useful to draw on a study of radio DJ monologues by Montgomery (1986) in which he deals with how sections of the audience are frequently addressed in direct terms. He explores *social deixis* as a means of addressing the audience (ibid.: 425) and he notes, in particular, the use of the pronoun *you* which can refer to the whole audience, part of the audience or one member of the audience, for example (see Montgomery 1986: 425, italics added for emphasis):

One person:	Yeh okay then *Bob Sproat* in er Worcestershire er . . . T-shirt on the way to *you*
One region:	Coming up for anyone listening in *Edinburgh*. Because I need *your* legs your hands *your* arms. And the rest of *you* tomorrow morning in Princes Street.
One occupation:	And *anyone who's a typist in a hospital*. And has to read that writing by doctors. Congratulations.
One event:	*If it's your birthday today* then *you* share it with all those people
By age, or other characteristic:	Now *if you're healthy and you're over ten years old*
By star sign:	*Hello Scorpio*. Although it takes a considerable amount of courage to realize a cycle or a chapter in *your* life . . .

Montgomery notes the descriptive lacuna in terms of accounting for the participation status of the 'left over' audience which is not being addressed at such moments. He concludes that the field of reference of audience is in a constant state of flux. It is instructive to note, according to Montgomery, that 'the audience, though directly addressed, is not identified in stable terms but in shifting ones' (1986: 427). By focusing on the language used to address or refer to the audience, we will not only get an indication of the existence of a transaction but also an insight into the interactional pattern within the participation framework.

Other research by Chang (2002) looks at an American phone-in show called *Cartalk* which involves two hosts (the Magliozzi brothers) who take calls about cars and car repair. In her analysis of pronouns within the participation framework of *Cartalk*, Chang finds that personal pronouns can take on a variety of referential meanings in a radio phone-in show owing to 'its ambivalent public–private nature' (ibid.: 148). Within this show, Chang identifies two participation structures: one where the interaction is between the two hosts (and not the caller), while the other option is the interaction between the caller and host(s). If we broaden this out to cover media interactions more generally we can map a number of possible participation frameworks, see figure 4.1.

Figure 4.1 Participation frameworks in media interactions, where P represents the presenter(s)/host(s)

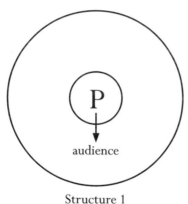

Structure 1
The presenter addresses the audience

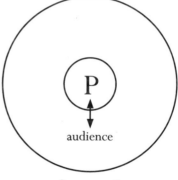

Structure 2
The presenter and the audience interact

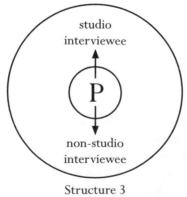

Structure 3
The studio interviewee, the presenter and the non-studio interviewee interact

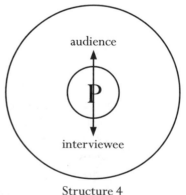

Structure 4
The interviewee addresses the audience

This phenomenon of changing alignments within participation frameworks was discussed by Goffman (1981), who, influenced by the work of Blom and Gumpertz (1972) and Cook-Gumpertz and Gumpertz (1976) on *code switching*, introduced the term *footing* to account for a form of code switching that does not actually involve a code switch, but where clearly there is some substantive change apparent in a conversation. Goffman notes that a persistent feature of natural talk is participants shifting 'alignment of speaker to hearers' and he calls this phenomenon *footing* (Goffman 1981: 128). In his words, it is a 'change in the alignment we take up to ourselves and the others present as expressed in the way we manage the production and reception of an utterance' (ibid.). A change in footing is 'another way of talking about a change in our frame of events' (ibid.). If a presenter wants to make the audience feel ratified and welcome within the participation framework, a deftness of footing is required. This can be realized both physically and linguistically (verbally and non-verbally) on television where a presenter can, for example, turn to a different camera to punctuate an alignment shift. On radio, it is more of a challenge as changes in footing can only be achieved through linguistic (verbal only) means. By way of illustration, let us look at how the presenter in the Irish radio phone-in show *Liveline* (see chapter 3) moves between addressing the audience and the caller (see extract 4.1). The bold print represents what is addressed to the audience and the unmarked script is addressed to the caller.

Extract 4.1

| Presenter: | **Hello there and a very good afternoon to you** <*theme music*> **well we were talking yesterday about ear piercing and nose piercing and piercing any other bits of you ah that may cross the mind** ah Breda your son got a nice little Christmas present pleased you no end anyway? |
| Caller: | Oh yes he did hello Marian . . . |

14 January 1998. Full transcript not available online.
Liveline website www.rte.ie/radio1/liveline/

If we look at this very closely, we can see (in table 4.1) how changes of speaker–addressee alignments are realized linguistically within the participation framework.

Table 4.1 Breakdown of footing pattern of extract 4.1

Item	Utterance breakdown	Function
Greeting	*Hello there*	Ratification of public listenership. This may be a fixed expression in this programme. It also serves as a spatial deictic, in the absence of personal pronoun(s) or vocatives, pointing to and aligning with anyone 'out there' who is listening and so bringing them into the participation framework.
Greeting	*a very good afternoon to you*	Greeting performs a standard opening ritual and the pronoun *you* refers to the ratified listenership. This use of pronoun simulates and defines the interpersonal level of the interaction.
Signature music of the show		Standard programme opening ritual which adds to familiarity of the encounter. The signature music acts as a *summons* in the same way as a telephone ringing in Schegloff's (1986) description of the organization of turns in telephone calls (see chapter 3).
Discourse marker	*well*	Discourse marker focusing the listener and signalling a deictic shift away from the audience and towards the talk so as to formulate background information.
Pronoun	*we*	Solidarity marker (*me here* + *you out there* = *we* in the participation framework). This marks an alignment between the presenter and the audience (for more on *we* see chapters 5 and 6).
Progressive aspect	*were talking*	Indicates incomplete or ongoing action (Quirk *et al.* 1985: 189). It reinforces the semiotic of ongoing dialogue with 'you out there' within the participation framework.
Temporal	*yesterday*	Gives temporal coherence by referring the listener back deictically to yesterday's programme. For those who did not hear yesterday's programme, this performs a different function. It signals that a 'display' or formulation of background knowledge is about to follow.

Formulation	*about ear piercing and nose piercing and . . .*	Fulfils the *responsibility for common ground* on the part of the presenter towards keeping and displaying the cumulative knowledge of the interaction and sets up the *common ground* record (cf. Clark and Carlson 1982: 334, see section 4.3).

Managing footing changes is a key function of the presenter and with it come distinct responsibilities, for example making sure that all participants are included and that all participants have enough background information on the topic of conversation. Let us look more closely now at the latter aspect of presenters' responsibility in managing the discourse, namely their responsibility for maintaining common ground.

4.3 Responsibility for common ground

In political interviews especially, the presenter usually aligns herself with the audience in the opening so as to frame the interview with necessary background information relating to his or her guest and/or to the substantive topic of the interview. This opening alignment serves to bring the audience into the participation framework (as discussed above), but it can also be used to frame the interview in a certain way as we shall explore through examples below. Once this is done, the presenter will normally change footing and align with the interviewee. Consider, for example, the opening of a BBC public interview hosted by Jeremy Paxman in February 2003 with British Prime Minister at the time, Tony Blair, as part of the *Newsnight* programme:

Extract 4.2

Jeremy Paxman: [*addressed to the audience*] Good evening, welcome to a *Newsnight* special in which we'll be cross-examining the Prime Minister on the confrontation with Iraq. After yesterday's performance at the UN America looks more determined than ever to go to war. Our government is George Bush's closest ally yet many here and around the world would not believe the case for war has been made. Tonight in the Baltic Centre in Gateshead we've invited the Prime Minister to face an audience of ordinary people from here in the north-east, all of whom are sceptical about the arguments for war with Iraq. Facing them is the Prime Minister. He has confessed himself worried he has not yet made the case for war. Tonight, taking questions from our audience and from me he'll have the chance to do so. [*change*

of footing, now addressing the interviewee] Prime Minister, for
you to commit British forces to war there has to be a clear and
imminent danger to this country – what is it?

Tony Blair: The danger is that if we allow Iraq to develop chemical,
biological and nuclear weapons they will threaten their own
region, there is no way that we would be able to exclude
ourselves from any regional conflict there was there as indeed
we had to become involved last time they committed acts of
external aggression against Kuwait.

6 February 2003. Full transcript and actual interview available at:
http://news.bbc.co.uk/1/hi/programmes/newsnight/2732979.stm

As we can see from this example, opening frames can be nuanced by the interviewer. In extract 4.3 from a BBC Radio 4 interview on the *Today* programme,
Sarah Montague interviews Rabbi Dr Jonathan Sacks about anti-Semitism in
Europe. Again the reporter brings the audience up to date with the context in
which this interview is set (the aftermath of two suicide attacks on synagogues in
Istanbul in which over 20 people died). This maintenance of common ground is an
important part of the presenter's genre role so that all who enter the participation
framework may have the 'means' to take part in the interaction as ratified hearers.

Extract 4.3

Sarah Montague: [*addressed to the audience*] Synagogues across Europe are
increasing their security after the suicide attacks in Istanbul at
the weekend. The Chief Rabbi here, Jonathan Sacks has been
warning of a rise in anti-Semitism recently and he joins us on
the line. [*change of footing now addressing the interviewee*] What
form have you noticed this rise in anti-Semitism taking?

Rabbi Dr Jonathan Sacks: Well obviously Saturday's attack was absolutely
devastating – an attack on worshippers at prayer, in a house
of prayer – and we've seen this phenomenon elsewhere.
Synagogues have been fire-bombed in France, in Belgium
there've been attacks, synagogue desecrations here in Britain.
It's a very worrying time.

17 November 2003. Full transcript available at
http://www.chiefrabbi.org/articles/other/today17nov.html

Without the background information which the interviewer provides in the first
turn, many listeners may not have had access to the interaction because they

would have lacked key information. In all forms of talk there is a certain obliga-
tion for speakers to take responsibility for the maintenance of common ground
in the interaction. However, in everyday conversations between intimates, this is
normally a shared activity. Clark and Carlson (1982: 334) refer to the *Principle of
Responsibility* whereby parties to a conversation generally adhere to the responsibility of keeping track of what is being said and are responsible for enabling everyone
else to keep track of what is being said:

> Each party keeps a cumulative record of what is being said that becomes part
> of everyone's *common ground* . . . With each contribution to the conversation,
> the current speaker presupposes the common ground already established;
> and all parties, the speaker included, add what is new in that contribution to
> their common ground.
>
> Clark and Carlson (1982: 334
> [italics replace block capitals used in the original for emphasis]

In the context of a media interaction, it is interesting to examine closely how
topics are framed relative to how the presenter chooses to position herself. In
extract 4.3 the interviewer aligns herself with her interviewee by assuming that
anti-Semitism is on the rise in Europe. Consider her alternative for example '*Is
there a noticeable rise in anti-Semitism in Europe?*' This would have placed her in a
more adversarial alignment with her interviewee and would have led to a dif
ferent type of interaction as illustrated in the Paxman Blair interview where
the opening question is 'Prime Minister, for you to commit British forces to war
there has to be a clear and imminent danger to this country – what is it?' (as
shown in extract 4.2). Compare extract 4.3 with extract 4.4, an infamous interview by Ireland's Radio Telefís Éireann reporter Carole Coleman with the US
president at the time, George W. Bush, in the White House on the eve of his
2004 visit to Ireland. The reporter starts by maintaining common ground but the
frame of events that she puts forward is very much at odds with her interviewee's.
This sets the adversarial alignment of this controversial interview from the very
beginning.

Extract 4.4

Carole Coleman: Mr President, you're going to arrive in Ireland in about 24
hours' time, and no doubt you will be welcomed by our
political leaders. Unfortunately, the majority of our public do
not welcome your visit because they're angry over Iraq, they're
angry over Abu Ghraib. Are you bothered by what Irish people
think?

George W. Bush: Listen, I hope the Irish people understand the great values of
our country. And if they think that a few soldiers represents
the entirety of America, they don't really understand America
then. There have been great ties between Ireland and America,
and we've got a lot of Irish Americans here that are very proud
of their heritage and their country. But, you know, they must
not understand if they're angry over Abu Ghraib – if they
say, this is what America represents, they don't understand
our country, because we don't represent that. We are a
compassionate country. We're a strong country, and we'll
defend ourselves – but we help people. And we've helped the
Irish and we'll continue to do so. We've got a good relationship
with Ireland.

24 June 2004. Full transcript available at http://www.whitehouse.gov/news/
releases/2004/06/20040625-2.html actual interview available at
http://www.rte.ie/news/2004/0624/primetime.html

So while presenters hold the responsibility for maintaining common ground within
interviews, they also have the power to frame that common ground and in so doing
may set up an adversarial or sympathetic alignment with the interviewee.

4.4 Institutional power roles and questioning

Institutional contexts such as political interviews, doctor–patient exchanges,
courtroom, and classroom interactions are typified by a pervasion of questions.
In all these cases, the speaker who has contextual status (e.g. lawyer in a courtroom, teacher in a classroom) normally controls the development of the discourse
through questioning (see Coulthard and Ashby 1975; Sinclair and Coulthard
1975; Blum-Kulka 1983; Drew 1985; Fisher and Groce 1990; Heritage and
Greatbatch 1991, among many others). The power-role holder, for example, the
doctor, the barrister, the interviewer, the teacher, decides whether to initiate an
exchange, when to initiate it and with whom. Much work has been done within
the CA model on questions (see chapter 3) and they are viewed as typically the
first part of 'adjacency pairs' (after Schegloff and Sacks 1973: 296) where the production of the first pair-part is followed by the second matching pair-part, setting
up a logical sequential relationship (for a criticism of this view see Tsui 1992;
1994). Sacks notes that in everyday conversation a person who asks a question 'has
a right to talk again afterwards' (1995: 49) and 'as long as one is in the position of
doing the questions, then in part one has control of the conversation' (Sacks 1995:
55). Atkinson and Drew (1979) coined the term 'turn-type pre-allocation', to
refer to how participants in institutional discourse, on entering an institutional

setting, are normatively constrained in the types of turns they may take according to their particular institutional roles. This has obvious relevance to the study of media discourse and in this section we will examine closely the forms and functions of questions in different media contexts.

Greatbatch (1988) provides an important account of the turn-taking system in news interviews. Using the Sacks, Schegloff and Jefferson (1974) description of everyday conversational turn-taking as a comparative, he notes that interviewers and interviewees generally confine themselves to a question–answer sequence respectively, that interviewers do not normally engage in the wide range of responses that questioners typically produce as reactions to answers in ordinary conversation, that if the interviewer uses a statement, it is normally a preface to a question, and so on. Thornborrow (2001c) points out that being in the role of answerer can limit the possibilities available to speakers (see also Drew 1992). Hutchby and Wooffitt (1998) tell us that institutional formats typically involve chains of question–answer sequences, in which the institutional figure asks the questions and the witness, pupil or interviewee is expected to provide the answers. This format is pre-established and normative rules operate which means that participants can be constrained to stay within the boundaries of the question answer framework. This is in contrast to casual conversation, where roles are not restricted to those of questioner and answerer, and where the type and order of turns in an interaction may vary freely (Hutchby and Wooffitt 1998). In an extract from a casual conversation (extract 4.5), we see how questions meander from speaker to speaker as the conversation evolves in real-time, without any pre-allocation of questioning turns or chains of question– answer sequences. This extract, a conversation between four female friends in a bar, is taken from the Limerick Corpus of Irish English (Farr, Murphy and O'Keeffe 2002).

Extract 4.5

[Note that *Twix* and *Snickers* are chocolate bar brand names]

Speaker 1:	I remember when I was in France ages ago when people were calling Twix Radars.
Speaker 2:	Radars?
Speaker 1:	Do you remember when Snickers were called Marathon?
Speaker 2:	Yeah.
Speaker 1:	And Twix were called Radars.
Speaker 3:	Were they called Radars? I never knew that.
Speaker 2:	Yeah the way they change the names of things like films.
Speaker 1:	They just translate them.
Speaker 2:	No they don't 'Analyse This' right, they called it 'Mafia Blues'. It was an English word why change the name?

Speaker 1:	They probably didn't know what analyse meant or something.
Speaker 3:	Yeah do you know the 'Runaway Bride' is that what it is called?
Speaker 2:	Yeah.
Speaker 1:	Yeah.
Speaker 3:	Am in France it was called 'Just married'.
Speaker 2:	'Just married' that was it.
Speaker 1:	What?
Speaker 3:	It was in English like.
Speaker 2:	Yeah you used to see it on buses and it was like 'Just Married' and I was like that's 'Runaway Bride'. And I was like 'oh my god'.
Speaker 3:	I wouldn't mind if they translated it into a French word but it was in English as well.

In institutionalized interactions on television and radio, the presenter is usually the questioner and this pre-allocates a high level of managerial control. The presenter can ask the questions and can decide when to intervene with the next question. However this power can be challenged, as in the extract from the aforementioned RTÉ interview by Carole Coleman with the then American President George W. Bush in 2004 (extract 4.6). When the presenter exerts her power to interrupt a long answer, the President admonishes her and resumes his answer on a number of occasions. He also flouts the question–answer norms in places by replying to her questions with his own questions.

Extract 4.6

Carole Coleman:	And they're angry over Iraq, as well, and particularly the continuing death toll there.
George W. Bush:	Well, I can understand that. People don't like war. But what they should be angry about is the fact that there was a brutal dictator there that had destroyed lives and put them in mass graves and had torture rooms. Listen, I wish they could have seen the seven men that came to see me in the Oval Office – they had their right hands cut off by Saddam Hussein because the currency had devalued when he was the leader. And guess what happened? An American saw the fact that they had had their hands cut off and crosses – or Xs carved in their forehead. And he flew them to America. And they came to my office with a new hand, grateful for the generosity of America, and with Saddam Hussein's brutality in their mind. Look, Saddam Hussein had used weapons of mass destruction against his own

people, against the neighborhood. He was a brutal dictator who posed a threat – such a threat that the United Nations voted unanimously to say, Mr Saddam Hussein +

Carole Coleman: Indeed, Mr President, but you didn't find the weapons of mass destruction.

George W. Bush: **Let me finish. Let me finish. May I finish?** He said – the United Nations said, disarm or face serious consequences. That's what the United Nations said. And guess what? He didn't disarm. He didn't disclose his arms. And, therefore, he faced serious consequences. But we have found a capacity for him to make a weapon. See, he had the capacity to make weapons. He was dangerous. And no one can argue that the world is better off with Saddam – if Saddam Hussein were in power.

Carole Coleman: But, Mr President, the world is a more dangerous place today. I don't know whether you can see that or not.

George W. Bush: **Why do you say that?**

Carole Coleman: There are terrorist bombings every single day. It's now a daily event. It wasn't like that two years ago.

George W. Bush: **What was it like September the 11th, 2001?** It was a – there was a relative calm, we+

Carole Coleman: But it's your response to Iraq that's considered+

George W. Bush: **Let me finish. Let me finish, please. Please. You ask the questions and I'll answer them, if you don't mind.** On September the 11th, 2001, we were attacked in an unprovoked fashion. Everybody thought the world was calm. And then there have been bombings since then – not because of my response to Iraq. There were bombings in Madrid. There were bombings in Istanbul. There were bombings in Bali. There were killings in Pakistan.

Carole Coleman: Indeed, Mr President, and I think Irish people understand that. But I think there is a feeling that the world has become a more dangerous place because you have taken the focus off al Qaeda and diverted into Iraq. Do you not see that the world is a more dangerous place? I saw four of your soldiers lying dead on the television the other day, a picture of four soldiers just lying there without their flight jackets.

George W. Bush: Listen, nobody cares more about the death than I do –

Carole Coleman: Is there a point or place+

George W. Bush: **Let me finish, please. Please. Let me finish, and then you can follow up, if you don't mind**. Nobody cares more about the deaths than I do. I care about it a lot. But I do believe the world is a safer place and becoming a safer place. I know that a free Iraq is going to be a necessary part of changing the world. Listen, people join terrorist organizations because there's no hope and there's no chance to raise their families in a peaceful world where there is not freedom. And so the idea is to promote freedom, and at the same time protect our security. And I do believe the world is becoming a better place, absolutely.

24 June 2004. Full transcript available at http://www.whitehouse.gov/news/ releases/2004/06/20040625-2.html actual interview available at http://www.rte.ie/news/2004/0624/primetime.html

Clayman and Heritage (2002) illustrate how interviewees can use response tokens as a means of asserting the right to intervene in the questioning process. They give the example from Dan Rather's 1988 CBS news interview with the then American Vice President George Bush Snr (see extract 4.7).

Extract 4.7

Dan Rather:	You said that if you had known this was an arms for hostages swap that you would've+
George Bush Snr:	Yes.
Dan Rather:	+opposed it. You also said that+
George Bush Snr:	⌊Exactly
Dan Rather:	+that you did not know that y+
George Bush Snr:	M= may may I May I answer that (0.4) thuh right
Dan Rather:	⌊that wasn't a question. It was a+
George Bush Snr:	⌊Yes
Dan Rather:	+statement
George Bush Snr:	it was a statement and I'll+
Dan Rather:	⌊Let me ask+
George Bush Snr:	+answer it. The President created this+
Dan Rather:	+the question if I may first
George Bush Snr:	+program has testified er stated publicly . . .

Adapted from Clayman and Heritage (2002: 113)

Clayman and Heritage note that this use illustrates the interviewee's abandonment of news interview turn-taking procedures and an incipient escalation into either disagreement with the interviewer and/or attempted interdiction of the interviewer's turn at talk. Clayman (1993) shows how reformulations of inter-viewers' questions by interviewees before responding to them can be used to shift the topical agenda, ignore the second part of a two-part question, agree with some embedded proposition in the question without engaging with the main propo-sition, and so on. In an extract from an RTÉ Radio 1 interview on the morning news programme *Morning Ireland* by radio presenter Cathal MacCoille with Ken Murphy, Director General of the Irish Law Society, we see the interviewee ini-tiate an answer that the presenter feels is moving off topic and he exerts his role-related power within the turn-taking structure to bring the interview back to the question (see extract 4.8).

Extract 4.8

Cathal MacCoille:	. . . Let's start with the easy question am and I'll I'll I'll put it to you Ken Murphy first. What I really want to see from this report today is what? For you?
Ken Murphy:	Ah I love it when you start with the easy questions Cathal. Am we would say that the ah the legal services market in Ireland is very competitive am concentration is ah low rivalry is high+
Cathal MacCoille:	Well could you please answer the question what I would really like to see from the report is what?
Ken Murphy:	What I would like to see is . . .

24 February 2005. Full transcript not available online. *Morning Ireland* website: http://www.rte.ie/radio1/morningireland/

It is interesting to note in this interview between a radio presenter and member of the legal profession, the institutionalized pre-allocation of questioning turns falls to the presenter, but if the context of the interaction were to be within court pro-ceedings, the situation would be reversed.

Beyond the CA paradigm, others have looked at structures of interaction in news and other media interviews within broader frameworks such as critical discourse analysis (Fairclough 1988, 1989, 1992, 1995a, 1995b, 2000; van Dijk 2001) and corpus linguistics (Carter and McCarthy 2002; Chang 2002; O'Keeffe 2002). Within the areas of pragmatics and discourse analysis there have been a number of significant studies that look at question and answer sequences beyond turn sequen-tiality level to address issues such as topic cohesion and coherence and pragmatic aspects, for example, how hedging can be used as a politeness strategy to reduce face threat (see for example Blum-Kulka 1983; Jucker 1986; Blum-Kulka and Weizman 2003; Weizman 2003). Blum-Kulka (1983) looks at the relationship between questions and answers within Burton's (1980) exchange structural model which includes categories such as supportive and challenging conversational moves. This is within the general three-part initiation→response→feedback exchange structure model as outlined by Sinclair and Coulthard (1975) (see chapter 3). In line with extract 4.8, Blum-Kulka notes that non-supportive responding moves by interviewees, according to Burton, are likely to result in challenging moves by the interviewer. Jucker (1986) provides a large-scale study of news interviews and, among other things, looks at topical cohesion, coherence as between question and answer, and vagueness in responses. He puts forward a scale of face-threatening question-types whereby the interviewee can be pressed to commit himself to action, to take responsibility for actions relative to a variety of syntactic types of questions (interrogative, declarative, imperative, moodless). Jucker (1986) also details the options for the interviewer for reducing the pragmatic force of questions by various types of prefaces. We will now look at question types in terms of their syntax and investigate whether there is a correlation between them, role-related power and asymmetry in media interactions.

Question types in context

Much research has been carried out into question types and functions, appropriate questioning strategies and their productivity, especially in relation to classroom discourse (see Perrott 1982; Long and Sato 1983; Brown and Wragg 1993; Farr 2002). Other classroom-related studies look at specific types of questions: for example display questions (Banbrook and Skehan 1989), referential questions (Brock 1986) and echo questions (Farr 2002). Merrit (1976) looked at questions in the context of service encounters within the CA model of question–answer adjacency pairs, where she sees them as integral to the coherence of the customer-request, server–response sequence. In a very different context, Pérez de Ayala (2001) looks at British Members of Parliament (MPs) parliamentary questions and she argues that politeness strategies (after Brown and Levinson 1987) serve to facilitate 'institutional hypocrisy' in that the face-threatening act is core to the genre yet the linguistic devices must be such that they do not cause threat to face. She finds that when an MP flouts 'the rules', he or she is often obliged to reformulate the face-threatening act with face redress. Yokota (1994) looks at questions in Japanese political discussion and argues that question–response sequences, though occupying considerable time, display no clear resolution nor true dispute. Her study shows how the general tendency to avoid overt control and conflict is reflected in the questioning strategies employed in the discourse, which she posits may be linked to a type of 'Japanese-like argumentation' (Yokota 1994: 353). Harris (2001) extends politeness theory beyond informal situations to adversarial political discourse, using Prime Minister's Question Time in the

British Parliament as data. She views the House of Commons as a 'community of practice' (Lave and Wenger 1991) and argues that this provides a way of exploring concepts of politeness and impoliteness against a set of member expectations.

Despite the many studies of questions, there is little consensus on their definition. They can be characterized as a semantic category, an illocutionary act, or to refer to requests or verbal directives, or simply as something that expects an answer (see Tsui 1992). Quirk *et al.* (1985) offer three semantic classes of questions based on the type of answer required:

1   questions requiring yes/no answers
2   wh– questions which require an answer from a range of possible answers
3   alternative questions which expect a reply from two or more options presented in the question.

O'Keeffe (2005) conducted a study of question forms and functions in the context of radio phone-ins. Based on an analysis of 100 questions from the Irish radio phone-in programme *Liveline*, she found the following breakdown (double questions were logged separately as they were seen to have a pragmatically distinct function; see table 4.2).

Table 4.2 Breakdown of distribution of question forms (O'Keeffe 2005)

Question type	Example	Percentage
Yes/no	Is it true that you figure it's associated with all sorts of seedy things like venereal diseases or prostitution or that kind of thing?	33
Wh–	What age is he ah Breda?	28
Declarative	You won't be seeing the match this weekend?	27
Double	How did you know? Did the bush telegraph tell you?	5
Tag	Eh that's the point isn't it?	5
Alternative	And in terms of changing a climate or an atmosphere ah within the course and within the community within society do you believe it's a legislative requirement or ah a debate requirement?	2

This analysis links question type to presenter roles. For example, her findings show that over 60 per cent of declarative questions occur when the presenter is in a 'management' role. Question types are also correlated in terms of the stage of the call in which they occur. Yes/no questions she finds, for example, occur more in *development of topics* (46 per cent) and *call opening* (24 per cent) stages.

It is useful to look at question types in context. The results in table 4.2 from

O'Keeffe (2005) are taken from one specific participation framework which has built up over time and around the discourse identity of the presenter. So as to investigate if there is any correlation between question type and interview type, we will now compare questions in other participation frameworks, firstly in the context of interviews where the presenter and the interviewee are both known personae. Using the same analytical model as used in O'Keeffe (2005), table 4.3 shows a breakdown of 100 questions from the well known BBC 1 *Panorama* interview by Martin Bashir of Diana, Princess of Wales (broadcast November 1995) and these are compared with 100 questions taken from the long-running British chat show *Parkinson* broadcast on ITV and hosted by Michael Parkinson (all from the same show involving interviews with five guests). We find that the question types differ considerably.

Table 4.3 Comparison of question types between Bashir–Diana interview and *Parkinson*

Question type	Bashir–Diana	Parkinson
Yes/no	25	23
Wh–	40	16
Declarative	31	39
Double	3	12
Tag	0	10
Alternative	1	0

Most striking here are the following:

1   Bashir asks 2.5 times more wh– questions than Parkinson (and 1.4 times more than in *Liveline*, see table 4.3)
2   Parkinson asks 4 times more double questions than Bashir (and 2.4 times more than *Liveline*, see table 4.3)
3   Possibly most strikingly Parkinson asks 10 times more tag questions than Bashir and this clearly marks the distinction between informality and deference in the respective interviews.

When we look qualitatively at this data we find that the questions in the Bashir interview appear to be more pre-scripted. The pervasion of wh– questions contrasts sharply with the more casual and seemingly less pre-scripted nature of Parkinson's questioning strategy. The Bashir interview (extract 4.9) appears much more 'controlled' (as much for the interviewer as for the interviewee).

Extract 4.9

Martin Bashir:	**What was the family's reaction to your post-natal depression?**
Diana:	Well maybe I was the first person ever to be in this family who ever had a depression or was ever openly tearful. And obviously that was daunting, because if you've never seen it before how do you support it?
Martin Bashir:	**What effect did the depression have on your marriage?**
Diana:	Well, it gave everybody a wonderful new label – Diana's unstable and Diana's mentally unbalanced. And unfortunately that seems to have stuck on and off over the years.
Martin Bashir:	Are you saying that that label stuck within your marriage?
Diana:	I think people used it and it stuck, yes.
Martin Bashir:	According to press reports, it was suggested that it was around this time things became so difficult that you actually tried to injure yourself.
Diana:	Mmm. When no one listens to you, or you feel no one's listening to you, all sorts of things start to happen. For instance you have so much pain inside yourself that you try and hurt yourself on the outside because you want help, but it's the wrong help you're asking for. People see it as crying wolf or attention-seeking, and they think because you're in the media all the time you've got enough attention, inverted commas. But I was actually crying out because I wanted to get better in order to go forward and continue my duty and my role as wife, mother, Princess of Wales. So yes, I did inflict upon myself. I didn't like myself, I was ashamed because I couldn't cope with the pressures.
Martin Bashir:	**What did you actually do?**
Diana:	Well, I just hurt my arms and my legs; and I work in environments now where I see women doing similar things and I'm able to understand completely where they're coming from.
Martin Bashir:	**What was your husband's reaction to this, when you began to injure yourself in this way?**
Diana:	Well, I didn't actually always do it in front of him. But obviously anyone who loves someone would be very concerned about it.

20 November 1995. Full transcript available at http://www. bbc.co.uk/politics97/diana/panorama.html

Notably, Parkinson uses far more double questions than Bashir. The first question serves more as a discourse marker, or 'starter' (Sinclair and Coulthard 1975) to create a topic boundary allowing the interviewee time to focus on the topic, while the follow-up question provides the interrogative focus. These occur in casual conversation and are associated with the 'online-ness' of speech (Carter and McCarthy 2006; see also Gardner 2004 for a discussion of the use of extended question sequences). These are in contrast with the formality created by the wh–questions in the Bashir interview and they give the impression of a less formal and less controlled interview (see extracts 4.10 and 4.11).

Extract 4.10   Parkinson interviewing American actor Renée Zellweger

Michael Parkinson: What part of [fame] don't you like? Is it just being recognized and all that?

Renée Zellweger: No, it's just the potential for humiliation is substantial you know! [*laughter*] I mean walking down a red carpet in shoes like this right here, with the video cameras on, to document every missed step, to haunt you forever, do you know? . . .

25 December 2004. Full transcripts available at: http://parkinson.tangozebra. com/guest_transcript.phtml?guest_id=55

Extract 4.11   Parkinson interviewing American actor Kevin Spacey

Michael Parkinson: You dedicated the film to your mother? What were the circumstances?

Kevin Spacey: Well since I last saw you my mother passed away, two and a half years ago, and my mother was the first person to introduce me to Bobby Darin. My parents had a pretty great record collection and Bobby was sprinkled in amongst you know Sinatra, Ella Fitzgerald, all the great big bands of that bygone era. And for some reason this movie was the one my mother wanted me to make more than any other film.

25 December 2004. Full transcripts available at: http://parkinson. tangozebra.com/guest_transcript.phtml?guest_id=55

Double and tag question types seem to be an indicator of informality and inter-activity in an interview. If we compare 100 questions in the context of political interviews by the same interviewer but in very different interview contexts, we find considerable difference in the distribution of the question types (see table 4.4). One interview is between BBC *Newsnight* presenter Jeremy Paxman and British

Prime Minister at the time, Tony Blair, in the lead up to the invasion of Iraq and the other is also with Jeremy Paxman in an interview with the author of the Harry Potter books, J.K. Rowling, on the eve of the release of a new book in the series.

Table 4.4 Question types in BBC *Newsnight* by Jeremy Paxman in two different interviews

Question type	Paxman–Blair	Paxman–J.K. Rowling
Yes/no	30	40
Wh–	24	18
Declarative	43	20
Double	3	15
Tag	0	7
Alternative	1	0

Compare an unhedged declarative question in extract 4.12 *And you believe American intelligence?* addressed to the British Prime Minister (leading to an argumentative phase of interaction) with a double question addressed to J.K. Rowling *And what about the money? A lot of people when they suddenly make a lot of money, feel guilty about it. Do you feel guilt?* where the more direct less negotiative alternative might have been: 'Do you feel guilty about all the money that you make?'

Extract 4.12

Jeremy Paxman:	**And you believe American intelligence?**
Tony Blair:	Well I do actually believe this intelligence –
Jeremy Paxman:	Because there are a lot of dead people in an aspirin factory in Sudan who don't.
Tony Blair:	Come on. This intelligence is backed up by our own intelligence and in any event, you know, we're not coming to this without any history. I mean let's not be absurdly naïve about this+
Jeremy Paxman:	Hans Blix said he saw no evidence of hiding of weapons.
Tony Blair:	I'm sorry, what Hans Blix has said is that the Iraqis are not co-operating properly.
Jeremy Paxman:	Hans Blix said he saw no evidence, either of weapons manufacture, or that they had been concealed.
Tony Blair:	No, I don't think again that is right. I think what he said was that the evidence that he had indicated that the Iraqis were not co-operating properly and that, for example, he thought that the nerve agent VX may have been weaponized. And he also said that the discovery of the war heads might be – I think I'm

quoting here – may be the tip of an iceberg. I think you'll find that in that report.

February 2003. Full transcript available at: http://news.bbc.co.uk/1/hi/
programmes/newsnight/2732979.stm

Extract 4.13

Jeremy Paxman: And what about the money? A lot of people when they suddenly make a lot of money, feel guilty about it. Do you feel guilt?

J.K. Rowling: Yes I do feel guilty about it. Definitely I feel guilty.

18 June 2003. Full transcript available at: http://news.bbc.co.uk/1/hi/
programmes/newsnight/3004594.stm

Results so far on question types in context (see tables 4.2, 4.3 and 4.4) show that profiling question types can give some indication as to the symmetric or asymmetric nature of an interview. From the results in tables 4.2, 4.3 and 4.4, we can say that the broader the distribution of question types, then the more symmetrical the alignment seems to be between interviewer and interviewee and the more interactive and informal the interview type. Question types in the more formal, controlled and less pseudo-intimate interviews that we have looked at seem to cluster around the more prototypical question type (yes/no, interrogative and declarative). We will now look at the lexico-grammatical and pragmatic aspects of questioning and control.

4.5 Management and control: within and beyond syntax

Following on from the comparison of question forms and how this correlates with the level of formality or informality in an interview, let us consider how there is variation within question forms. Interviewers can ask questions in many ways, for example, this yes/no question asked by David Frost in a BBC interview with American Secretary of State at the time, Donald Rumsfeld, could have been asked in a number of ways (extract 4.14).

Extract 4.14

The interviewer is referring to the American forces in Iraq

David Frost: Tell me Mr Secretary. Are you where you hoped to be 14 months ago when the war came to an end, or not?

27 June 2004. Full transcript available at: http://news.bbc.co.uk/1/hi/
programmes/breakfast_with_frost/3844047.stm

Here the interviewer chose quite a direct syntactic form which begins with a directive *Tell me* which is followed immediately by a deferential form of address *Mr Secretary*. This use of an honorific title mitigates against the face threat of the directive. Such directives are common in media discourse (as discussed in chapter 2 they are pragmatically specialized in the context of media interactions) and are normally only used by the power-role holder. The use of the honorific title mitigates to some degree what seems a direction (consider the effect of leaving out the honorific title: *Tell me. Are you where you hoped to be 14 months ago when the war came to an end, or not?*), however, the interviewer could have taken a less direct and less confrontational route if he chose to use the inclusive pronoun *we* instead of *you* (. . . *are we where we hoped to be 14 months ago when the war came to an end, or not?*). Compare extract 4.14 with the question in extract 4.15, where the more inclusive pronoun, *our*, is used. This example is taken from an interview by Dorothy McRae McMahon of the Australian Broadcasting Corporation (ABC) with the Archbishop of Sydney, Cardinal Edward Clancy. Here we see a much less direct question which begins by taking responsibility for common ground (as discussed earlier) before posing the question.

Extract 4.15

Dorothy McRae McMahon: Talking of history, I'd often thought that the Catholic church, because of its history in this country, has a special connection with average struggling sort of people; it's never really been seen as the establishment church. Do you think that the church has learned things from that relationship it would have to pass on in terms of **our** understanding of the Australian people and **our** culture?

1 April 2001. Full transcript available at: http://www.abc.net.au/sundaynights/stories/s809819.htm

This question is less direct than the previous example in a number of ways. As we mentioned it uses the inclusive *our understanding of the Australian people and our culture*. It also uses a less face-threatening structure to direct the question to its addressee *do you think* as opposed to *Tell me. Are you where you hoped to be . . .?*. It hedges with vague language such as the pro-form *things*, the structure *in terms of* and the conditional form . . . *would have to pass on* . . . (see Farr and O'Keeffe 2002).

These examples show us how the power-role holder can choose whether to ask direct questions or to hedge the directness of the question. Hedging is an interactional strategy that speakers and writers use in communication, and they do so in a variety of ways and for different reasons (for various definitions see Fraser 1975;

1980; Holmes 1984; Markannen and Schröder 1997; Farr and O'Keeffe 2002). It can involve downtoning, approximating or boosting utterances through lexico-grammatical choices. O'Keeffe (2005) finds frequent examples in her analysis of radio phone-in calls where the presenter chooses structures that are pragmatically softened versions of more direct forms, for example the tag question 'Now you've a few other craft shops *I gather?*'.

Asking one's interviewee difficult questions or challenging what they have said is face-threatening, especially where the interviewee is of higher social status than the interviewer. Confrontational questions are often mitigated or downtoned lexico-grammatically so as to hedge the impact of the challenge as in the first example (extract 4.16)from an interview by Jeremy Paxman with British Prime Minister at the time, Tony Blair.

Extract 4.16

Jeremy Paxman: **You seem to be suggesting or implying, perhaps I'm being unfair to you, but you seem to be implying** there is **some** equivalence between democratically elected heads of state like George Bush or Prime Ministers like Tony Blair and regimes in places like Iraq.

7 February 2003. Full transcript available at: http://news.bbc.co.uk/1/hi/
programmes/newsnight/2732979.stm

Extract 4.17 is an example from Martin Bashir's interview with Diana, Princess of Wales.

Extract 4.17

Martin Bashir: **It's been suggested** in **some** newspapers that you were left **largely** to cope with your new status on your own. **Do you feel** that was your experience?

20 November 1995. Full transcript available at http://www.bbc.co.uk/
politics97/diana/panorama.html

The next extract (4.18) is from an NBC interview with US First Lady Laura Bush [name of interviewee not provided on White House website, 1 February 2005]. Here again notice the use of downtoning forms such as *Privately, if you will*.

Extract 4.18

Interviewer: The Iraq elections this week, they're called a resounding
                 success by your husband. About 60 percent of the Iraqi people
                 went to the polls. **Privately, if you will**, how nervous was he
                 about the turnout for those elections?

> 1 February 2005. Full transcript available at http://www.whitehouse.gov/
> news/releases/2005/02/20050201-12.html

As we saw above in the case of double questions, the choice of question form can
also be a hedge. Tag questions are more associated with casual conversation yet
we find them in media discourse. For example in the comparison between question forms used by the BBC's Jeremy Paxman (see table 4.4) with British Prime
Minister Tony Blair and the author J.K. Rowling, we see that there are seven tag
questions in the latter interview and none in the former (extract 4.19).

Extract 4.19

Jeremy Paxman: That really would be killing the Golden Goose **wouldn't it?**
J.K. Rowling: Yeah well. I'm supposed to be richer than the Queen what do I
                 care?

> 18 June 2003. Full transcript available at: http://news.bbc.co.uk/1/hi/
> programmes/newsnight/3004594.stm

Downtoning can also take place within the turn structure. As we saw in extract
4.7 earlier from the interview between Dan Rather and George Bush Snr, the
interviewee can attempt to subvert the question–answer turn pre-allocation
format so as to contest the institutional power (usually leading to argumentation);
however, this can work the other way. In this light-hearted Paxman–Rowling
interview, Paxman, who is known for direct and tough questioning routines,
flouts the turn pre-allocation conventions by providing follow-up moves leading to
bantering phases during the interview (extract 4.20). At a turn level this downtones the institutional structure making it more resemble a casual conversation
and we even see the interviewee asking questions.

Extract 4.20

Jeremy Paxman: So this is it? [*referring to the next book in the Harry Potter series*]
J.K. Rowling: This is it.
Jeremy Paxman: Are we allowed to look inside it?

J.K. Rowling: Hmmmm. Yes a bit. You can have a look there . . . yes so, that's
                   it.

Jeremy Paxman: How many pages?

J.K. Rowling: 766 . . . All with writer's block, which I think you'll agree is a
                   bit of an achievement.

Jeremy Paxman: But do you find the whole secrecy issue, the need for secrecy, a
                   bit ridiculous?

J.K. Rowling: No.

Jeremy Paxman: Why not?

J.K. Rowling: No not at all. Well, a lot of it comes from me.

Jeremy Paxman: **Really?**

J.K. Rowling: Yeah definitely. I mean, of course one could be cynical, and I'm
                   sure you would be disposed to be so and say it was a marketing
                   ploy, but I don't want the kids to know what's coming. Because
                   that's part of the excitement of the story, and having – you
                   know – sweated blood to create all my red herrings and lay all
                   my clues . . . to me it's not a . . . this is my . . . this is my . . .
                   I was going to say this is my life, it's not my life, but it is a very
                   important part of my life.

Later in the interview . . .

Jeremy Paxman: Is Harry going to become a bolshy teenager?

J.K. Rowling: He's a lot, lot, lot angrier in this book. He really is quite angry
                   a lot of the time and I think justifiably so, look at what he has
                   gone through. It is about time he started feeling a little bit
                   miffed at the hand life has dealt him.

Jeremy Paxman: **Well when you look at a lot of that marketing stuff,
                   that merchandise, when you look at things like the
                   Harry Potter Ice Pumpkin Slushie maker and all that
                   junk.**

J.K. Rowling: **Is that a real thing or have you made it up?**

Jeremy Paxman: **I'm serious. There's a list of about 50 of these things.
                   Harry Potter Embroidered Polo Shirts, the Late Night
                   Ride Towel, Harry Potter and Ron Weasley alarm
                   clock. I mean it goes on and on.**

J.K. Rowling: I knew about the alarm clock. How do I feel about it? Honestly,
                   I think it's pretty well known, if I could have stopped all
                   merchandising I would have done. And twice a year I sit
                   down with Warner Brothers and we have conversations about
                   merchandising and I can only say you should have seen some

of the stuff that was stopped: Moaning Myrtle lavatory seat alarms and worse.

Jeremy Paxman: **I thought that sounded rather fun.**

J.K. Rowling: I knew you were gonna say that. It's not fun. It was horrible, it was a horrible thing.

18 June 2003. Full transcript available at: http://news.bbc.co.uk/1/hi/ programmes/newsnight/3004594.stm

4.6 Conclusion

This chapter has looked at the discourse role of the presenter or host in a media interaction and within this role, the responsibilities that must be assumed within the many alignments that can be found within the participation framework of a media interaction. This power-role holder must ratify the audience at the opening of an interaction by directly addressing them and most importantly by supplying background information to fulfil their responsibilities towards maintaining common ground. Here we also looked in detail at the question forms and strategies and how lexico-grammatical form is linked to interview type. The more prototypical the question types, the more formal and controlled the interview and, conversely, the wider the distribution of question types, the more interactive and informal the interaction. Tag questions and double questions were particularly linked to informality.

We also looked at how the power-role holder can use linguistic devices such as hedges to downplay the force of a question. Finally, we saw how the exchange structure itself can also be a vehicle for downtoning the institutionalized nature of an interaction when the expected initiation→response sequence is replaced with the three part initiation→response→feedback structure (this will be examined in greater detail in chapter 5) and where the interviewee flouts the rules by taking up the initiation move by asking a question. The next chapter will look in great detail at how the power-role holder sometimes seeks to redress the institutional asymmetry by creating pseudo-intimacy with the audience and interviewee. This usually leads to a more intimate type of interaction which can involve greater disclosure on the part of interviewees. We will now examine how this is achieved and sustained through linguistic means.

5 Creating and sustaining pseudo-relationships

. . . a new type of performer: quiz-masters, announcers, 'interviewers' in a new 'show-business' world – in brief, a special category of 'personalities' whose existence is a function of the media themselves. These 'personalities' usually, are not prominent in any of the social spheres beyond the media. They exist for their audiences only in the para-social relation.

Horton and Wohl (1956: 186)

5.0 Introduction

In the previous chapter we focused on how interactions are managed and controlled by various means, here we are interested in a feature of media discourse at the other end of the relational cline, that is how pseudo-intimate relationships are created and sustained. We use the term 'pseudo'-intimate because the participants do not normally know each another and if they do, it is only at the level of public persona, for example when a well known host interviews a well known actor. In particular, we will look at material from television and radio talk shows to identify the linguistic markers of pseudo-intimacy. We will show how lexico-grammatical features more commonly associated with everyday conversation between friends, such as vocative use, response tokens and other pragmatic markers, are often exploited in media interactions so as to simulate and maintain a sense of pseudo-familiarity within the participation framework between the presenter, the interviewee and the audience.

5.1 Simulating intimacy between strangers in media discourse

Let us begin by looking at the notion of intimacy. According to Brown and Ford (1961: 132), it is the horizontal line between members of a dyad (two people speaking) that results from shared values, which may derive from kinship, social identity, gender, nationality or some other common fate, as well as frequent contact. They also note that among the behavioural manifestations of intimacy is a relatively complete and honest level of self-disclosure. In the context of media interactions, we frequently find a level of intimacy that is counter-intuitive to that which should exist between strangers in an interaction, as in the extract (5.1) from *The Gerry Ryan Show*, an Irish morning radio talk show broadcast on Radio Telefís Éireann.

Extract 5.1

Gerry Ryan:	Generally you wouldn't turn away a fella?
Caller:	No absolutely no way.
Gerry Ryan:	And do you get many of them coming over to you in these places that you go to?
Caller:	They usually are married.
Gerry Ryan:	Married men?
Caller:	Yes.
Gerry Ryan:	And do they make it is it abundantly clear that they are only looking for the wild thing?
Caller:	Yes yes.
Gerry Ryan:	Umm.
Caller:	Yes.
Gerry Ryan:	And are you keen on the wild thing?
Caller:	Absol= of course as keen as anybody else.
Gerry Ryan:	Right but under the right circumstances says you.
Caller:	⌊Under the right circumstances and certainly not on the first night.
Gerry Ryan:	Absolutely not well you know don't don't give it away love.
Caller:	Yes yes exactly.
Gerry Ryan:	No.
Caller:	So would you put out the call for me?
Gerry Ryan:	I will. Would you like to describe yourself?
Caller:	Would I like to describe myself?
Gerry Ryan:	Yeah.
Caller:	Five nine.
Gerry Ryan:	Umhum.
Caller:	In in in a very good job not highly paid am I love traditional music I love dancing I love travelling I like good food occasionally.
Gerry Ryan:	Umhum.
Caller:	Am what else is there to say I'm slim built.

Gerry Ryan: Slim?
Caller: Slim yeah.
Gerry Ryan: Yeah.

> Exact date unknown, 2000. Full transcript not available. *The Gerry Ryan Show*
> website: http://wwww.rte.ie/2fm/ryanshow/index2.html

In order to reach such a level of disclosure, there must be some pre-existing pseudo-relationship of trust established between the presenter and callers/guests who are, in reality, strangers. There must be a sense of security that those who are listening are also 'friends'. However, in the absence of kinship relations, this pseudo-intimacy must be based on some sense of common identity and nationality or some other familiarity built up through frequent 'contact' on daily radio. Central to creating and sustaining pseudo-relationships is the development of a sense of co-presence when the show is on air. Given that the 'interaction' between the presenter and the audience is not one of physical co-presence (that is to say, the audience of a chat show or radio phone-in is 'out there'), a sustained sense of commonality must be simulated to transcend physical distance.

The role of daily or regular contact with the audience, bracketed by the same rituals of theme music and familiar greetings are not to be underestimated in the process of constructing pseudo-relations within the participation framework of a programme. Familiarity of routines, small talk about the weather or everyday events, and so on, bridge the relational gap between stranger and friend. In extract 5.2 from an opening of the American talk show *The Oprah Winfrey Show*, we can see how the host, a well known public persona, pitches her level of intimacy as very close and personal by aligning herself with great empathy towards her audience, addressing them directly and sincerely.

Extract 5.2

Oprah Winfrey: Well you know I've often said this. I believe it. It's why I don't
                 have any children myself. It's because I believe that being a
                 parent is just the world's toughest job. Today we are going to
                 meet mothers and fathers who were put to the ultimate test . . .

> (taken from Gregori-Signes 1998b: 319)

Horton and Wohl (1956/1979)[1] were one of the first to write about the way the media and media performers create the illusion of an interpersonal relationship. They referred to it as a 'para-social' relationship because it is based on an implicit agreement between the performer and the audience that they will pretend the relationship is not mediated and is carried on as though it were face-to-face. In their study of *The Johnny Carson Show*, Horton and Wohl found that many viewers, in 1950s America, claimed that they 'knew' Johnny Carson better than their next-door neighbour:

> a new type of performer: quiz-masters, announcers, 'interviewers' in a new 'show-business' world – in brief, a special category of 'personalities' whose existence is a function of the media themselves. These 'personalities' usually, are not prominent in any of the social spheres beyond the media. They exist for their audiences only in the para-social relation.
>
> Horton and Wohl (1979: 186)

Horton and Wohl note that television and radio personae can claim and achieve an intimacy with what are literally crowds of strangers, and this intimacy, even if it is an imitation of the real thing, is 'extremely influential with, and satisfying for, the great numbers who willingly receive it and share it' (1979: 187).

Simulating co-presence

A key factor in the creation of pseudo-intimacy is the simulation of co-presence. Scannell (1991) notes that while the central fact of the communicative context of broadcasting is that it speaks from one place and is heard in another, the design of talk in radio and in television recognizes this and attempts to bridge the gap by simulating co-presence with its listeners and viewers. To set this within our participation framework model, we have made the case in chapter 2 that the audience must be seen as ratified hearers. We will now look at how this is brought about through recurring patterns of interaction and language use. Though the interaction between the television or radio host (as speaker) and the audience (as addressees) is a unidirectional one, it is fundamental to the study of media interactions to acknowledge that a collective sense of 'co-presence' is something that all participants are complicit in, and as such its construction is a generic activity. Duranti (1986: 242), referring not just to media genres but to talk in general, points out that audience co-authorship 'represents the awareness of a partnership that is necessary for an interaction to be sustained, but it is often denied by analysts and participants alike'.

One of the means of bridging the co-presence gap between presenter and audience, particularly on radio, is where the presenter tries to add authenticity to his persona, as in the example from *The Nick Abbot Show* (LBC), a London-based talk radio show, where the presenter's phone rings with a personal call while he is on air (extract 5.3).

Extract 5.3

Kev:	One of the guys who works here said 'I've always listened to Nick but one thing about him lately [*phone rings in background*] is that he's gone effects crazy.'
Nick Abbot:	Hang on a minute, my phone's ringing!
Kev:	What! [*laughs*]
Nick Abbot:	How unprofessional.
Kev:	Find out who it is.
Nick Abbot:	Blimey, it's my best mate. [*answers phone*] Hang on. Steve? [*Steve in background: Hello Nick?*] Steve, I'm on the air, are you mad? [*Kev laughs, you can hear Steve mumble in the background*] Yeah and you're on the air as well. I work till 10 on Friday. [*Steve in background: 'Oh, I'm so sorry.' Everyone laughs*] You're on the air now, national radio . . . [*laughs*] So what have you been up to? [*Steve says something*] Why is my phone switched on, I don't know that's a good question. [*Steve in background: I thought you finished at 9*] No, I finish at 10. So can you call me back later because I'm busy now. I get paid a lot of money to do this. [*Laughter*] [*Steve in background: Can people hear me?*] Can people hear him?

Exact date unknown, 1998. Full transcript available at
http://www.w2s.co.uk/nick-abbot/transcripts/lewis15.html
(see also http://www.w2s.co.uk/nick-abbot/transcripts/indexfrm.html)

This makes for greater authenticity in terms of building up a persona that is more than just a public one. The notion that the presenter's mobile phone could ring while he is on air and that he has a friend who wants to know what time he is off work makes the presenter seem more like 'one of us', someone who is an ordinary person with a job, and so on, thus helping to endear the audience to the presenter and break down the public persona. This is further exemplified in another extract from the Irish morning radio talk show *The Gerry Ryan Show* (extract 5.4) on RTÉ where the presenter gives domestic details which most of his audience can relate to; again this serves the function of constructing a persona of the presenter as 'one of us'. He is someone you can call, someone who will understand.

Extract 5.4

Gerry Ryan:	It's Wednesday morning. Anna Good morning to you.
Caller:	Good morning Gerry how are you?
Gerry Ryan:	Oh well <*yawning*> I'm good. A little bit of sunshine this morning.

Caller:	Oh well that's good.
Gerry Ryan:	It's had a positive effect on me anyway dunno about every=.
Caller:	Well I think it has on everybody hasn't it?
Gerry Ryan:	It took me feckin well half an hour to put out the bins this morning that was the only thing that depressed me and then do you know do you ever have one of these ones where you know everything is going well Ryan then decides that he is going to put five or six of plastic sacks up on top of one bin that I'm wheeling right?
Caller:	Yeah.
Gerry Ryan:	And then puuf.
Caller:	And they all fall.
Gerry Ryan:	No one of them explodes all over me
Caller:	Stop.
Gerry Ryan:	<*laughter*>
Caller:	That's horrible.
Gerry Ryan:	<*laughter*> and I know you know that one or two of me neighbours are looking out at going 'look at the big eejit I knew that was going to happen to him'.

Exact date unknown, 2000. Full transcript not available. *The Gerry Ryan Show* website: http://www.rte.ie/2fm/ryanshow/index2.html

Another common way of building co-presence is for presenters/hosts to refer to their physical surroundings so as to bring the audience closer. A concordance search of the word *right* in the media corpus yields many examples of this. Figure 5.1 shows some.

Figure 5.1 Concordance lines of *right* in the media corpus exemplifying reference to physical surroundings as a means of creating a sense of co-presence

Mark: Right. She's actually **right behind me** warming up,

remont at Leatherby's and **then right here at Lake Elizabeth**. Lovely spot. Kind of a

women. Kristi: Right. Doug: **Right here in Fremont**, you got Leatherby's Ice Cream.

oxide and **I got the tablespoons right here**, I got Bob in a headlock, and I'm ready to

n a red carpet **in shoes like this right here**, with the video cameras on, to document

activities. **And you roller blade right here**. Kristi: Yes! It's been a lot of fun.

sing. He's a tall man. Well, **he's right here**. You can see for yourself. CARSON: You

ve three but you know, but **we're right outside of the city limits** so we can have more.

Footing as audience ratification

In chapter 4 we looked at footing and presenter alignment in the context of management and control. Changes in footing can also serve to ratify the audience as addressees within the participation framework of a programme. A presenter's ability to move between the audience and interviewee as addressees is one of the most core means of making the audience feel part of the participation framework of a television or radio talk show. Most television and radio show hosts begin and end a show by aligning with their audience as part of the communicative ritual of the interaction. Chat shows usually open with the presenter addressing the audience directly and not the guest. Extract 5.5 is an example from the ITV television chat show *Parkinson* where actor Barbara Windsor is the guest.

Extract 5.5

Michael Parkinson: [*addressing the audience*] My next guest is part of our national
                      life like Big Ben and jellied eels. To describe her simply as
                      an actress misses the point. To the public she's a national
                      treasure. Welcome please, Barbara Windsor. [*applause*]

25 December 2004. Full transcript available at http://parkinson.tangozebra.
com/guest_transcript.phtml?guest_id=55

In an extract (5.6) from *The Ricki Lake Show*, an American talk show, we see another example of inclusive alignment within the participation framework. The guests are aligned with the presenter and each other, then the presenter, using the pronoun *we* and the temporal reference *today* pivots her alignment to include the studio and non-studio audience and, following applause, she re-aligns so as to address all of the audience directly.

Extract 5.6

Valery: She does a hundred miles an hour driving down the highway
               [*studio audience reaction*] when it's like thirty-five.
Ricki: And I'm scared that your two kids are never gonna have a
               mother to see them grow up.
Valery: I've tried to tell her that.
Patsy: I feel that the only love that I do have is with my children and I
               admit I have a problem and that I do need help.
Ricki: Well hopefully **we** can get that help for you **today** alright?
               [*audience applause*] **Next up we will meet a girl who says**

**that when she gets drunk she likes to just get in her
car and drive. Don't go away.**

(taken from Gregori-Signes 1998b: 343)

Let us now look at other linguistic markers of pseudo-intimacy common to certain
types of radio and television interactions.

5.2 Markers of pseudo-intimacy in media discourse

Here we will focus in particular on how pronouns, vocatives and some pragmatic
markers (response tokens and discourse markers) can be used in media discourse
to create an illusion of an interpersonal relationship between strangers by drawing
on linguistic features that are normally used in casual conversation between real
friends and intimates.

Pronouns

Pronouns, according to Wales (1996: 50) are characterized by a diversity of
ever-changing roles and functions and 'their flexibility in the minds and mouths
of the users of English are often ignored by grammarians'. Because the proto-
typically human referents of pronouns have a wide variety of possible social roles
and stances, she maintains, interpersonal pronouns are therefore rarely neutral
in their reference (for other work on pronouns see McCarthy 1994; Pennycook
1994; Wales 1996; Wortham 1996; Chang 2002; O'Keeffe 2002). Pronouns can
be used to include as well as exclude since by referring to oneself, one's world and
that which is in it, one does so by reference to that which is not. As Pennycook
(1994) notes, pronouns can set up exclusions and construct 'others', as we shall
explore in chapter 6. In media interactions, inclusive pronoun choices, however,
can help create and sustain the illusion of an interpersonal relationship between
strangers (after Horton and Wohl 1979).

O'Keeffe (2002) and Farr and O'Keeffe (2002) show that the frequency distribution of the pronouns *I*, *you*, *he*, *she*, *we* and *they* in a corpus of Irish radio phone-in
programmes is very similar to the distribution pattern for pronouns in casual conversation as detailed in Biber *et al.* (1999: 334). This suggests, quantitatively at
least, that media encounters (on chat shows, news interviews, phone-ins, etc.)
display an interpersonal rather than representational level of interaction (that is,
reciprocity between *I*, *you*, and *we* are more prevalent than *she*, *he*, *it* and *they*).
This is also consistent with the findings of Montgomery (1986) who notes that DJ
radio monologue operates more frequently along the axis between the first and
second person (*I* and *you*). As he explains, it is interpersonal and socio-relational

rather than representational (ibid.: 423–5). Radio monologues are an interesting focus of study for pronoun use. The presenter must assume non-present participants and single-handedly create a sense of commonality within the programme's participation framework (see Montgomery 1986 for an example of this).

When we compare the frequency of the pronouns *I* and *you* in our corpus of media interactions with their rank order in other spoken corpora, we also find that it most resembles interactions from casual conversations. This again suggests that a high level of interpersonal (*I/you*) interaction is achieved. Compare also the position of the representational pronoun *it*. Here we use data from the following sources:

1   the media corpus, a 271,553-word corpus of media interactions including chat shows, news interview, phone-ins, etc. (see chapter 3).
2   the Limerick Corpus of Irish English (LCIE), a one-million word corpus of spoken Irish English designed according to the same matrix as CANCODE (see McCarthy 1998; Farr, Murphy and O'Keeffe 2002).
3   the Limerick-Belfast Corpus or Corpus of Academic English (LIBEL), a one-million word corpus of academic interactions in a university context. Note that only 500,000 words of LIBEL are used here.
4   the Cambridge and Nottingham Corpus of Discourse in English (CANCODE), a five-million word corpus of mostly British English casual conversation (see McCarthy 1998). The CANCODE results here are taken from Carter and McCarthy (1997a).

Table 5.1 Comparison of top ten word lists frequencies across spoken corpora and sub-corpora

	Media	*Shop (LCIE)*	*Academic (LIBEL)*	*LCIE*	*CANCODE*
1	the	**you**	the	the	the
2	and	of	and	**I**	**I**
3	**I**	is	of	**you**	and
4	to	thanks	**you**	and	**you**
5	**you**	it	a	to	it
6	a	**I**	to	it	to
7	that	please	in	a	a
8	of	the	that	that	yeah
9	it	yeah	it	of	that
10	in	now	is	yeah	of

Pronouns such as *we*, *our* and *us* are central to the process of establishing and maintaining a sense of commonality and inclusion in everyday casual conversation between people who have a real common bond. In extract (5.7) from the LCIE, in a conversation between three former school friends, the use of *we* reinforces the bond that still exists between them. Three female speakers are reminiscing about a teacher in their former school.

Extract 5.7

Speaker 1:	Do you remember the leather jacket he had for
Speaker 2:	⌊twenty years
Speaker 1:	And his briefcase. Is he still there?
Speaker 3:	No he's gone.
Speaker 1:	Is he gone? Why what is he doing?
Speaker 2:	He was going out with my aunt's friend.
Speaker 3:	He left after **we** left.
Speaker 1:	Really.

Even though a television or radio talk show host does not normally know the audience as individuals, an inclusive 'we' relationship is carefully built up through consistent pronoun use. Figure 5.2 shows some random examples from our media corpus.

Figure 5.2 Extract of concordance lines of *we* use by television and radio hosts

you stay with us me for a second Monica **we**'ve another caller on the line ah I be
MP: Now, here to the left is a guy that **we** all know, Don Bleu. K: Oh sure
        Oh, it's a pleasure.   D: **We**'ll see you on December 17th.
d I think she's excited about doing it. **We**'ll let her catch her breath and talk
s head) . . . **we**'ll talk about this while **we** look at some more music. Jabba talk
excessive prejudice against tattoos but **we**'ll see **we**'ll see okay?
    Now **we** move ah north interesting **we**'re just talking to somebody in Belfast
a dozen times, but I'll ask them when **we** come back. Kate: That's okay. Sure.
skate or are skating already over here. **We**'ll show you how you can come down her
ive a live performance also later. And **we**'ll be back with more on Morning on 2
ed shows on American television . . . Can **we** talk about your dog?   JM: Yes   E
I even want to do this any more. Look **we** got all these calls backed up here, a

Random samples of *us* (Figure 5.3) also show consistent use of the pronoun to reinforce inclusion within the participation framework of the presenter and audience as a group familiar to each other over time.

Figure 5.3 Sample concordance lines of *us* from the media corpus

in anti-semitism recently and he joins **us** on the line: What form have you noti
been on this programme and talking to **us** before.   Yeah   These a
      Mel Brooks.(*Applause*) M: Tell **us** about this West End show that you've
            Keri, can you tell **us** about the changes your character is g
those little video bits. Can you give **us** a little
      s and applauds] D: Come on, fill **us** in, come on!   Kristi: You guys have
      it in this country. Well give **us** a hint.   Well it's to do with
thank you for sharing that story with **us**.   Alright Gerry.   If yo
a miniDisc machine that would allow **us** to do this. Put it in and it's a simp
where how, etc. And that's all from **us** for today back with you tomorrow at t
            hunters and the Examiner tells **us** that two thousand eight hundred was t
of the matter is that they talk to **us** here on the radio and elsewhere and t
Okay what do you want to talk to **us** about?   Am I'm ringing about s
            I will do.   Tell **us** how   Well he has feelers out a
unique job?   Yes.   Ah give **us** a hint.   There is nothing else

When we look at *our*, we again find examples of consistent inclusion. It is worth noting that the referential ambiguity of the pronouns *we*, *us*, *our* in English facilitates such inclusion.

Figure 5.4 Sample concordance lines of *our* from the media corpus

ng anywhere.   M: Well that's to **our** benefit. Kevin Spacey, thank you.
EW CALL   Now yesterday ah one of **our** callers referred to the fact that he
      ike your country and it won't look like **our** country. But it will certainly look
s came home and you would not convince **our** first caller that it was a good idea
                  Our guest is Roberta Pearson, editor of
Stephanopoulos: Good morning, everyone. **Our** guest this morning, fresh off the co
      e small screen and into the subculture. **Our** guests include Joss Whedon, the crea
hi, whose won an Olympic gold medal and **our** hearts ice skating all over the world
.um, www.mns . . . uh, I forgot it. It's on **our** hotline. Scott, thanks for being her
t.   Okay just for the benefit of **our** listeners lets backtrack a little bi
            Donny: **Our** next guest fell in love with ice-ska
mbering up for her performance later on **our** show and of course getting ready for
g icon. We have seen her grow up before **our** very eyes into a mature person, on a

Let us turn now to the role of vocatives in pseudo-intimate media discourse.

Vocatives

Vocatives are closely related to 'address terms' (Jefferson 1973) or 'forms of address' (Brown and Gilman 1960; Brown and Ford 1961; Wood and Kroger 1991), but as Leech (1999) points out, a term of address is any device used to refer to the addressee of an utterance, while a vocative is just one particular type of address term. Vocatives can take many forms: endearments (*honey*), kinship terms (*Daddy*), familiarizers (*dude*), first name familiarized (*Johnny*), first name full form (*John*), title and surname (*Mr Smith*), honorific title (*Sir*), nickname (*Oggmonster*), and even elaborated nominal structures such as: *those of you who have brought your own sandwiches* (see Biber *et al.* 1999). Additionally, impersonal vocatives may occur in utterances such as 'someone get that phone, will you!' (see McCarthy and O'Keeffe 2003; Carter and McCarthy 2006). An addressee can potentially be referred to using any of these forms (gender and age and institutional hierarchies being the only restriction in the case of titles). Choice of vocative form therefore provides an index of (projected or assumed) relationship between speaker and addressee and for this reason they play a crucial role in creating and sustaining pseudo-intimacy (or distance) within media interactions.

Brown and Gilman (1960) conducted a study of great significance and influence which looked at forms of address and included seminal work on pronouns (particularly the *tu–vous*, or T–V, opposition exemplified in languages such as French, which marks social intimacy and distance, respectively). Their study was framed in terms of power semantics. Zwicky (1974) looked at the range of nouns and noun phrases that can be used vocatively in English. She suggests that English vocative forms are both idiomatic and sociolinguistically marked and she notes that 'there is virtually no affectively neutral vocative' (ibid.: 796). In the field of pragmatics, Wood and Kroger (1991) argue that the research in this area needs to be integrated with a more general theory of language use, such as Brown and Levinson's politeness theory (1987). In an attempt to address this they applied Brown and Levinson's theory in their study of forms of address and their relationship to politeness. They conclude that negative politeness in Brown and Levinson's terms (i.e. the need to protect the recipient from coercive threats to face) outweighs positive politeness (the need to avoid threats to face that suggest lack of esteem), and that status commonly takes precedence over solidarity, all of which is reflected in choice of address terms. Positive politeness, on the other hand, which requires the achievement of closeness and common identity, can be attended to by 'personalization' and by the use of so-called identity markers. The mutual use of first name (FN) signals that the speaker and hearer 'belong' (ibid.: 147). In addition, Wood and Kroger (1991) note that forms of address have specific pragmatic functions: they open communicative acts and set the tone of the interchange that follows and they establish the relative power and distance of speaker and hearer.

Jaworski and Galasiński (2000) examine TV political debates and make some interesting observations on how socio-political changes in societies can alter the range of acceptable forms of address. They quote research showing how the address-forms *brother* and *comrade* emerged after the Iranian and Chinese revolutions, respectively (see also Minaeva 1998 on how similar changes happened in the post-Soviet period in Russia). The data in Jaworski and Galasiński's study involved Poland's former trade union leader Lech Wałesa, and they show how marked choice of working-class-style vocatives by one of his debating opponents is used to claim political membership and intimacy with the recipient, Wałesa. On the other hand, the use of a distancing form of the vocative in return by Wałesa 'contributes to positive self-image building' (ibid.: 80), projecting himself as a strong national leader. Jaworski and Galasiński conclude, with regard to the use of vocatives, that 'the speaker does not use the vocative to attract the attention of his addressee, but to define the interpersonal space between them' (ibid.: 79).

Wilson and Zeitlyn (1995) investigate a wide range of person-referring expressions, including vocatives. Their analysis is based on a small-scale corpus of family dinner table conversations (consisting of 1,242 utterances which yielded 1,100 person-referring expressions). The vocatives in their corpus are realized as just simple names (no titles) or kinship terms, while a range of complex person-referring expressions are used to refer to non-present referents. They note that vocatives are common at topic boundaries, with some 27.5 per cent of topic-changing utterances being accompanied by vocatives. Leech (1999) carried out a corpus-based study of vocative use (see also Biber *et al.* 1999). He used a combined British and American spoken English corpus totalling 100,000 words, with 50,000 words from each variety. Leech's study considers vocatives formally, functionally and semantically/pragmatically. He identifies semantic categories based on degree of familiarity (e.g., familiarized FN such as *Jackie*; honorific titles such as *Prof.*; others such as *silly*, *lazy*, and so on). Notably, he identifies three discrete functions of the vocative: (1) summoning attention, (2) addressee identification and (3) establishing and maintaining social relationships.

McCarthy and O'Keeffe (2003) compared vocatives in a corpus of radio phone-in calls to the Irish radio phone-in *Liveline* and casual conversation data taken from the spoken corpus CANCODE. They classified vocatives in both datasets according to the contexts in which they occurred and arrived at functional headings connected with topic and turn management, face concerns, general relational concerns, humour/badinage and summons. Overall, they found that the casual conversation data revealed a preference for vocatives in relational, topic management, badinage and face-saving contexts, while the radio data revealed a tendency for vocatives to be used more in the management of phone calls, turn-taking, topic management and face-saving contexts. In the radio data they noted that vocatives occurred with greater frequency at initial position in an utterance, whereas in the casual conversation data, final position vocatives were most common. They also found that in neither dataset did vocatives seem to be necessary except in a small number of cases where they were needed to summon a speaker. Overwhelmingly, they concluded that the vocative serves pragmatic functions.

Vocatives are frequently used in casual conversations between friends as markers of intimacy and solidarity as in the extract (5.8) from a conversation between two close friends taken from LCIE where one is telling the other about how she and her boyfriend broke up.

Extract 5.8

Mary:	. . . 'so it's over' I said 'I don't love you'. I said 'I care for you very much' I said 'but there's nothing going on'. I said 'you're more than welcome' I said 'to come to John's wedding as long as you come' I said 'knowing that there is no hope for us getting back together'. I said 'It's over Joe. Finito'.
Susie:	Fair play to you. You wouldn't have done that ah even a couple of months ago.
Mary:	No I wouldn't **Cathy** I'm as strong as an ox. <*laughing*>
Susie:	How did that come out of the blue?
Mary:	**Cathy** it was just the way he was crying down the phone sobbing like a baby and I was there bluh give me a bucket will you for God's sake after all I've been through . . . do you know what I mean?
Susie:	Yeah.

McCarthy and O'Keeffe (2003) provide the following example from CANCODE where again the vocative is not required in the utterance other than to serve a relational function. In extract 5.9 a group of female young friends are discussing weight problems (<$X> marks speaker turns).

Extract 5.9

<$3> You're not fat **Jane.**
<$1> I will be if I'm not careful.

As McCarthy and O'Keeffe have noted, vocatives can be used to mitigate face threat. In the next example (5.10), a tense moment where a caller refuses to answer a very awkward question is defused by her pragmatic choice to use the presenter's name (Marian) to downtone the threat to face. In this interview (from an Irish phone-in show, *Liveline*) an Irish nurse, Monica Hall, was wrongly accused of murdering her colleague, Helen Feeney, in Saudi Arabia some years earlier. Here in the body of the call, having heard the arduous tale of how Monica Hall was forced to confess to the murder (along with her then husband), the presenter focuses on the specifics of the crime. The absence of the vocative and the repeated use of the distancing device *I understand that* would have risked making the caller's response more adversative.

Extract 5.10

Presenter:	What did happen to Helen Feeney?
Monica Hall:	Am **I understand that** she was battered to death.
Presenter:	How where when why?
Monica Hall:	I have no answers for those for those questions **Marian**. Ah **I understand that** it was in her apartment that's where her body was found.

20 May 1998. Transcript not available online. *Liveline* website
www.rte.ie/radio1/liveline/

In another extract from the same show (5.11), we see the mitigating function of vocative use where the presenter and a caller get into an argument. The caller is claiming that marital breakdown is becoming fashionable and even desirable in Irish society. The presenter contradicts the caller. The caller then interrupts (marked +) with a challenge. The vocative tagged onto this challenge is crucial in mitigating the face threat at this fraught moment.

Extract 5.11

Caller:	. . . but as time goes on it's cool these days ah and pardon me for using that word because it's a slang word I don't like. But as they say it's cool to say 'I'm separated'. It's attractive.
Presenter:	Is it?
Caller:	It's attractive to ah men and women.
Presenter:	Well now I've interviewed a fair number of separated people down through the years and I don't think anybody ever found it cool or a great experience. I mean there was an awful lot of pain and that kind of+
Caller:	How long+
Presenter:	+thing.
Caller:	+ago is that **Marian**?
Presenter:	Well on and off over the years.

2 April 1998. Transcript not available online. *Liveline* website
www.rte.ie/radio1/liveline/

In examining the use and role of vocatives in marking intimacy, it is interesting to focus on how their form and function differ according to the speaker relationship and interaction type (for example whether it is symmetrical or asymmetrical). Firstly, let us look at the most formal situations, that is, where the interviewer and interviewee are both known as public personae and where the interviewee is of high status. In these situations, we find that the interviewer shows deference by using the honorific title which is in line with the findings from Wood and Kroger (1991) that negative politeness (i.e. the need to protect the recipient from coercive threats to face) outweighs positive politeness (the need to avoid threats to face that suggest lack of esteem), and that status commonly takes precedence over solidarity. Extract 5.12 shows opening and closing extracts from an infamous interview (referred to in chapter 4) which took place in the Library of the White House, in 2004 between Irish reporter for RTÉ, Carole Coleman, and the President of the United States of America at the time, George W. Bush.

Extract 5.12

Opening

Carole Coleman: **Mr President,** you're going to arrive in Ireland in about 24 hours' time, and no doubt you will be welcomed by our political leaders. Unfortunately, the majority of our public do not welcome your visit because they're angry over Iraq, they're angry over Abu Ghraib. Are you bothered by what Irish people think?

Closing

Carole Coleman: **Mr President,** thank you very much for talking to us.

George W. Bush: You're welcome.

> 24 June 2004. Full transcript available at http://www.whitehouse.gov/news/releases/2004/06/20040625-2.html actual interview available at http://www.rte.ie/news/2004/0624/primetime.html

This interview was confrontational at times and there are further examples where the interviewer resorts to vocative use in an attempt at negative politeness so as to mitigate face-threatening moments where she interrupts and contradicts the President of the United States in the White House (extract 5.13).

Extract 5.13

George W. Bush: Look, Saddam Hussein had used weapons of mass destruction against his own people, against the neighborhood. He was a brutal dictator who posed a threat – such a threat that the

United Nations voted unanimously to say, Mr Saddam Hussein+

Carole Coleman: Indeed, **Mr President**, but you didn't find the weapons of mass destruction.

George W. Bush: Let me finish. Let me finish. May I finish? He said – the United Nations said, disarm or face serious consequences. That's what the United Nations said. And guess what? He didn't disarm. He didn't disclose his arms. And, therefore, he faced serious consequences. But we have found a capacity for him to make a weapon. See, he had the capacity to make weapons. He was dangerous. And no one can argue that the world is better off with Saddam – if Saddam Hussein were in power.

Carole Coleman: But, **Mr President**, the world is a more dangerous place today. I don't know whether you can see that or not.

George W. Bush: Why do you say that?

Interviewer: There are terrorist bombings every single day. It's now a daily event. It wasn't like that two years ago.

24 June 2004. Full transcript available at http://www.whitehouse.gov/news/ releases/2004/06/20040625-2.html actual interview available at http://www.rte.ie/news/2004/0624/primetime.html

In another famous interview broadcast on November 1995 on BBC 1's *Panorama* programme, Martin Bashir interviews Diana, Princess of Wales (extract 5.14). Here again the interviewer shows negative politeness to his higher status interviewee by using the honorific title.

Extract 5.14

Opening

Martin Bashir: **Your Royal Highness**, how prepared were you for the pressures that came with marrying into the Royal Family?

Diana: At the age of 19, you always think you're prepared for everything

. . .

Closing

Martin Bashir: **Your Royal Highness**, thank you.

20 November 1995. Full transcript available at http://www.bbc.co.uk/ politics97/diana/panorama.html

On the long-running BBC Sunday morning television programme *Breakfast with Frost*, we find two contrasting patterns of vocative use which clearly reflect the level of projected relationship that the interviewer wishes to achieve with his respective guests. Compare his vocative use in an interview with Donald Rumsfeld, US Government Secretary of Defence (extracts 5.15 and 5.16), where he uses the honorific form throughout, with the first name reciprocation in the interview with British Member of Parliament Charles Kennedy, then leader of the Liberal Democrats (extract 5.17).

Extract 5.15

David Frost:	Tell me **Mr Secretary.** Are you where you hoped to be 14 months ago when the war came to an end, or not?

27 June 2004. Full transcript available at: http://news.bbc.co.uk/1/hi/ programmes/breakfast_with_frost/3844047.stm

Later, similar to the example from the earlier extract (5.13), we see the presenter's mitigating use of the vocative when challenging his guest in extract 5.16.

Extract 5.16

Donald Rumsfeld:	But it will certainly look an awful lot better than the Saddam Hussein killing fields and mass graves, and shoving people off the tops of buildings to kill them, and cutting off their hands and pulling out their tongues with pliers and chopping them off, which is what that repressive regime did.
David Frost:	But people do all say **Mr Secretary**, at the same time, that we were responsible, partially, for the security situation.

27 June 2004. Full transcript available at http://news.bbc.co.uk/1/hi/ programmes/breakfast_with_frost/3844047.stm

David Frost, interviewing Charles Kennedy a few months later on the same show, displays a very different pattern of vocative use (extract 5.17). Note how the first name vocative reciprocation is followed by banter and small talk and it is seven turns before the first topic is raised.

Extract 5.17

David Frost:	Now we zoom, we zoom to Fort William and the local laird himself. How are you **Charles**?
Charles Kennedy:	**David** I'm very well indeed thank you. A beautiful morning, winter's morning up here, frosty and chilly but very, very attractive.

David Frost: Very good, and let me ask you one question from the last time
                you were with us – how's the New Year resolution to give up
                smoking going?

Charles Kennedy: Well I anticipated, I thought you might get round to that at
                some point in our discussion. Well, if you remember, the
                pledge that I gave in your programme just towards the end
                of last year was to try and give up smoking. That's exactly
                what I'm doing. I've made, rather like the Liberal Democrats,
                substantial progress as we head into 2005.

David Frost: Very good – substantial progress. But you have had one or two
                cigarettes since January 1st I discern?

Charles Kennedy: That would be the case although I've actually had quite
                substantial periods without any, so I'm heading in the right
                direction, just like the party itself I hope.

David Frost: Very good, well let me just ask you the subject that has become
                the big subject this morning, or the big news subject this
                morning – Michael Howard's policy on putting immigration at
                the front of his programme, the ad in *The Sunday Telegraph*. Do
                you welcome that, or do you think it is playing to the lowest
                common dominator?

23 January 2005. Full transcript available at http://news.bbc.co.uk/1/hi/
programmes/breakfast_with_frost/3844047.stm

In an infamously confrontational interview between BBC's Jeremy Paxman and
the British Prime Minister, Tony Blair (extract 5.18), we see the deferential form
Prime Minister used by the interviewer when he is being highly adversarial, whereas
the FN *Jeremy* is used by the higher status interviewee (the Prime Minister of
Great Britain) when he wants to reject outright what the interviewer has said.

Extract 5.18

Jeremy Paxman: Well you said of those UN resolutions and the sanctions
                which followed them in the year 2000, you said that they had
                contained him. What's happened since?

Tony Blair: I didn't actually, I said they'd been contained him up to a point
                and the fact is –

Jeremy Paxman: **I'm sorry Prime Minister** – we believe that the sanctions
                regime has effectively contained Saddam Hussein in the last ten
                years, you said that in November 2000.

Tony Blair: Well I can assure you I've said every time I'm asked about
                this, they have contained him up to a point and the fact is

the sanctions regime was beginning to crumble, it's why it's subsequent in fact to that quote we had a whole series of negotiations about tightening the sanctions regime but the truth is the inspectors were put out of Iraq so —

Jeremy Paxman: They were not put out of Iraq, **Prime Minister, that is just not true**. The weapons inspectors left Iraq after being told by the American government that bombs will be dropped on the country.

Tony Blair: I'm sorry, that is simply not right. What happened is that the inspectors told us that they were unable to carry out their work, they couldn't do their work because they weren't being allowed access to the sites. They detailed that in the reports to the Security Council. On that basis, we said they should come out because they couldn't do their job properly.

Jeremy Paxman: That wasn't what you said, you said they were thrown out of Iraq —

Tony Blair: Well they were effectively because they couldn't do the work they were supposed to do.

Jeremy Paxman: No, effectively they were not thrown out of Iraq, they withdraw.

Tony Blair: No I sorry **Jeremy, I'm not allowing you away with that, that is completely wrong**. Let me just explain to you what happened.

Jeremy Paxman: You've just said the decision was taken by the inspectors to leave the country. They were therefore not thrown out.

6 February 2003. Full transcript available at http://news.bbc.co.uk/1/hi/
programmes/newsnight/2732979.stm

Moving to other types of interactions, when we look at our sub-corpus of *known* interactions, typically chat shows, where the host and the interviewee are known in the public domain and where the interviewee is not of higher status, but is usually a celebrity, we can summarize that there is generally limited and patterned vocative use at openings and closings of shows.

Start of the interview

- At the opening of a show or at the point of introducing a new guest, the host simultaneously addresses the studio and non-studio audience and introduces the guest referring to them by their full name — first name (FN) and surname (SN) for example in extract 5.19 Michael Parkinson introduces actor Mel Brooks. Note here because the presenter is aligned with the audience the FN

+ SN is not a vocative because it is not addressed to Mel Brooks. Its use marks a change in footing from the audience to the interviewee.

Extract 5.19

Michael Parkinson: My final guest is one of the select few who have won all four major entertainment honours, Oscar, Tony, Emmy and Grammy. In cinema terms he's a true godfather of comedy, now his talents have reached out to theatre where a musical version of his classic movie *The Producers* is a smash Broadway hit and is destined to do the same here in the West End. Ladies and gentlemen, **Mel Brooks**. [*applause*]

25 December 2004. Full transcript available at http://parkinson.tangozebra. com/guest_transcript.phtml?guest_id=55

During the interview

As the interview develops, no vocative reciprocation normally takes place and the only other occurrence is at the closing where the FN + SN forms are again used by the presenter so as to reinforce the public persona level of the relationship (extract 5.20). As in this example of the closing of the Parkinson interview with Mel Brooks where he uses the FN + SN vocative and then changes footing to address the audience, here again he refers to his guest using the FN + SN forms marking the end of the encounter.

Extract 5.20

Michael Parkinson: **Mel Brooks** thank you very much indeed! [*addressing audience*] **Mel Brooks.** [*applause*]

25 December 2004. Full transcript available at http://parkinson.tangozebra. com/guest_transcript.phtml?guest_id=55

Though both presenter and guest are known persona, vocative use seems to be related to role where it is normally only the talk show host who uses vocatives.

We find much the same pattern in other talk shows where public personae are interviewed. In this extract (5.21) from an American chat show transcript of *The Donny and Marie Show* where the interviewee is figure skater Kristi Yamaguchi, we find the same opening and closing FN + SN address pattern and there is no other vocative use between opening and closing.

Extract 5.21

Opening

Donny Osmond: Our next guest fell in love with ice-skating at the age of six and
                won an Olympic gold medal at the age of twenty. And right now
                she's touring the country in a show called 'Discover Stars on Ice
                (SOI) presented by Smuckers'. Take a look at this. [*a short clip is
                shown*] Will you please welcome **Kristi Yamaguchi**!

Extract 5.22

Closing

Donny Osmond: And thank you for coming to our show. [*the audience claps and
                cheers*]
Kristi: Oh, it's a pleasure.
Donny Osmond: We'll see you on December 17th. **Kristi Yamaguchi**!

> 4 January 1999. Full transcript available at http://www.geocities.
> com/amyc521/article/dmtranscript.html

In an interview with Christina Applegate on American chat show *The Tonight Show
with Jay Leno* (NBC) (extract 5.23) while the opening conforms to what we have
described above and there is no reciprocation of vocative use during the interview,
we find a slight lapse into FN use at the very end of the closing. This might be seen
as a personal 'off record' use by the presenter where the interview is officially over
and he makes an evaluative comment to his guest on how it went, seemingly off
microphone.

Extract 5.23

Opening

Jay Leno: My next guest played 'Kelly Bundy' for eleven years on
                'Married . . . with Children', currently starring in a film
                called 'The Big Hit' which comes out this Friday. Please
                welcome **Christina Applegate**! [*she is handed a microphone*]
                Here you go. Can you put that on?
Christina Applegate: Thank you! [*she tries to put it on*]

Closing

Jay Leno: Well, that's terrific.
Christina Applegate: That's how to get them into the theatre, right?
Jay Leno: Well, this is great! Congrat . . . The film opens when? [*he
                looks on his card on the table*] This . . . uhm . . . this Friday.

Christina Applegate: Friday!

Jay Leno: Friday. Alright. **Christina Applegate**! Thank you,
                        Christina [*he shakes hands with her. To her*] Alright, that was
                        easy!? [*to the camera*] Be right back with Randy Travis, right
                        after this.

> 21 April 1998. Full transcript available at
> http://www.bundyology.com/leno.html

When we look at media interactions from the *unknown* sub-corpus of our data (see
chapter 3), that is between a presenter (public persona) and a guest or caller who
is from the private domain, we find that though as participants they are essentially 'strangers', vocative use sometimes projects a level of intimacy that is more
akin to people who are very familiar with each other. This is especially the case
in shows that are dependent on 'strangers' calling in to disclose personal issues.
Radio phone-in is a genre that is particularly associated with pseudo-intimate vocative use. In extract 5.24 we see that the presenter and caller are instantly on FN
terms, though they have never met. Note also the reciprocity of vocative use. This
example comes from the Irish talk radio show *The Gerry Ryan Show* (RTÉ).

Extract 5.24

Gerry Ryan: **Mary** good morning to you.
Mary: Good morning **Gerry**.
Gerry Ryan: How are you?
Mary: I'm great and yourself?
Gerry Ryan: I'm excellent **Mary**.
Mary: Good.
Gerry Ryan: Excellent if I got any better well it's a family show I can't use
                the words to describe it.

> Exact date unknown, 2000. Full transcript not available online. *The Gerry Ryan*
> *Show* website http://www.rte.ie/2fm/ryanshow/index2.html

Both the presenter and the caller are complicit in the reciprocal use of first names
and the construction of a pseudo-intimate relationship. This not only projects an
intimate level of relationship, but appears to play a role in creating and sustaining
such relations in the interaction and in future interactions with others who are listening and who may in the future decide to call the show.

   Let us now look at the role of pragmatic markers in the creation of pseudo-
intimate relations in media interactions.

Pragmatic markers

Apart from hedging which we have looked at in chapter 4, there are other important features typical of casual conversation worth considering when we focus on how the illusion of an interpersonal relationship is created and sustained in media interactions. Pragmatic markers, according to Carter and McCarthy (2006), are a functional class of items which operate outside the structural limits of the clause and which encode speakers' intentions and interpersonal meanings. As well as hedges, they include discourse markers, which indicate the speaker's intentions with regard to organizing, structuring and monitoring the discourse, stance markers, which indicate the speaker's stance or attitude vis-à-vis the message, and interjections, items which indicate affective responses and reactions to the discourse. Here we will look at 'interjections' in the form of response tokens and the use of discourse markers.

Response tokens

Carter and McCarthy (2006) note that some adjectives and adverbs are many times more frequent in spoken language than in written language because of their frequent use as response tokens. These include *absolutely, certainly, definitely, fine, good, great, indeed, really* (see also McCarthy 2002, 2003). Tottie (1991: 255) tells us that these devices 'grease the wheels of the conversation but constitute no claim to take over the turn'. These interactive devices are referred to by a number of different but related terms: backchannels, minimal and non-minimal responses and listenership responses (see Fries 1952; Dittman and Llewellyn 1967; Yngve 1970; Duncan 1974; Zimmerman and West 1975; Fishman 1978; Heritage 1984; Jefferson 1984a, 1993; Coates 1986; S.K. Maynard 1989, 1990, 1997; White 1989; Drummond and Hopper 1993a; 1993b; Mott and Petrie 1995; Fellegy 1995; Schegloff 1982; Gardner 2002; McCarthy 2002, 2003). In the context of spoken grammar, Carter and McCarthy (2006) see the term *response token* as better describing their function of referring to a whole preceding utterance rather than their word-class identity as adjectives or adverbs, as in this example from McCarthy (2003: 49) where *lovely* is best described as a response token than an adjective (extract 5.25).

Extract 5.25 Telephone call between friends, arranging a barbecue

A: I would love it if you could bring a salad.
B: Yeah.
A: It would be very nice.
B: I will do then. I'll do that this afternoon then yeah.

A: **Lovely**.
B: What time do you want us then?
A: When were you planning?
B: Well you said about fiveish didn't you.
A: Yeah.
B: Yeah.
A: **Lovely**.

In symmetrical interactions of genuine intimacy between friends such as this, we frequently find that when someone is talking, other participants add vocalizations (*mmm, umhum*) and short utterances (*yeah, really*) to show that they are listening, that they are interested, that they agree (*exactly, absolutely*), that they are surprised (*you're not serious!*), shocked (*I don't believe it!*) saddened (*how awful!*), and so on. These short utterances are seen as not constituting turns and are not attempts by the addressee to take over the floor. If anything, they are signals to the speaker to continue. Here is an extract (5.26) from a conversation between friends (taken from LCIE) where speaker 1 is telling a story and speaker 2 is feeding back signals that she is listening and in agreement.

Extract 5.26

Speaker 1:	. . . it just goes to show you can't take people at face value.
Speaker 2:	**No.**
Speaker 1:	And you don't know what's going on either.
Speaker 2:	**Exactly.**
Speaker 1:	But am seemingly she knew what she was doing as well . . .

These features are found in some types of media interactions. For example, in extract 5.27 a caller to the Irish radio phone-in *Liveline* is telling a story about how, when she was young many years ago, a neighbour used to do home ear-piercing, the presenter shows that she is listening by repeatedly using the minimal response token *yeah*.

Extract 5.27

Caller:	The way this was done was a Scottish lady who lived across the road from us.
Presenter:	**Yeah**.
Caller:	And she would soak some grey wool. A length of grey wool in a saucer with olive oil.
Presenter:	**Yeah**.

Caller:	And then she'd thread it through an extremely large darning needle.
Presenter:	**Yeah.**
Caller:	Then there was a cork held together. It was a perfectly clean cork a new cork held behind your earlobe and she just threaded the needle with the wool straight through your ear and into the cork. Then she took the cork away pulled the wool and tied it in a little knot so you had your little ring of grey wool with olive oil on it hanging out of both ears.

14 January 1998. Full transcript not available online. *Liveline* website:
http://www.rte.ie/radio1/liveline/

When we examine interviews where a power differential prevails such as the BBC interview between Martin Bashir and Diana, Princess of Wales, we do not find any follow up response tokens (extract 5.28). These more formal interactions are structured around two-part exchanges comprising initiations + responses in the form of interviewer questions and interviewee answers.

Extract 5.28

Martin Bashir:	Were you overwhelmed by the pressure from people initially?
Diana:	Yes, I was very daunted because as far as I was concerned I was a fat, chubby, 20 year-old, 21-year-old, and I couldn't understand the level of interest.
Martin Bashir:	At this early stage, would you say that you were happily married?
Diana:	Very much so. But, the pressure on us both as a couple with the media was phenomenal, and misunderstood by a great many people. We'd be going round Australia, for instance, and all you could hear was, oh, she's on the other side. Now, if you're a man, like my husband a proud man, you mind about that if you hear it every day for four weeks. And you feel low about it, instead of feeling happy and sharing it.
Martin Bashir:	When you say 'she's on the other side', what do you mean?
Diana:	Well, they weren't on the right side to wave at me or to touch me.
Martin Bashir:	So they were expressing a preference even then for you rather than your husband?
Diana:	Yes which I felt very uncomfortable with, and I felt it was unfair, because I wanted to share.
Martin Bashir:	But were you flattered by the media attention particularly?

Diana: No, not particularly, because with the media attention came
                      a lot of jealousy, a great deal of complicated situations arose
                      because of that.

                           20 November 1995. Full transcript available at http://www.bbc.co.uk/
                                                            politics97/diana/panorama.html

Extract 5.29 is a similar example from an American interview on *ABC* with US
Secretary of Defence, Donald Rumsfeld.

Extract 5.29

Stephanopoulos: But as a practical matter, if there is no 'smoking gun', can
                      you get the coalition you need to fight this war?
Donald Rumsfeld: Oh, it's already there. There are a large number of countries
                      that have already said they're willing to participate in a
                      coalition of the willing. And there will be more at that
                      point in the event that cooperation is not there from Iraq. I
                      mean, the hope is that – the last thing anyone wants is to use
                      force. War is your last choice, not the first choice. The hope
                      is that Iraq will be cooperative. If they're not, the hope is
                      that Saddam Hussein will leave the country. And there are
                      countries in that region that are hoping that's the case. If not,
                      the hope is that the people of the country will take back their
                      country and their government from this vicious regime.
Stephanopoulos: How about the argument that with the inspectors there
                      right now, US forces in the region, Saddam Hussein is
                      effectively contained, so you don't need to take quick
                      military action?
Donald Rumsfeld: Well, what we know is that containment hasn't worked. If
                      you think of what the international community has done for
                      a decade – they have tried economic sanctions, we've tried
                      diplomacy, they've tried the use of limited military force in the
                      northern and southern no-fly zones, they have now gone to the
                      UN to get a resolution, and the only reason there are inspectors
                      in there at all is because of the threat of the use of force. I mean,
                      that is what's supporting the diplomacy that exists.
Stephanopoulos: In the last few days, the inspectors have come across some
                      finds. A dozen empty chemical warhead shells. A cache of
                      nuclear documents. What do you make of these findings?
Donald Rumsfeld: Well, if you think of the fact that there have been no
                      inspectors there for four years, I guess it's been, three or

four years, that you've got a country and a regime that is very skillful at denial and deception – they are actively trying to deceive the inspectors and the world. One has to almost think that anything that's found, quote, 'discovered,' has to be something that Saddam Hussein was not uncomfortable having be found. I mean, how else would it be found? The country's enormous.

19 January 2003. Full transcript available at http://www.defenselink.mil/transcripts/2003/t01192003_t19sdabc.html

In contrast, where there is an attempt to achieve pseudo-intimacy in a media inter-action, one finds, particularly, the presenter providing a feedback move which deviates from the more formal *initiation + response* format as seen in the examples above. For example:

Extract 5.30

Caller:	. . . my story goes back to am February it was actually on Valentine's Day.
Gerry Ryan:	**Umhum**.
Caller:	And what happened was that I was actually two weeks due at that stage to give birth I was thirty-eight weeks pregnant.
Gerry Ryan:	**Yeah**.
Caller:	And you might hear her in the background there.
Gerry Ryan:	I can hear the results of your labour.
Caller:	⌊Yes <*laughter*> Basically what happened was that about two weeks previously my husband who is big into toys as husbands tend to be+
Gerry Ryan:	Toys?
Caller:	+am Absolutely got <*laughter*> a caller i.d. machine.
Gerry Ryan:	**Umhum**.
Caller:	So he he got it basically not to not necessarily for cranks calls because we hadn't had any crank calls.
Gerry Ryan:	He just liked the idea of having it.
Caller:	Absolutely what he wanted.
Gerry Ryan:	⌊Yeah I know that's a bit like me <*laughter*>.
Caller:	Yeah I mean like we would get a call like his mother would ring him or something and he would pick up the phone 'Hi Mum how are you?' cause he'd see her machine or her number on the machine.
Gerry Ryan:	**Yeah yeah I know**.

Caller:	That was the whole idea anyway . . . I was completely against it because I was I mean I let him off. I couldn't understand it at all and he was saying to me constantly 'Look at this now I can do this and blah bah blah' but+
Gerry Ryan:	**Umm**.
Caller:	+ I let him off anyway so . . .

> Exact date unknown, 2000. Full transcript not available online. *The Gerry Ryan Show* website: http://www.rte.ie/2fm/ryanshow/index2.html

O'Keeffe and Adolphs 2002 look at response tokens in 20,000 words of calls to the Irish radio phone-in show *Liveline* and find a total of 245 tokens. From this analysis they propose four main functions of response tokens in radio phone-ins (see also O'Keeffe and Adolphs in press).

1   *Continuer tokens* – these maintain the flow of the discourse, with forms such as *yeah*, *mm* as the most typical exponents.
2   *Convergence tokens* – these cluster at points of agreement and understanding in a conversation and also include convergence around common knowledge or known information.
3   *Engagement tokens* – these are response tokens which register high on the affective scale where a listener is responding at an affective or relational level to the content of the message. They manifest in many forms (for example single-word forms such as *excellent*, short repetitions, echo questions). They express genuine emotive responses such as surprise, shock, horror, sympathy, empathy, and so on.
4   *Information receipt tokens* – these responses are highly organizational and associated more with managing interactions, where they can serve as global acknowledgement tokens at points in the discourse where adequate information has been received. These responses can coincide with the onset of boundaries in the discourse and can co-signal points of topic transition or closure (and so can have a discourse marking function). In this analysis *right* was used most frequently in this role.

O'Keeffe and Adolphs (2002) compared these functions across similar-sized datasets from British and Irish casual conversation (20,000 words from CANCODE and LCIE respectively) and found that in intimate conversations between real friends, response tokens are used most for agreement and convergence (around 50 per cent in both cases) whereas in the radio phone-in conversations, around 50 per cent of their usage was as continuers (table 5.2). Also, in real casual conversations, we normally do not need to use a high number of information receipt tokens.

Table 5.2 Percentage functional breakdown of response tokens

	Radio	LCIE	CANCODE
Continuer	52	11	19
Convergence	9	47	52
Engaged	19	4	28
Information receipt	20	0	0

Further analysis of the radio data (table 5.3) shows us that it is the presenter almost exclusively who uses response tokens (O'Keeffe and Adolphs in press).

Table 5.3 Percentage breakdown of presenter–caller use of response tokens for each functional category as detailed in table 5.2

	Presenter	Caller
Continuer	98	2
Convergence	95	5
Engagement	59	41
Information receipt	100	0

Discourse markers

Many commonly-used words and phrases function as discourse markers (see Schiffrin 1987, 1999, 2001) for example, adverbs and adjectives such as *anyway*, *well*, and *right* or phrases and clauses such as *as I was saying, you know, you see*. Extract 5.31 is an example from LCIE.

Extract 5.31

Speaker 1:	. . . **anyway** I had emailed a youth hostel I think it was called 'Backpackers rest' **right** I was supposed to stay there and they never answered me back but I just assumed it was booked anyway, they got into Paris about half eight and it took about two hours to find it, the youth hostel +
Speaker 2:	Yeah because the one time when we got into a taxi, he wanted the exact address . . .
Speaker 1:	[*many taxi drivers*] are not even from Paris a lot of them aren't even French, they don't actually know. You have to have the exact address or they won't know. **As I was saying** we were looking for this youth hostel . . .

As we can see from this example, discourse markers help to organize the discourse. They can also give an indication of the degrees of formality and people's feelings towards the interaction (see Carter and McCarthy 2006). In a call to *The Nick Abbot Show*, LBC talk radio show (extract 5.32), we see liberal and symmetrical use of discourse markers suggesting that the male caller is complicit in his being ridiculed for cleaning his flat twice a week.

Extract 5.32

Nick Abbot:	**Wait a minute**, who do you live with?
Caller:	I live on my own.
Nick Abbot:	You live on your own and you clean your flat twice a week.
Caller:	I'm afraid I do, I'm a bit different.
Nick Abbot:	You certainly are. Can you clean your flat once a week then come over to my place and clean mine? **You know** you won't go cold turkey or anything because you'll still be doing the same amount of cleaning but you'll be doing something worthwhile with your life.
Caller:	Yeah, it just baffles me why I bring in a couple of carrier bags of stuff every week and I send out, **you know**, four or five bin-liners of stuff twice a week.
Nick Abbot:	**Well that's true, yeah. You know** I threw out a load of stuff the other day and I thought maybe I should er . . . 'cause **you know** when you catch Blue Peter or one of these programmes that always goes on about recycling and I thought maybe I should go through this stuff and recycle it but then I just thought no to hell with it let's just throw it away.
Caller:	That's what I would say stuff the recycling I prefer a tidy flat **actually**.
Nick Abbot:	[*laughs*] That's it sod the earth let's just get this crap out of here.
Caller:	That's right.
Nick Abbot:	**Okay well** good luck with your French polishing or whatever the hell it is that you're doing.
Caller:	**Okay**.
Nick Abbot:	I don't believe that, he lives on his own and he cleans his flat twice a week. That's weird. **Wait a minute.** Are you still there ?
Caller:	Yeah.
Nick Abbot:	Do you iron as well?
Caller:	Don't be stupid that's my mum's job.

Nick: [*laughing*] **Okay**. Just checking.

        Exact date unknown, 1994. Full transcript available at
        http://www.w2s.co.uk/nick-abbot/transcripts/lewis5.html

In this interview between Michael Parkinson and Lily Savage (a well known British comedian in drag played by Paul O'Grady), we also see how copious use of discourse markers makes the conversation very interactive and, similar to the above example, often marks humour and irony.

Extract 5.33

Michael Parkinson:	**Now** tell us about this come back.
Lily Savage:	Come back? I hate that word. It's return, return, return to the people who never deserted me. **Sorry about that Michael. Well,** I thought . . . The excesses of show business got the better of me. **You know**, when you find yourself at a skip at five o clock in the morning with one of the Bay City Rollers on your back. **You know what I mean** . . . So I went back up to Liverpool **you see**.
Michael Parkinson:	And what did you do there?
Lily Savage:	**Well** I worked for one of me friends who has got an agency . . . **And then** there was all that business with Wayne Rooney, **you know what I mean**. [*laughter*] . . . Now he's playing for Manchester. Fifty quid and it wasn't worth it, **believe you me** . . .
Michael Parkinson:	Anything else you've been doing that we should know about?
Lily Savage:	I've been doing lots, **well**, then I decided**, I thought**, you've still got a womb Lil. [*laughter*] Cheap audience in here tonight. **So** I thought I'd carry another woman's eggs for her. I don't mean I had a market stall. No, for lesbian couples who couldn't have children, I had eighteen babies in a period of three year. I was prolific, I had to have me pelvic floor laminated. [*laughter*] **I'm telling you**. They shot out, **seriously**. There's lesbian couples all over the country delighted because of me. I had to sell two on ebay. **I tell you what**, her video saved my life. [*laughter*] I did the buttock clenching exercises. I can pick a pencil up now with my bum. [*laughter*] I'll show you later.

Michael Parkinson: **Now** what's this rumour about Mr O'Grady killing you off?
Lily Savage: **Don't talk to me about that four-eyed fruit.** I've
had enough of him. I never watch the Paul O'Grady Show.
I know he's a pal of yours Babs and I don't want to speak
ill of him, I'm a Richard and Judy girl. **And I'll tell you
why . . .**
Michael Parkinson: **Let's talk a bit about the panto**. Because you've back in
panto now. **So tell me**, is it an original panto?

25 December 2004. Full transcript available at http://parkinson.tangozebra.
com/guest_transcript.phtml?guest_id=55

Discourse markers can indicate power-relations (see chapter 4) in that the power-role holder in a media interaction usually manages the discourse and so will use markers such as *right let's turn to . . .*, *okay*, and so on. They can be used as a means of both structuring and controlling the discourse. In figure 5.3, for example, we see concordance lines of the discourse marker *right* (from the media corpus), a very common discourse marker in media discourse, which is normally used by the presenter to confirm information, create topic boundaries and close calls.

Figure 5.5 Concordance lines of discourse marker *right* from media corpus

Confirming information
        it was a sister and friend.   Oh **right** okay.   But ah he collected
            nless they ask for it. Now one+ **Right**. Okay. So y=   +and once thi
        old and a five year old.   Right **right** and am   so lot   o= you s
        a   raki   practitioner. **Right**. I know your marriage subsequently
    ot no an academic doctor.   I see **right** cos I was wondering from which per
            ly but I hope not   . **Right** okay so basically you want to know
        course as keen as anybody else. **Right** but under the right circumstances
        where we should put the tattoo. **Right**. Anyway you're delighted with it?
Create topic boundaries
            ill have a record because of it **Right** well you're fairly certain of that
        y ah see themselves as British. **Right** okay. I suppose yeah and I suppose
    ng from England from Cheshire. **Right** can I ask you your opinions here of of a
            right to be Irish.   Yes. **Right**. Consider all the implications for the
        eed to as in my job I'm active. **Right** do you run for a living?   I don't
    orse and become irretrievable. **Right**. So you wouldn't be completely pes
        st run as day schools you know. **Right** well certainly that's what's happe
Call closings
            in our criminal courts. **Right** okay Michael McDowell thank you ve
        daughter I think it's cute. **Right** okay Thank you very much indeed fo

with Helen Feeney's murder. **Right**. Okay. Listen thank you very much
little twinge of jealousy. **Right** Okay Joe. Okay thanks a million
th it right to the very end. **Right**. Okay. Okay well that's a good a news

As we saw in chapter 4, discourse markers can be found in situations of conflict
as we see in this example from a well known public forum interview with British
Prime Minister at the time, Tony Blair, on BBC *Newsnight* hosted by Jeremy
Paxman (extract 5.34).

Extract 5.34

Jeremy Paxman:	And you believe American intelligence?
Tony Blair:	**Well** I do actually believe this intelligence –
Jeremy Paxman:	Because there are a lot of dead people in an aspirin factory in Sudan who don't.
Tony Blair:	**Come on.** This intelligence is backed up by our own intelligence and in any event, **you know**, we're not coming to this without any history. **I mean** let's not be absurdly naïve about this
Jeremy Paxman:	Hans Blix said he saw no evidence of hiding of weapons.
Tony Blair:	**I'm sorry**, what Hans Blix has said is that the Iraqis are not co-operating properly.

6 February 2003. Full transcript available at http://news.bbc.co.uk/1/hi/
programmes/newsnight/2732979.stm

When we conduct a cluster analysis of the first 50 discourse markers in the media
corpus using *Wordsmith Tools* (Scott 1998) searching for two-, three-, four-, five-
and six-word clusters, we find patterns most frequently operating as multi-word
discourse markers (see table 5.4).

Table 5.4 Most frequent multi-word clusters used in media corpus as
discourse markers

Two word	*Three word*	*Four word*	*Five word*	*Six word*
you know	at the time	at the same time	you know what I mean	at the end of the day
I mean	first of all	I have to say	I have to tell you	
and then		as I was saying	as far as I know	

Using this data from the media corpus, we can quantify the frequency and distribution of multi-word discourse markers according to the three prevailing types of the data in our media corpus: interviewee *unknown* to public, interviewee *known* public persona, and political interview. This analysis is very telling in terms of the impact of the type of interaction on the use of language. It shows clearly that in interactions involving a presenter and people who are not known in the public domain, there is greatest distribution and frequency of multi-word discourse markers and in political interviews, it is the reverse. In table 5.5, we also compare the media results with casual conversation (using the LCIE) and find that the interactions involving a presenter and a non-public persona most resemble the results from casual conversation (note that in order to compare the results, they have been normalized, that is converted to occurrences per million words).

Table 5.5 Comparison of frequency and distribution of multi-word discourse markers

	Unknown	*Known*	*Political*	*LCIE*
you know	5220	3022	219	4758
I mean	3090	1581	310	1438
and then	775	1000	64	1124
first of all	157	172	59	92
at the same time	67	118	21	59
I have to say	112	43	0	28
as I was saying	56	0	0	4
you know what I mean	45	75	0	221
I have to tell you	34	32	0	5
as far as I know	34	0	0	16
at the end of the day	79	54	11	33
Total	**9669**	**6097**	**684**	**7778**

From this data, we can summarize that political interviews are least pseudo-intimate in their use of multi-word discourse markers and show less than 10 per cent the level of discourse marking found in everyday conversation between friends. It is also interesting to note from this that some forms have become pragmatically specialized to media contexts, for example *I have to tell you*, *I have to say*, *at the time*. Another interesting distinction to note here is between items which mark given/shared information versus those which mark new/non-shared information. Markers of given/shared information include *you know*, *you know what I mean* and project of higher intimacy than markers of new/non-shared information such as *I have to say*, *you see*. The latter are a marker of lower intimacy than the former.

5.3 Conclusion

In this chapter we have focused on the notion that some media interactions are more intimate than others and that this intimacy is something that is created over time through routines such as signature turns, opening gambits with the audience, inclusive use of pronouns and simulation of co-presence. We also found that presenters can project themselves as seemly, ordinary people, for example people who put out the rubbish bins every Wednesday. This serves to create an 'everydayness' about the persona of the presenter that builds trust with the audience. The audience over time can feel that this is someone that they can relate to and ultimately someone that they could phone if they had a problem or issue to discuss, almost like a real friend. Pseudo-intimacy such as this is crucial to the success of shows such as radio phone-ins and chat shows.

We noted that the language items that help create and sustain this illusion of an interpersonal relationship in media interactions include the use of vocatives. However we found that their use varies relative to the context of the media interaction. Where the interviewee is of high status, the full honorific title + FN + SN is used by the interviewer, whereas the high status interviewee may use the FN form when addressing the interviewer. In the case of chat shows, where the interviewer and interviewee are both known public personae, the interview consistently uses FN + SN forms referentially (rather than vocatively) at the openings and closings of the show and in-between vocatives are generally avoided by both the participants. In the case of radio phone-ins as McCarthy and O'Keeffe (2003) have shown, and in talk shows, FN reciprocation proliferated and this mirrors vocative use in everyday conversation between friends and intimates.

We also looked in detail at the effect of using the three-part initiation→response→feedback exchange structure in media interactions where there is a feedback move which provides a response token from the presenter. This is an atypical structure in media interactions, especially in formal news interviews. However, it is found in more intimate media interactions such as chat shows and especially radio phone-in shows. It is notable that the absence of the visual channel in the context of radio phone-ins must add to the necessity to use such tokens so as to create the sense of intimacy needed for this type of programme in the absence of visual cues such as eye contact and head nods. The pragmatic effect of the use of response tokens is to help create and sustain a sense of pseudo-intimacy, something more akin to a cosy chat between friends. Another pragmatic marker that we looked at here was discourse markers and we noted that they are an indicator of interactivity. We found considerably more discourse marking in media interactions in the *known* and *unknown* sub-corpora than in the political interview data. The use of discourse markers in the non-political interview data very much resembled casual conversation patterns.

In chapter 6, we will also look at inclusive language but in relation to how it can be used to create a sense of commonality and identity, while at the same time creating an 'other'. Here we looked at how pronouns were used to create a sense of intimacy and co-presence within the participation framework of a programme, for example. In chapter 6 we will see how they can also serve to mark common identity and be indices of socio-cultural information, as well as marking who is inside and outside the participation framework.

6 Creating identities

> ... in the daily consumption of broadcast discourse, the public and private are increasingly interconnected
>
> Tolson (1991: 196)

6.0 Introduction

The notion that media interactions take place within a shared space, or a participation framework, between a presenter, an interviewee and an audience has been stressed throughout the book. Within this collective of participants, there is an understanding of:

- a range of shared space
- a cache of shared knowledge
- a sense of common identity.

These features are marked through language use. For example, extract 6.1 is from a radio interview from the Australian Broadcasting Corporation (ABC) radio station Radio National, where the presenter, Robert Bolton, is talking to Professor David Flint, Chair of the Broadcasting Authority of Australia. Notice how the interviewee does not need to make his references to *the Parliament* and *our jury system* explicit. He assumes that within the range of shared space of the interaction, these references will be interpreted within local shared knowledge in an Australian frame of reference.

Extract 6.1

David Flint: I think it would be dangerous to give a regulator too much immediate power. That would be unwise. You have to have some system which ensures that in no way can the regulator be used to suppress the free circulation of ideas and thoughts in the media. And that obviously is the reason why **the Parliament** has adopted this approach. It's rather like **our jury system** I suppose, that the general view is it's better to allow a hundred guilty people to go free than one innocent person to be condemned . . .

15 July 1999. Full transcript available at http://www.abc.net.au/rn/talks/8.30/mediarpt/mstories/mr990715.htm

Again in this example below from the BBC 2 television programme *Newsnight* involving a public interview with British Prime Minister Tony Blair, the Prime Minister sees no need to be explicit about whom *our* and *we* refer.

Extract 6.2

Tony Blair: This intelligence is backed up by **our own intelligence** and in any event, you know, **we're** not coming to this without any history.

6 February 2003. Full transcript available at http://news.bbc.co.uk/1/hi/programmes/newsnight/2732979.stm (accessed 18 January 2005)

Linguistic markers of shared space, knowledge and identity such as these prove very interesting in the study of media discourse. They can provide indices of commonality which are embedded in language within the shared social space of the participation framework. These indices are also telling as to where the participants locate themselves in space, how much knowledge they assume as shared and how they position themselves relative to what they are not. In this chapter we will focus on linguistic indices such as ad hoc vague categories (*the rugby season and the Cup and everything*), pronoun use, deictic referencing (*those people*) and self-reference tokens (*here in Britain, on this island*). In everyday casual conversation between friends, these features of language also locate and position participants and reinforce their shared world and common identity, as in extract 6.3 taken from the Limerick Corpus of Irish English. The speakers can be very inexplicit when referring to people and places because they have a high level of shared knowledge, some of which may emerge within the ongoing conversation but much of which is amassed over time through being in frequent contact as friends.

Extract 6.3

A: And what's **he** going to be doing **in there**?
B: I think **they're** training **him** as a trainee manager.

A: Frying chips?

C: You mean **he**'s frying chips. Basically. <*laughs*>

B: **He** says 'I'm going to do **everything**. Fry chips and wait tables **and stuff'**.

A: . . . there's no way **he**'ll be able for **that** like. <*laughs*>

In the case of media interactions, this is also the case but it happens on a much larger scale and so points of shared reference will normally be broader so as to be inclusive within the participation framework. For the analyst, they offer an interesting insight into the identity of the collective of participants since they are markers of membership. Let us begin by looking at the vague categories that can be invoked collaboratively in the process of discourse within a stable group or participation framework.

6.1 Vague categorization as indices of shared knowledge

Vague categorization refers to the setting up of categories that are ad hoc or non-lexicalized, for example *places to look for antique desks* (Barsalou 1983, 1987). These are in contrast with lexicalized categories which pre-exist within the lexicon and which encode a single lexical item, for example, *bird, furniture* (Rosch *et al.* 1976; Rosch 1978; Mervis and Rosch 1981). Ad hoc categories are dynamic in nature because they are created spontaneously by a speaker relative to a lexical need at a moment in a conversation. A speaker can make up a vague category which will be inexplicit in form but which will be within the range of shared knowledge of the addressee(s). In such examples, categorization is non-lexicalized and this challenges the notion that categories are stable, easily recognizable and arrived at 'pre-textually' (Overstreet and Yule 1997b). Let's look again at an example from extract 6.3 from casual conversation: *He says 'I'm going to do everything. Fry chips and wait tables and stuff'*. The speaker came up with this category *fry chips and wait tables and stuff* at the moment of speaking relative to what she knows is within the shared cultural knowledge of the other participants in the conversation. There is no one word that encompasses the sum of activities that the ad hoc category suggests, yet for those participating in the conversation this inexplicit category proved perfectly adequate and suggested a collection of tasks that working in a fast food restaurant in Ireland would entail. This vague categorization would not work in every culture, and that is why they are of interest to the analyst in terms of how they display assumed shared cultural knowledge. Overstreet and Yule (1997b: 85–6) also note that insights can be gained from looking at the discourse processes involved in categorization when a single lexical item is not available to the discourse participants for the referential category. They stress the spontaneity of categorization and the context-dependent nature of the categories themselves when one looks at examples from actual discourse, as opposed to stylized examples. Here are some more examples from casual conversation (LCIE) where speakers choose to make up a category as they speak rather than draw on a pre-textual lexical item (if one exists):

- . . . I'm normally **a very nervous person and that kind of thing**
- . . . the [*name of university*] crowd were around and they had **a camera crew and everything**
- . . . he's going to the gym a lot to do **weights and stuff**
- [*referring to a friend who has just had a baby*] I suppose she's very busy at the moment having **sleepless nights and all that**.

There are a number of terms used to refer to the forms such as *and that kind of thing, et cetera, and stuff*, which construct these ad hoc categories, for example, 'general extender' (Overstreet and Yule 1997a, 1997b), 'generalized list completer' (Jefferson 1990), 'tag' (Ward and Birner 1992), 'terminal tag' (Dines 1980; Macaulay 1991), 'extension particle' (DuBois 1993) and 'vague category identifier' (Channell 1994) and 'vague category marker' (O'Keeffe 2003). Here we will use the term 'vague category marker'. O'Keeffe (2003) refers to vague category markers as recognizable chunks of language that function in an expedient way as linguistic triggers employed by speakers and decoded by participants who draw on their store of shared knowledge. She argues that the meanings of vague categories are socio-culturally grounded and are co-constructed within a social group that has a shared socio-historic reality. This is consistent with Overstreet and Yule (1997b) who point out that the process of establishing categories is locally contingent in discourse and it is this that makes them interesting as indices of identity.

O'Keeffe (2003) provides a detailed analysis of vague categories in a corpus of five programmes (55,000 words) from the Irish radio phone-in show *Liveline*. In total, she found that 138 categories were created over the five programmes in her sample. Here are some examples:

- . . . a lot of **undesirables, criminals and people like that . . .**
- . . . conviction about **social justice, and so on**
- . . . buy a bar of chocolate or something . . .
- . . . the expense of insurance and ah people for instance organizing voluntary sporting activities now find that you know if you have **a gymkhana or whatever . . .**
- . . . maybe they are like **the wise virgins and all that jazz**.

Each category was analysed in terms of what it referred to or its 'reference domain' and the findings, as detailed in table 6.1, locate the participation framework of the programme within a predominantly Irish range, with 64 per cent of all categories having Irish reference domains.

Table 6.1 Reference domains of 138 vague categories in the Irish radio phone-in *Liveline*

Reference domain	Percentage
Irish	64
Global	33
European	2
Biblical	1

In the context of this programme, the references which are Irish provide the narrowest point of socio-cultural reference and are also at the core of the shared cache of knowledge within this participation framework. When these Irish references are further broken down, they give more insight into the participants of this programme and what they assume as shared uncontested knowledge (table 6.2).

Table 6.2 Breakdown of Irish vague categories

Category	Example of what is referred to	Percentage
Social practices and attitudes	The process of 'word of mouth' in Ireland	37
Social responsibilities and realities	Negative social realities that come with the Celtic tiger economy	32
Work, financial and consumer practices	Car rental companies in Ireland	23
Social types	Irish criminals and social undesirables	14

The categories in table 6.2 reflect largely middle class concerns about Irish society and very often draw on stereotypes, see extract 6.4, for example.

Extract 6.4 Talking about why people send their children to boarding schools

Presenter: . . . some people were there saying oh well sending [*children*] away **unhappy homes all that kind of thing**.

For the majority of people listening at the time, we can only assume that they deconstruct the meaning of the category *unhappy homes all that kind of thing* based on a stereotype, as opposed to direct first-hand experience and this is the case for many of the examples found in the data.

Within the context of the work of Louw (1993) and Sinclair (1996) on semantic prosody, we could say that vague category markers cluster with lexis which has negative prosody. Semantic prosody refers to how a word or expression can associate with a particular semantic environment, for example, a positive or negative one. Carter and McCarthy (1999), for instance, looked at the *get* passive construction (*get robbed, get knocked down, get followed*) and observed that it showed a tendency to co-occur with a negative prosody (most typically encoding unfortunate or undesired events). As figure 6.1 illustrates, O'Keeffe (2003) finds that there is a similar tendency in the use of vague category markers.

Figure 6.1 Samples of negative semantic prosody associated with categorization in O'Keeffe (2003)

ell sending them away **unhappy homes** all that kind of thing.   Mm I know
     mean there was an awful lot of **pain** and that kind of   thing   .
  ools are from **unhappy families** there is that kind of element I suppose but mo
ke **venereal diseases or prostitution** or that kind of thing?   Well I I
        der.   And had he been subject to that kind of **physical torture**?
     n't I. And you know Marian if you're in that kind of am **hostile environment**

        ld is going to be, and so on I mean that that sort of **issue** I think we need to
   create **divisions and conflicts** and all that sort of thing.   Yeah.
        react quite strongly to **stress** and all that sort of stuff so I have I'm now

 g out of this ah situations of **hardship**, and so on I think we wouldn't say tha
xecuted and the other was to get **lashes**, and so on and so forth. Yo= yo= did y
ing through ah this system and the **pain**, and so on, and so on. But having said
h ah this system and the **pain**, and so on, and so on. But having said that let me

        it's associated with all sorts of **seedy** things like **venereal diseases** or
        Won't that be the most **subversive** thing that has been done to both
      e the point of **road rage** ah this is the thing I'm concerned with where loc
    or you know the the the **danger** is these things get worse and worse and be
 t okay so let people be **beware** of these things. Okay?   Yeah. But the
h am **tough-minded** view would say 'these things happen. It's too bad''.
     roller coaster you know I mean I think **things are moving very fast** but
     yes   ah of doing **unspeakable** things to one another ah to come

Vague category markers in the above study were identified manually by reading through all of the transcripts (55,000 words in total). In order to look at vague category markers in a larger corpus of data, software that calculates lexical chunks can be used (see chapter 3 for details of core corpus analysis functions). For example, below is a sample of the vague category marking chunks that occur in the first 500 most frequent three-word chunks in the media corpus. As in previous chapters, these are broken down across the three sub-corpora:

- *known personae:* e.g. chat shows where a celebrity host interviews a celebrity
- *political interviews:* e.g. news interviews
- *unknown personae:* e.g. radio phone-ins or television interviews where the interviewee is from the private sphere.

As outlined earlier, here, as a sample, we are only focusing on the three-word vague category marking chunks and the following data is used in the analysis:

- the media corpus, a 271,553-word corpus of media interactions including chat shows, news interview, phone-ins, etc. (see chapter 3)
- the Limerick Corpus of Irish English (LCIE), a one-million word corpus of spoken Irish English designed according to the same matrix as CANCODE (see McCarthy 1998; Farr, Murphy and O'Keeffe 2002)
- the Cambridge and Nottingham Corpus of Discourse in English (CANCODE), a five-million word corpus of mostly British English casual conversation (see McCarthy 1998)
- the Limerick-Belfast Corpus of Academic English (LIBEL), a one-million word corpus of academic interactions in a university context. Note that only 500,000 words of LIBEL are used here.

Note that the results from CANCODE and LCIE (table 6.3) are taken from McCarthy, Walsh and O'Keeffe (2005).

Table 6.3 Three-word chunk analysis of vague category markers

Media corpus	LCIE and CANCODE	LIBEL academic corpus
Known persona		
things like that	do you know	and so on
and all that	and you know	and so forth
something like that	sort of thing	
and so forth	things like that	
	something like that	
	you know like	
political interviews		
and so on	and all that	
	kind of thing	
	and so on	

unknown persona

and so on	and so forth
anything like that	
sort of thing	
and so forth	
and all that	
something like that	

Though only three-word chunks are being compared, here again the findings are consistent with our other comparisons in earlier chapters where the discourse features in the corpus of unknown personae interacting on air are closest to those found in casual conversation, whereas political interviews are the least similar. In this comparison, the results from the political interviews corpus most resemble those from the institutional setting of academic discourse from the LIBEL corpus.

6.2 Pronouns as indices of audience identity

As detailed in chapter 5, many researchers agree on the non-canonical nature of pronoun use (see McCarthy 1994; Pennycook 1994; Wales 1996; Wortham 1996; Chang 2002; O'Keeffe 2002), however, the main focus for grammarians has been on sentence-level pronoun form. As Wales (1996: 50) notes, pronouns have a wide variety of social roles and stances and, therefore, interpersonal pronouns are rarely neutral in their reference. To view pronouns as neutral, according to Pennycook (1994: 174), assumes that there is 'some unproblematic, uncontested world out there that is referenced by language'. In the context of media interactions in established participation frameworks, the speakers, that is the presenters, interviewees and audience members (in the case of radio and television talk shows), make systematic choices about how they refer to themselves, their world and others in it relative to what it is not. Speakers' choices in pronoun use in media interactions offer another viable index of socio-cultural identity in the study of media interactions. Central to this is the concept of *deictic mapping* (after Wortham 1996) whereby pronouns can either be centring (e.g. *me, we, us*) or othering (e.g. *they, those, them*).

Deictic mapping: centring and othering

Wortham (1996) uses the term *deictic mapping*, whereby he analyses 'participant deictics' in the context of a classroom interaction by looking at personal pronouns. According to Wortham (1996: 331) 'deictics systematically index aspects of the context, and these forms often sketch the framework of the interactional event'. When we apply this notion to the situation of media discourse, we can make assertions about deictic markers as indices of the context at a societal level, especially in

respect to how a presenter, interviewee and audience collectively position themselves in relation to 'others', in other words, how participants locate themselves
politically, socially and interactionally within a participation framework. Crucially
this central position is collaboratively negotiated over time within this group.
Extract 6.5 is from an interview with an American bishop on Australian television.
It gives an example of how pronouns position the speaker and those participating
in the programme. The interview is with Bishop Shelby Spong, former Episcopal
Bishop of Newark, New Jersey, on the Australian religious and ethics programme
Sunday Nights with John Cleary (Australian Broadcasting Corporation).

Extract 6.5

Bishop John Shelby Spong: . . . treat the Aboriginal people as if **they** are holy
people to God and to do whatever **you** can to enhance **their**
being, and to call **them** into a deeper sense of self worth, is
a positive thing . . . I would say that the gay rights movement
is of God, and the homophobic opposition to the gay rights
movement which is so often masked in quotations from
Leviticus, is not of God, it is of the negativity towards human
life, because the gay movement is an attempt to say Yes, **that**
percentage of the population who happens to be gay or lesbian
is also holy, and **we** want to call them into living fully and
loving wastefully, and being all that **they** can possibly be.
Remember 100 years ago **we** persecuted left-handed people
because **we** thought **they** were abnormal, and **we** tied **their**
left hands behind **their** backs in **our** ignorance, and tried to
make **them** into normal right-handed people. I think **we**'re in
the danger of trying to do the same thing to the gay and lesbian
population.

17 June 2001. Full transcript available at
http://www.abc.net.au/sundaynights/stories/s815368.htm

The inclusive pronouns *you* (generic) and *we* are used to be inclusive but the pronouns *they, them, their* reinforce the reality of otherness, as does the choice of *that*,
as opposed to *this* as a deictic (pointing) reference (see below). Though there is
positive sentiment being expressed towards the Aboriginal people and the gay
community in this extract, they are clearly not included within the assumed range
of the participation framework nor are they part of the collaboratively negotiated
centre. By way of comparison with another institutional context, that of academic
discourse at university level, we find a similar centring and othering process displayed in extract 6.6, an economics lecture on taxation taken from the LIBEL

corpus. Here *we* centres those within the participation framework of the academic field of economics (including the students attending the lecture) whereas *they* refers to those who are outside this.

Extract 6.6

> So under both systems the rich person and the poor person end up the same.
> **They** still get four thousand . . . But **we** know that **we** know the focus from
> an economic perspective tends to be on marginal rate or average rate. But
> **we**'re just looking at average rate here. And the average rate is calculated then
> on the basis of ah total tax revenue divided by total income. Okay? Twenty
> percent. The average tax rate is twenty percent if **we**'re taking the ordinary
> system. And sixty percent if **we** take the basic income. Alright?

When we look at the distribution of person-referring pronouns (i.e. not including *it*) in the media corpus, we find again that the forms vary depending on the type of interaction. Table 6.4 also shows the distribution of these pronouns in the institutional setting of academic discourse.

Table 6.4 Distribution of person-referring pronouns in media corpus compared with academic discourse (results displayed as per 1,000 for ease of comparison)

	Media corpus			*Academic discourse LIBEL*
	Known	*Political*	*Unknown*	
I	40	20	37	15
you	30	20	29	29
he	5	4	9	4
she	3	1	3	2
we	7	10	9	9
they	7	10	10	7
Totals	92	65	97	66

Consistent with the findings above in relation to three-word vague category marking chunks (table 6.3), the results for political interviews strongly resemble those in academic discourse.

Montgomery (1986), referring to DJ monologues, distinguishes between the *interpersonal/socio-relational axis* (I–you) and the *representational axis* of interaction (see chapter 5). Within this terminology, we could say that the *known* corpus data (chat shows and interviews with celebrities and public personae) and the *unknown* data (interactions with callers from the private sphere, e.g. radio phone-ins) operate more on the *interpersonal/socio-relational axis* as represented by the distribution of *I–you* pronouns. Biber *et al.* (1999) also find that first and second person pronouns typify casual conversation and occur with far greater frequency when compared with the registers of fiction, news and academic prose. They note that this is to be expected since conversational participants normally deal with matters of immediate mutual concern. Chang (2002) adds that this also hints at the common context shared between participants, not only in space and time, but also in social, cultural and institutional background knowledge. In her analysis of a corpus of *Cartalk*, a US weekly phone-in on National Public Radio, involving two brothers, Ray and Tom Magliozzi, who answer questions about cars and car repair posed by listeners, Chang finds that the use of pronouns in the radio show closely parallels their distribution in a comparable corpus of casual conversation (the Cambridge-Cornell corpus of American English, a one-million word component of the Cambridge International Corpus).

It is also worth noting the more or less equal result for *we* and *they* shown in table 6.4. For every *we* there is a *they*, which supports Pennycook's assertions about the inherent dichotomies of *we*, which he says is 'always simultaneously inclusive and exclusive, a pronoun of solidarity and of rejection, of inclusion and exclusion' (Pennycook 1994: 175). *We* claims both authority and communality (ibid.: 176) and it also constructs an I/we, we/you and we/they dichotomy, 'the two pronouns must always be understood with reference to other assumptions about who is being defined as the "we" from which the "you" and the "they" differ' (ibid.: 176).

Let us take a more detailed look at *we* in media interactions in terms of its indexical information about the identity of the participation framework of a programme. *We* is chosen as the focus here as it encompasses the participation framework and can be used by the presenter or the interviewee to appropriate speaking authority on behalf of the audience. This uncontested appropriation further substantiates a tacit participation framework range. Chang (2002) analysed all of the *we* references in her corpus of over 31,000 words of *Cartalk* and she found the following referents for the hosts' (the Magliozzi brothers) and the callers' use of *we* (table 6.5).

Table 6.5 Breakdown of hosts' and callers' use of *we* in US radio phone-in *Cartalk* (Chang 2002)

Hosts		*Callers*	
We the Magliozzi brothers	169	Caller + spouse	12
One of the hosts + staff	6	Caller + family/spouse/partner (?)	14
One of the hosts + caller	2	Caller + a third person	3

Both hosts + caller	12	Caller + the hosts	2
Both hosts + friend	1	Caller + one host	1
Hosts + listeners	6	Quoted *we*	2
We Americans	8	*We* in the area	7
We car mechanics	2	Impersonal *we*	1
Other generic *we*	7	Caller + ?	3
Impersonal *we*	4		
Roleplay/quoted/echoed	8		
Total	225		45

O'Keeffe (2002) profiles all of the generic uses of *we* in her corpus of 55,000 words from the Irish radio phone-in *Liveline*. In these uses of *we*, the speaker employs the pronoun in a collective way on behalf of all those who share the social space of the radio programme. It is a claim to authority, but also a claim to membership of this group.

Table 6.6 Profile of generic *we* values across *Liveline* data

We referent	Example	Percentage
We with a democratic right to vote for our political future	. . . get on and address what we are voting on	42
We Europeans	We are within Europe	15
We with a legal right	. . . we are a bit inclined to ah see opportunities to compensate people . . .	10
We part of the majority Roman Catholic Republic of Ireland	. . . Don't tell me you think we should change our respect for Good Friday	8
We media consumers	. . . by subscribing to Sky that we can we can watch these things . . .	7
We with moral obligations within society	. . . we do need to stop and ask ourselves what's important to us . . .	6
We the ordinary mainstream people	. . . what we call marriage . . .	5
We a sporting nation	. . . much as we did against France . . .	3
We economically successful	. . . what we want to do with all this wealth	3

| *We* part of the United Nations | . . . we operate within the United Nations we are Ireland | 1 |

In these results from O'Keeffe's study we can see an indexing of socio-cultural identity and it is one which is also bound to a time and a place. The data used for this study comes from 1998, when some of the Republic of Ireland's main concerns included how to vote in two major referenda: the European Union Referendum on The Treaty of Amsterdam and the Good Friday Referendum on Northern Ireland.[1] In addition, Irish people spoke out about the issue of thousands of Irish army deafness compensation cases being taken against the state and there was growing awareness of Ireland's rapid economic growth and success and its social consequences. These generic *we* values could be said to hold residual socio-historic information and it would be interesting to check the same type of data in the future to index the extent of any referential shifts.

Let us look now at the counter-side of *we*, that is the *other* which it creates. *Othering* is a by-product of positioning and centring. The notion of positioning is normally associated with research into power semantics in dyadic interactions, where concepts such as footing, alignment and framing (see chapters 4 and 5) can be linked (Goffman 1974; Goffman 1981; Davies and Harré 1990; Tannen 1993; Tannen and Wallat 1993; Gavruseva 1995; Antaki, Díaz and Collins 1996). Here we will look at how 'otherness' is constructed through pronoun choice. The use of the demonstrative pronoun *that* occurs in an interesting example (extract 6.7) from the *Liveline* data (the context is *tattoos*).

Extract 6.7

Caller: . . . sailors had them done . . . I think there's um a lot of undesirables criminals and people like **that** . . .

14 January 1998. Full transcript not available online. *Liveline* website
www.rte.ie/radio1/liveline/

On the surface, *like that* appears to be a straightforward vague category marker as discussed earlier, which could be substituted by *and so on*. On closer examination, this use of *that* is far from neutral and the speaker's choice to use it intentionally positions her in a separate set within society in relation to sailors, undesirables and criminals who collectively form the *other* set. The caller clearly wants to distance herself from sailors, undesirables and criminals.

There are many encodings of enmity and *otherness* to be found in media interactions. Chang provides an interesting example of the construction of *other* through stereotypes (in this case French people) from the American radio phone-in *Cartalk* (extract 6.8).

Extract 6.8

Host 2	. . . I mean as many bad things we've said about the French. **They** know how to sit down, and have a cup of coffee, four, five times a day in the middle of the day.
Host 1	Yeah.
Host 2	And **they** know how to go on strike.
Host 1	**They** sure do.
Host 2	Work ain't one of the ethics that **they** have.
Host 1	No.
Host 2	And that's what **we**'ve got to get rid of this Protestant work ethic is killing **us**.

(Chang 2002: 133)

This is consistent with examples provided by O'Keeffe (2002: 106–7), again from the Irish radio phone-in *Liveline* in the context of callers in the Republic of Ireland constructing otherness in relation to Protestants in Northern Ireland (extract 6.9).

Extract 6.9

Presenter:	But the problem is I mean this was an agreement where **we** were trying to ah all bring sides on board. The Unionists would not sign up to the concept that **they** were Irish. **They** don't want to be Irish.
Caller:	Course **they** don't. The Unionists don't want to be anything but Unionists.
Presenter:	**They** want to be British.
Caller:	Oh come on **they** don't want to be British.
Presenter:	Well **they** tell you **they** want to be British.
Caller:	Marian the Unionists want to be Unionists **they** want to be a separate little empire all to **themselves** getting attention from Dublin and attention from England and answerable to nobody.
Presenter:	Well now I ga= I've gather from your tone that you're not a great admirer of Unionists but the simple fact of the matter is that **they** talk to **us** here on the radio and elsewhere and **they** say **we** are British and **we** want to remain British.
Caller:	**They** say all of **those** things ah yo= I'll go back to that lady in a second. **They** say all of **those** things ah what **they** want is for

the British to pay for **their** welfare **their** social welfare system and all of the rest but not to interfere with **them** or anybody else to interfere with **them**. **They** have a nice little empire running have it running for many many years and **they** want to keep it going+

Presenter: Are you+

Caller: +of course they do.

> 2 April 1998. Full transcript not available online.
> *Liveline* website www.rte.ie/radio1/liveline/

Immediately in the next turn of this *Liveline* extract we find a very interesting contrast between the presenter's use of *this* and the caller's use of *that* to refer to the same issue (extract 6.10).[2]

Extract 6.10

Presenter: Are you going to vote for **this** change?

Caller: I haven't fully considered **that** yet. I'll wait until I see the agreement.

Presenter: Right.

Caller: I haven't I haven't am as I said I haven't paid much attention to what was going on. I have no faith in in in ah Unionists am in what **they** say nothing whatsoever. It as I said earlier **they** talk only to God and **they** talk down to him.

Presenter: Right.

> 2 April 1998. Full transcript not available online.
> *Liveline* website www.rte.ie/radio1/liveline/

The shift here from the presenter's *this change* to the caller's use of *that* indexes a position of self-distancing on the part of the caller in relation to the proposed constitutional change. The caller chose *that* as a distancer rather than *it*, which would have been a more neutral choice in this case as a topic continuer in this exchange. This variation between *this* and *that* is in line with research by McCarthy (1994) who looks at *it*, *this* and *that* in written texts (see also McCarthy 1998). He tells us that *this* regularly functions to signal that the topic focus is shifting or has shifted to a new one. While *that* also functions in this way, it can also refer to entities or foci that are non-current, non-central or other-attributed (after Halliday and Hasan 1976) and so it can marginalize, or reject validity or importance. Looked at in terms of speaker positioning, we can say that *this*, by its focusing function, can show affiliation while *that*, through its distancing function, can indicate enmity or have an *othering* effect.

Extract 6.11 is an example from an interview from the Sunday morning BBC television show *Breakfast with Frost*, in 2004, with US Government Secretary of Defence at the time, Donald Rumsfeld. When the topic of interrogation techniques used by US army personnel is raised, notice how pronoun choice is used as a distancing device.

Extract 6.11

David Frost: And in terms of the famous Major General Miller, the hard
                man of Guantanamo who was sent to improve the record
                of the flow of information on his first trip just for a few
                days, people say that in those few days he affected the whole
                climate, that he sent lists of what he did in Guantanamo
                to battalion commanders, and so on, and your Brigadier
                General, or then Brigadier General, Janis Karpinski said that
                Major General Miller insisted that prisoners should be treated
                like dogs. Now the FT say this, and I don't know, this is the
                FT, the *Financial Times*, says 'one fact remains undisputed –
                less than two months after his departure from Iraq the first
                of the shocking photographs were taken. Whether one event
                helped cause the other, is the question that could decide the
                fate of an administration'.

Donald Rumsfeld: Well, I've not seen the article you're referring to. I think the
                reality is that the administration has seen **those** photographs
                . . . We have not yet determined in any connection at all
                between **that** abuse and an interrogation process. Indeed,
                the majority of the people in **those** pictures engaged in **that**
                abuse were individuals who were not even security detainees,
                that is to say **they** were not people that were even being
                interrogated for the most part. Some may very well have been
                being interrogated but not necessarily in **those** photographs.
                They may have been detainees that people wanted information
                from. But that, **those** activities I think it would be a mistake
                to suggest represented interrogation techniques. Now, we're
                going to know as the trials proceed, precisely what happened
                . . .

27 June 2004. Full transcript available at http://news.bbc.co.uk/1/hi/
programmes/breakfast_with_frost/3844047.stm

Deictic references used to locate speakers geographically offer more indices of identity in media data. As well as pronouns, deictic adverbs tell us a lot about how the group of language users position themselves. Below we compare the use of *over there* from a number of different sources. *Over there* creates an *other* because it is not *here*. As examples from the media corpus illustrate, these reference points are very arbitrary (see table 6.7).

Table 6.7 Examples of deictic references from the media corpus

Centre	Other	Example
Australian Catholic church	Rome/ Catholic curia	Well I came away feeling that our brethren in Rome didn't fully understand the situation in real life as we have it here. I would think that this group that you speak about did exercise an undue influence in forming opinions and convictions **over there**.
Kerry, a county in the south-west of Ireland	Leinster, an eastern Irish province	Maybe it just shows . . . Leinster hurling maybe it's not just a one horse race **over there**.
Ireland	Arab world	I fell for a Moroccan and the whole relationship was complicated from the start because he was from **over there** and to make it worse then he was a Muslim
Europe	Arab world	I know here if you cross the red light it's your fault that's the end of it [*Yeah*] **over there** all foreigners are infidels.
Western world	Iraq	So why wasn't that information given to Hans Blix and his team, to say go and look **over there?**

Other interesting examples can be found by looking at items which locate participants relative to where they are not for example *up there*, *down here*, *down there* (see O'Keeffe 2002).

6.3 Self-reference

Here we will look at the lexical and lexico-grammatical choices made by media participants when they refer to 'themselves' as a place or group, for example collective references such as *Britain*, *America*, *this country*, *this island*, or *our nation*, and so on. Participants' self-reference tokens provide us with further indices of identity because they are markers of self-definition and they reflexively position participants within the participation framework. *Reflexive positioning* is a term introduced by Davies and Harré (1990) to refer to how interactants position themselves in relation to 'others', who, using Davies and Harré's terms, are positioned interactionally. Positioning is a useful concept in the study of media discourse as it allows us to look at the language participants use to locate themselves politically, socially and interactionally. The central position which is arrived at within any participation framework is collaboratively negotiated over time and reflects a collective identity.

Single lexical items are a good starting point when looking at self-reference. As Sinclair (1996: 82) points out very few words have 'terminological tendencies', that is a 'fixed meaning in reference to the world'. Carter (1987: 71) tells us that 'lexical items in discourse require to be constantly interpreted and reinterpreted by the language user' and that, when analysts go beyond constructed examples to consider real texts, 'the "values" of lexis become of significance'. Within the relatively stable and collaboratively achieved sense of range in a participation framework of media texts, it is predicted that unmarked stable patterns of meaning or *values* will emerge and that these values may be specific to particular participation frameworks and so will be revealing in terms of the socio-cultural identity of the participant cohort.

The starting point for a lexical analysis using corpus techniques (as discussed in chapter 3) is to generate a word frequency list. Here we looked at the first 200 words in the list from the media corpus (see chapter 3) and then selected all the lexical items that had potential as self-reference tokens. The next step was to concordance these lexical items to check if they were in fact being used by participants in media interactions in this way and to eliminate any non-self-reference uses (e.g. delete any instances of *united nations* from the count of *nation*). Table 6.8 shows the list of single word tokens that were identified from the 200 most frequent words in the media corpus.

Table 6.8 Self-reference tokens from first 200 most frequent words in media corpus

Word	Total frequency
country (199)/countries (71)	270
world	204
community	155
government	133
British (62)/Britain (52)	114
American (55)/America (50)	105
States (US: 65)	85
Australia (43)/Australian (39)	82
society	71

English (35)/England (29)	64
state	58
national	57
island	51
nation	41
Europe	36

Each of these items merits a detailed analysis within the context of the interviews in which they occurred. Here we will scan just a sample to exemplify how they have indexical information in the overall context of media discourse.

Country

This is by far the most frequently used self-reference token in our dataset. Across the three sub-corpora of unknown, known, and political interactions we find that, not surprisingly, it is used mostly in political interviews (see table 6.9).

Table 6.9 Breakdown of the distribution of *country* in media corpus

Sub-corpus	Percentage
Political	60
Unknown	22
Known	18

The well known BBC interview from 1995 between Martin Bashir and Diana, Princess of Wales, provides an interesting illustration of its use in context. In this interview Diana famously expressed her wish to be 'the queen of people's hearts' as opposed to being the future queen of Great Britain. She strategically refers to Britain as a country many times in the interview invoking a sense of collectiveness, solidarity and common identity. Notice also how she creates opposition between *this country* and *abroad* in the examples in extracts 6.12, 6.13, 6.14 and 6.15.

Extract 6.12

Diana: If I'd been on what I call an awayday, or I'd been **up part of the country** all day, I'd come home feeling pretty empty, because my engagements at that time . . .

Extract 6.13

Martin Bashir:	What role do you see for yourself in the future?
Diana:	I'd like to be an ambassador **for this country**. I'd like to represent **this country abroad**. As I have all this media interest, let's not just sit **in this country** and be battered by it. Let's take them, these people, out to represent **this country** and the good qualities of it **abroad**. When I go **abroad** we've got 60 to 90 photographers, just **from this country**, coming with me, so let's use it in a productive way, to help **this country**.

Extract 6.14

Diana:	I'd like to be a queen of people's hearts, in people's hearts, but I don't see myself being Queen **of this country**. I don't think many people will want me to be Queen.

Extract 6.15

Martin Bashir:	What was your reaction when you learnt that the child was a boy?
Diana:	Enormous relief. I felt **the whole country** was in labour with me. Enormous relief. But I had actually known William was going to be a boy, because the scan had shown it, so it caused no surprise.

20 November 1995. Full transcript available athttp://www.bbc.co.uk/
politics97/diana/panorama.html

Compare this call for sympathy and compassion by Diana, Princess of Wales, with the invocation of purpose and duty in time of imminent war in an interview with the US Secretary of Defence in the lead-up to the invasion of Iraq, Donald Rumsfeld (extract 6.16). Notice how the uses of *country* here position the presenter, the interviewee, the nationwide audience and the enemy country.

Extract 6.16

Donald Rumsfeld:	. . . notwithstanding the fact that [Hitler] was engaged in a holocaust against the Jews. It was a classic debate **in our country**, in the pre-World War II period, and it was the attack on Japan, by Japan on Pearl Harbor that brought us in.

Extract 6.17

Presenter: I'm a big fan of your moral clarity, your inner strength and
                        understanding of what appeasement would do **for the
                        country**. You have helped defend the freedom throughout
                        most of your adult life and we owe you a debt of gratitude.

            21 January 2004. WNDB 1150 radio station, Daytona Beach, Florida.
            Full transcript available at: http://www.defenselink.mil/transcripts/
                                          2004/tr20040121-secdef0361.html

Extract 6.18

Presenter: How are you doing? I'm a big fan of yours. I love what you've
                        done **for this country** and for the cause of liberty, my
                        friend.
Donald Rumsfeld: Thank you. I appreciate that. I must say, life's been good. I'm
                        healthy, I feel that the work we're doing is important **for the
                        country**. It's a delight to work for this President . . .

            21 January 2004. WABC, New York. Full transcript available at:
                                    http://www.defenselink.mil/transcripts

World

World is used predominantly in the corpus of political interviews as table 6.10
illustrates.

Table 6.10 Breakdown of the distribution of *world* in media corpus

Sub-corpus	Percentage
Political	76
Known	16
Unknown	8

In the non-political discourse of the 'known' and 'unknown' data, *world* is mostly
used as an intensifier (41 per cent of all uses in the known corpus and 27 per cent
in the unknown data). Figure 6.2 gives some examples.

Figure 6.2 Example of uses of *world* as an intensifier in the known and unknown sub-corpora of the media corpus

> And there is **no way in the world** that any nurse would murder another nurse.
> He is **the soundest man in the world** I know him for over forty years
>   **Never anywhere else in the world that I've travelled.**
> **the best female skater in the world**. She is certainly one of the busiest.
> **the most exclusive club in the world** – the college of cardinals.
>   I watch **every game in the world** basketball cricket soccer you name it rugby . . .
>   It'll do **anything in the world for her.**
>   found **nowhere else in the world** and that's Killarney Shad
> **one of the most famous in the world**. In the studio where the Beatles . . .
>   **the worst director in the world**, you know, he didn't get it.

The political corpus, on the other hand, refers to various 'worlds' reflecting many different positions which participants take up in news interviews. Here are some examples:

- a post-September 11th world
- a post-Copernican world where we can still think of God as a being who sits above the sky and periodically invades the world in a supernatural way
- a world where the technology available is in such a scale, you could solve, not all, but many of the problems
- a world that is not always an easy place to live
- a world, which seems to be passing
- the world is just a world in which things like that happen, accidents happen, tragedies occur, sicknesses occur
- I'm not going to live in a world where the United States, which has bombed 19 countries since the war, and has weapons of mass destruction . . .
- a world where any country can attack any other country because of its civil rights record
- my own Arab world
- That's the nature of our world. We're an interdependent world. We tend to try to avoid having single suppliers so that we have relief valve.
- Well definitely the terrorists and the evil forces are trying to break our world, they are trying to stop democracy from happening in Iraq. They are trying to undermine the political process.
- a pluralist world, that the rhetoric of exclusivism, the rhetoric of consigning everybody else to hell.

Island

On the surface *island* appears to be a neutral token as a geographical reference. One dictionary definition is 'a mass of land that is surrounded by water and is smaller than a continent' (*Collins Concise Dictionary*, 1989). However, O'Keeffe (2002) looks at the word in the context of her radio phone-in data from *Liveline* which was recorded on the island of Ireland. She finds that the core value of *island* is in reference to the island of Ireland and the second most frequent usage is to refer to one of the Aran Islands, a group of small islands off the west coast of Ireland. She compares the occurrence of *island* across spoken data collected on other islands, namely, Britain and New Zealand, and finds that the results from the London-Lund Corpus (Britain), the Lancaster/IBM Spoken English Corpus (Britain) and the Wellington Spoken Corpus (New Zealand) (data from ICAME corpus on CD – Hofland, Lindebjcrg and Thunestvedt 1999[3]) are at odds with the Irish data. Only occurrences of *island* (or *islands* in the case of New Zealand) that referred to the respective countries or island composites were counted and all results have been normalized to occurrences per million words (see table 6.11).

Table 6.11 Occurrences of *island* across spoken data from other island countries compared with occurrences in *Liveline* (O'Keeffe 2002)

Corpus	Data	Occurrences of island per million words
London-Lund Corpus	500,000 words of British English	0.8
Lancaster/IBM Spoken English Corpus	55,000 words of British English, mostly BBC recordings	18.0
Wellington Spoken Corpus	1 million words of New Zealand English	70.0[4]
Liveline	55,000 words of Irish English, all spoken radio phone-in data	873.0

We see from these results that the word *island* occurs with a strikingly high frequency in the *Liveline* data and indeed it is very interesting to note how low the occurrence is in the British data. The high result in the Irish data is partly accounted for by frequent discussions that took place during the 1998 sample period about the question of Irish identity in the lead up to the Referendum on the Good Friday Agreement in Northern Ireland, and the vote to amend the

Republic's constitutional claim on Northern Ireland in articles 2 and 3 of the Irish Constitution in May 1998 as discussed above (see also footnote 1).

The use of the word *island* to refer to Ireland is politically fraught and so proves an interesting item to study in this media context. The Republic of Ireland is only part of the island of Ireland while the six counties of Northern Ireland are part of the United Kingdom and so to use *island* to refer to Ireland as a country is tantamount to a political aspiration for a united Ireland. This is borne out by the research of Coperías Aguilar and Besó (1999) who assembled two corpora of written data from diametrically opposing political parties in Northern Ireland: a 15,440 word corpus of Sinn Féin[5] data and a 9,800 word corpus of Ulster Unionist Party (UUP)[6] data (see table 6.12).

Table 6.12 Occurrences of *island* across Sinn Féin and Ulster Unionist Party written data 1997–8 (Coperías Aguilar and Besó 1999) compared with occurrences in *Liveline* (O'Keeffe 2002) – results per million words

Corpus	No. of occurrences of island
Sinn Féin	2072
Liveline	873
Ulster Unionist Party	714

O'Keeffe (2002) notes that the most frequent patterns that co-occur with *island* in the *Liveline* corpus are *of the island*, *in the island* and *on the island* in that order of frequency. Interestingly, the literal or geographic pattern *on the island* is the least frequent.

Table 6.13 Frequency distribution of colligation patterns for *of the island*, *in the island* and *on the island* in *Liveline* corpus. All results are per million words.

Pattern	No. of occurrences
of the island	109
in the island	72
on the island	36

This patterning points to a preference for metaphoric as opposed to literal (or geographic) usage in the participation framework of *Liveline*. If the lesser-used phrase *on the island* locates Irish speakers geographically, the majority patterns: *of the island* and *in the island* locate participants metaphorically. This lexico-grammatical choice profiles the identity of a group of people who very much see themselves metaphorically as living *in* an island country or being part *of* a whole island (something that is not found in the British or New Zealand corpora referred to above). In further support of this assertion, we can substitute the word *island* in the *of* and *in* patterns with words such as *country* or *society* (in the/of the *country* or *society*).

Self-reference using proper nouns

England/Britain

England is used for two purposes in the media data. Firstly, by British speakers as a means of referring to England as opposed to other parts of Britain, namely Wales or Scotland. For example, extract 6.19 is from a BBC *Newsnight* interview on the subject of British alcohol licensing laws, recorded in July 2003, with the then Minister for Sports and Tourism, Richard Caborn.

Extract 6.19

Richard Caborn: We have evidence to show where we have relaxed **in England** on Sundays, in Scotland when we allowed the opening hours to extend, there was a reduction in the problems related to nuisance through drink. Also you can cite many other countries that you don't get those problems on the Continent.

Tuesday 8 July 2003. Full transcript available at http://news.bbc.co.uk/1/ hi/programmes/newsnight/3055548.stm

However, 79 per cent of all uses of *England* come from the known and unknown corpora (chat shows and radio phone-ins) and are all used by non-British speakers (American, Australian and Irish). It seems that these speakers use *England* to refer to Britain as a whole. Some examples are provided below:

- Well, you know, 'Buffy [the Vampire]' is enormously popular in Europe. In **England**, it's a major thing. Actually, in Germany the soundtrack to the musical sold as much in Germany . . .
- You're not meant to say things like that when you're in **England**.
- I still have family here. I still harbour a dream of retiring here. You can take the boy out of **England**, but you can't take **England** out of the boy. And um, yes, I feel a huge emotional attachment to **England**.
- Is it true that Bishop Casey is not going to be allowed back to either Ireland or **England**?

Britain, on the other hand is widely used in political/news interviews and rarely used in the known and unknown sub-corpora (table 6.14).

Table 6.14 Breakdown distribution of *Britain* in media corpus

Sub-corpus	Percentage
Political	94
Unknown	4
Known	2

Focusing more closely on the use of *Britain* in the political and news interviews, we can divide it into two meanings or 'values' (to use the term from Carter 1987) (table 6.15).

Table 6.15 Values of *Britain* in political/news interview data

Value/meaning	Example from media corpus	Percentage
a nation-state	the interests of Britain	59
literal use, as a country	I am a Muslim and I live in Britain	41

The majority of *nation-state* uses are by British politicians and the literal references are mostly by non-politicians. Thirteen per cent of all *nation-state* uses are metaphoric where Britain is given agency:

- . . . about five years ago as **Britain faced up to** the prospect of a national general election.
- Because **Britain occupied** Egypt in 1882 and we were still there in 1945. You know, you have to know a little bit of history . . .
- Those are **choices Britain has to make**.

America

When we scrutinize the occurrences of *America* in the media corpus, we find the following breakdown across the 47 occurrences (table 6.16).

Table 6.16 Distribution of *America* in media corpus

Sub-corpus	Percentage
Political	64
Known	30
Unknown	6

All but two of the occurrences in the known and unknown data are in the literal sense of the country as a geographical location. In the political/news interviews (table 6.17), the situation differs.

Table 6.17 Uses of *America* in political/news interview data

Pattern of use	Percentage
a nation-state	90
literal use, as a country	10

Here are some examples:

America – the nation-state

- I think he'll talk about how Ronald Reagan believed in **America**. I think that's why Americans loved him so much.
- . . . in 1983 when Saddam was a huge ally of **America**, and they were arming him . . .
- And if they think that a few soldiers represents the entirety of **America**, they don't really understand America then.

America – literal use as a country

- . . . could they be tried under American trial rules in **America**.
- And the black people in **America** were the first people who made this very clear to me.
- And he flew them to **America**. And they came to my office . . .

Australia

Again when we look at *Australia* in Australian media interactions we find that political interviews provide the most occurrences.

Table 6.18 Distribution of *Australia* in media corpus

Sub-corpus	Percentage
Political	69
Known	18
Unknown	13

In contrast to the earlier findings in relation to the breakdown of meaning values of the item, here we find that in the political corpus there is a much larger percentage of literal usage, referring to the country as opposed to the nation-state. This could be due to the nature of the political interviews which were examined. A more in-depth study of Australian data would be needed in order to draw more concrete conclusions from this:

Table 6.19 Uses of *Australia* in political/news interview data

Pattern of use	Percentage
literal use, as a country	82
a nation-state	18

Below are some examples.

Australia – literal use as a country

- What do the political leaders in **Australia** need to do to actually begin to give effect to that?
- . . . such as the Columbine massacre in the United States, the Port Arthur massacre in **Australia**, the massacre in Scotland ten years ago at Dunblane.
- I think that South African Muslims have a lot to teach other people in a country like **Australia**.

Australia – the nation-state

- . . . they're questions, which are looming larger than ever, and perhaps as **Australia** faces a federal election in the next month or so . . .
- . . . there are 100,000 abortions each year, each year, John, and that's a tragedy for **Australia**.
- . . . but faced with a government prepared to push **Australia** to a race-based election, I had to make some trade-offs.

To summarize, we have found generally that people refer to countries using the proper noun more in political interviews and that when they do so, they encode metaphoric meaning more than literal meaning. At a lexico-grammatical level we can suggest the following tendencies:

- when speakers are being literal they are most likely to use the prepositional phrase 'in + name of country' or 'to + name of country' (e.g. What do the political leaders in Australia need to do?; I am a Muslim and I live in Britain; he flew them to America).
- when speakers are being metaphoric they are likely to use verb phrases (e.g. those are choices Britain has to make; Australia faces a federal election; America is not the enemy).

6.4 Conclusion

In this chapter we looked at how a collection of participants in a media interaction draw on shared knowledge, shared worlds and shared socio-cultural identities. These identities can create a positioning of the participation framework of a programme, an identity, and those who listen and watch the show feel part of that identity because it represents their positioning. We also note that many may watch or listen to a programme and reject its position and not feel included or represented when the presenter or interviewee says *we know that . . .*, *in our country*, or *our state . . .* Even at a subtle level identities and enmities are created in the way that we use pronouns to refer to *others* who are *out there*, and set up categories based on shared assumptions about the cultural range of our co-participants in the case of vague categorization, for example *undesirables, criminals and people like that.*

We also looked at some of the items of self-reference in the media corpus. From these superficial examples of analysis, the rich potential for further studies into self-reference and the indexical information it conveys is obvious. We have seen that it is most productive to use corpus-based techniques, as shown, for example, in Coperías Aguilar and Besó (1999), McCarthy (2002) and O'Keeffe (2002), in this type of analysis and that it has enormous scope for the study of socio-cultural representation and identity in media discourse. However, in order to undertake such a study a larger sample would be needed.

Overall, this chapter set out to explore the collective understanding of (1) a range of shared space, (2) a cache of shared knowledge and (3) a sense of common identity that prevails within the participation framework of a media interaction. From the brief analyses that we have conducted here, it is clear that media interactions do not take place in an ethereal vacuum. They are grounded in social space and they are driven by shared knowledge and a sense of common identity.

7   Conclusion

> Presenter: Okay well listen thank you very much indeed for talking to us.
> Caller: Thank you for having me.
>
> Extract from *Liveline* radio phone-in, Radio Telefís Éireann, 2 April 1998

7.0 Introduction

Let us now draw together our investigation of media discourse. The book started out with a theoretical investigation about the nature of spoken interactions in the media and how they could best be described. That led us to the notion of a participation framework. We also raised the question of genre and how it can be applied to this type of spoken language. The second major stage of the book (chapter 3) involved looking at what types of interactions there are and how these have been looked at from different perspectives. We saw the contribution of a number of methodologies, particularly conversation analysis, and we put forward the notion of using corpus linguistics as a complementary tool. The remaining chapters of the book involved actual analysis using data which is mostly available on the internet in the form of transcripts. We looked at three facets of media interactions:

1   how they are controlled and managed within the participation framework
2   how some interactions draw on pseudo-intimacy and
3   how identities are encoded in the language of media interactions.

Let us bring together what we have found and reflect on some issues that arise out of these findings as a whole and suggest possible further research.

7.1   Media interactions take place within a participation framework

The main theoretical assertion of this book has been that the traditional dyadic model of interaction between a speaker and a hearer is not adequate for the description of media interactions. In its place we proposed a participation framework model within which we can say that all media interactions take place between a presenter/host, one or more interviewee/guest and an audience. The interviewee/guest and the audience may be co-present but not always. There will be a non-present audience who listen to or view the interaction and this cohort is fully ratified within the participation framework. We have asserted throughout this book that the study of media interactions needs to take cognisance of the participation framework, but within this framework there is also scope for further research.

Firstly, we have not mentioned another layer of the interaction, that is the pre-interaction stage. In advance of most media interactions, there is an interplay between a producer (or production team), a researcher, the presenter and the interviewee. The researcher plays the conduit role between producer, presenter and interviewee. Most interviewees are contacted in advance of a programme by a researcher. The interviewee briefs and is briefed by a researcher. The researcher very often prepares questions and suggests topics that may be raised and provides these as background to the presenter and interviewee in advance of an interview. The media interaction that we see/hear therefore is the culmination of interactions between producers, researchers, the interviewer and the interviewee. It would be fruitful to study the totality of programme making, that is to record and analyse all of the interactions that lead up to an interview: the production meetings, the researcher's interaction with the interviewer and interviewee as well as auditing the written sources that are consulted by the researcher, the interviewer and the interviewee.

Secondly, participation frameworks can take place in different modes. Some are televised and some are on radio. The former has both a visual and sound component while the latter only has sound. This must have an impact on the interaction, not least of all on how the message is packaged differently for these two contexts. In-depth research is also needed on the impact of medium on the interaction, that is to compare interactions on television versus on radio. Many interesting questions arise, for example: are non-verbal responses such as head nods and shoulder shrugs substituted on radio by vocalizations? what is the effect of camera angle on meaning?, and so on.

7.2 Media interactions require an eclectic approach

Because, as we have seen, media interactions are not straightforward dyadic interactions, it is very difficult to apply any one method to investigate the interaction adequately. Conversation analysis provides an excellent focus on the turn-by-turn unfolding of the interaction and the significance of sequentiality and placement within it. Discourse analysis helps us understand the effect of certain moves and exchange structures, and how certain features such as the use of discourse markers, deixis, hedging, and so on, operate within the participation framework of the programme. A pragmatics framework and an interactional analysis focus us on the interplay of power semantics within this asymmetrical interaction and on how power can be downplayed, challenged or redressed. Corpus linguistics adds to the analysis of the interaction by allowing us to look at the totality of the data and see consistent patterns of use. As we saw in chapter 6, this can be particularly illuminating when looking at the shared space that is created within the participation framework of a programme. The language we use in media interactions encodes indexical socio-cultural information that draws on and reinforces the commonage of the participation framework. This aspect of the study of media interactions is understudied and corpus linguistics can contribute in this area by allowing for the scrutiny of large amounts of data and the systematicity therein.

The main methodological point of this book has been to show the benefits of an eclectic approach to analysing and interpreting media data. Because media interactions need to be understood from different perspectives, they can only be investigated adequately by employing different methodological tools to suit different aspects of the interactions. At turn and exchange level, methods such as conversation analysis and discourse analysis are crucial. When examining the power relations at play within an interaction, a pragmatic interpretation is also required. Corpus linguistics can look at large amounts of data and give statistical support to qualitative findings and can also show semantic patterns of use which can be very informative from a socio-cultural perspective, but in order to account for features and statistics that recur in a corpus, the analyst in this applied context needs to return to existing models such as conversation analysis, discourse analysis and pragmatics.

7.3 Media interactions are not homogeneous

Finally, let us return to the notion of spoken genres. By looking closely at media interactions, we have found that they are not homogenous as a genre. Variation is apparent relative to the context and speaker relationship, which is also the case with casual conversation. Casual conversation is not one uniform type nor is media discourse. We have found that television and radio interactions differ relative to (1) the participants, that is, whether they are known or unknown in the public sphere and (2) the context of the interaction, whether is it a radio phone-in, a chat show or a political interview. Political interviews were found to be most institutionalized and their features were closest to other institutional contexts, such as academic discourse, whereas radio phone-ins and chat shows were found to have features and patterns that more resemble casual conversation. The notion that all spoken genres are in some way linked in a chain of communication is a powerful notion and this is something that is very important in the study of media interactions, especially those which draw on the pseudo-intimacy of casual conversation. By emulating patterns of familiarity, for example by routine greetings, using first name vocatives, hedging and inclusive pronouns, a shared world can be simulated and closeness and intimacy can be created between strangers who feel over time that they belong within the participation framework of certain programmes and not part of others. The broadcast media engage in a 'conversation' with their audiences. In this book, we have seen how banal, everyday conversation provides us with a benchmark for understanding the mediated conversations that are beamed into our homes 24 hours a day. Over the decades, as we have observed, this conversational relationship between media and audience has become less formal, less distant and more like the conversations that we have in everyday life. One can only suppose that this trend will continue in a future where communication technology globally transcends time and space.

Notes

1 Introduction

1   A term borrowed from Goffman (1981) to refer to the rituals of openings, greetings, small talk, leave-takings and closings.

2 A framework for analysing media discourse

1   When we use the term *hearer*, we also refer to viewers.
2   This view, which attributes the origins of higher order psychological processes of the individual to external social interaction, is a notion which links to the work of Austin, Bakhtin, Malinowski, Wittgenstein, Buehler and Vygotsky, among others (Duranti 1986: 239). Verbal communication seen as an achievement of individual social actors, has a far-reaching impact on the study of a linguistic system, running counter to the Chomskyian means of documenting a linguistic system via individual competence (Duranti 1986: 239–40), and so external empirical evidence is valued over invented internal intuitions about language use.
3   Whenever 'utterance' is used henceforth in the Bakhtinian sense, it will be italicized.
4   Note that when 'discourse' is used by Candlin and Maley (and others when stated), as a countable noun, I am interpreting it in the spirit of Fairclough (1995a: 18–19) who says in addition to being used as an abstract noun for a general view of language in social use, discourse is used as a count noun as a category alongside genre in the analysis of texts.

3 Review of methodologies for analysing media discourse

1   In the interest of consistency, Hopper and Drummond's terminology is used (1992).
2   It is worth noting that since Cameron and Hills' research was conducted, it is much more prevalent for phones to have caller identification devices and this, too, has an impact on turn sequentiality and placement.
3   Hutchby (1991: 121) also asserts that 'call validations' are always caller-initiated. He defines call validations as: 'substantive production of news, and . . . the necessary and autonomous work of the caller alone'. He sees this as an institutional reality.

4   LCIE is a one-million word corpus of Irish English which has been built using the
     design matrix as detailed in McCarthy (1998) (see Farr, Murphy and O'Keeffe
     2002).

4 Managing the discourse

1   *Bradmanesque* refers to the famous Australian cricketer in the 1920s to 1940s, Sir
     Donald Bradman.

5 Creating and sustaining pseudo-relationships

1   Horton and Wohl (1956) is reprinted in Gumpert and Cathcart (1979). Henceforth
     references to this paper will be Horton and Wohl (1979).

6 Creating identities

1   The Good Friday Agreement was evolved within the Northern Ireland peace process
     in 1998. Among other things it included constitutional amendments to the constitu-
     tion of the Republic of Ireland, relinquishing territorial claims to the six counties of
     Northern Ireland. In order to fulfil this, a referendum was held in the Republic of
     Ireland on the same day as the referendum on the Treaty of Amsterdam in May 1998.
     The constitutional change was carried by a 94.4 per cent majority.
2   Note: 'this change' refers to the referendum in the Republic of Ireland on the Good
     Friday Agreement, which also included constitutional amendments relinquishing
     territorial claims to the six counties of Northern Ireland. See also footnote 1.
3   For further information on the ICAME CD see http://www.hit.uib.no/icame/cd
4   This figure includes all instances of North Island and South Island.
5   An Irish republican political party, predominantly Catholic, with elected repre-
     sentatives in the parliaments and assemblies of the UK, Northern Ireland and the
     Republic of Ireland. Sinn Féin literally means *ourselves* and the party has commonly
     been referred to as 'Sinn Féin/IRA' (Irish Republican Army) because of its links with
     this organization.
6   The Ulster Unionist Party (UUP), predominantly Protestant and loyalist, is one of
     the largest political parties in Northern Ireland. It is perceived as a more moderate
     unionist party than its rival the Democratic Unionist Party (DUP).

Bibliography

Aijmer, K. and Altenberg, B. (eds) (1991) *English Corpus Linguistics: Studies in Honour of Jan Svartvik*, London: Longman.

Antaki, C., Díaz, F. and Collins, A.F. (1996) 'Keeping your footing: conversational completion in three part sequences', *Journal of Pragmatics*, 25: 151–71.

Armbruster, B. (1996) 'Schema theory and the design of content-area textbooks', *Educational Psychologist*, 21: 253–76.

Atkinson, J.M. (1979) 'Sequencing and shared attentiveness to court proceedings', in G. Psathas (ed.) *Everyday Language: Studies in Ethnomethodology*, New York: Irvington-Wiley, pp. 257–86.

Atkinson, J.M. and Drew, P. (1979) *Order in Court: the Organization of Verbal Interaction in Judicial Settings*, London: Macmillan.

Bakhtin, M. (1986) 'The problem of speech genres', in C. Emerson and M. Holquist (eds) *Speech Genres and Other Late Essays*, Austin, TX: University of Texas Press, pp. 60–102.

Banbrook, L. and Skehan, P. (1989) 'Classrooms and display questions', in C. Brumfitt and R. Mitchell (eds) *Research in the Language Classroom*, London: Modern English Publications and the British Council, pp. 141–52.

Barsalou, W.L. (1983) 'Ad hoc categories', *Memory and Cognition*, 11: 211–77.

Barsalou, W.L. (1987) 'The instability of graded structure: implications for the nature of concepts', in U. Neisser (ed.) *Concepts and Conceptual Development*, Cambridge: Cambridge University Press, pp. 101–40.

Baynham, M. (1991) 'Speech reporting as discourse strategy: some issues of acquisition and use', *Australian Review of Applied Linguistics*, 14: 87–114.

Baynham, M. (1996) 'Direct speech: what's it doing in non-narrative discourse?', *Journal of Pragmatics*, 25: 61–81.

Benwell, B. (1996) 'The discourse of university tutorials: an investigation into the structure and pedagogy of small-group teaching across a range of academic disciplines', unpublished thesis, University of Nottingham.

Bhatia, V.K. (1993) Analysing Genre: Language Use in Professional Settings, London: Longman.

Biber, D. (1988) *Variation across Speech and Writing*, Cambridge: Cambridge University Press.

Biber, D., Conrad, S., and Reppen, R. (1998) *Corpus Linguistics: Investigating Language Structure and Use*, Cambridge: Cambridge University Press.

Biber, D., Johansson, S., Leech, G., Conrad, S. and Finegan, E. (1999) *Longman Grammar of Spoken and Written English*, Harlow: Longman.

Blom, J.P. and Gumpertz, J.J. (1972) 'Social meaning in linguistic structure code-switching in Norway', in J.J. Gumpertz and D. Hymes (eds) *Directions in Sociolinguistics: The Ethnography of Communication*, Oxford: Basil Blackwell, pp. 407–34.

Blum-Kulka, S. (1983) 'The dynamics of political interviews', *Text* 3(2): 131–53.

Blum-Kulka, S. and Weizman, E. (2003) 'Misunderstanding in political interviews', in J. House, G. Kasper and S. Ross (eds) *Misunderstanding in Social Life: Discourse Approaches to Problematic Talk*, London: Pearson, pp. 107–28.

Boden, D. (1994) *The Business of Talk*, Cambridge: Polity Press.

Boxer, D. and Pickering L. (1995) 'Problems in the presentation of speech acts in ELT materials: the case of complaints', *ELT Journal*, 49: 99–158.

Brock, C.A. (1986) 'The effects of referential questions on ESL classroom discourse', *TESOL Quarterly*, 20(1): 47–59.

Brown, H. (2000) 'Finucane can, but she sometimes can't', *The Irish Times*, 2 December, p. 11.

Brown, R. and Ford, M. (1961) 'Address terms in American English', *Journal of Abnormal and Social Psychology*, 62: 375–85.

Brown, R. and Gilman, A. (1960) 'The pronouns of power and solidarity', in T. Sebeok (ed.) *Style in Language*, New York: John Wiley and Sons, pp. 253–76.

Brown, P. and Levinson, S.C. (1987) *Politeness: Some Universals in Language Usage*, Cambridge: Cambridge University Press.

Brown, G. and Wragg, E.C. (1993) *Questioning*, New York: Routledge and Kegan Paul.

Burton, D. (1980) *Dialogue and Discourse*, London: Routledge and Kegan Paul.

Button, G. (1987) 'Moving out of closings', in G. Button and J. Lee (eds) *Talk and Social Organisation*, Clevedon: Multilingual Matters, pp. 101–51.

Cameron, D. and Hills, D. (1990) '"Listening in": negotiating relationships between listeners and presenters on radio phone-in programmes', in G. McGregor and R. White (eds) *Reception and Response: Hearer Creativity and the Analysis of Spoken and Written Texts*, London: Routledge and Kegan Paul, pp. 53–68.

Candlin, C.N. and Maley, Y. (1997) 'Intertextuality and interdiscursivity in the discourse of alternative dispute resolution', in B.L. Gunnarsson, P. Linell and B. Nordberg (eds) *The Construction of Professional Discourse*, London: Longman, pp. 201–22.

Carbaugh, D. (1988) *Talking American: Cultural Discourses on Donahue*, Norwood, NJ: Ablex Publishing Corporation.

Carbaugh, D. (1996) 'Mediating cultural selves', in D. Grodin and T.R. Lindoff (eds) *Constructing the Self in a Mediated World*, London: Sage, pp. 84–106.

Carter, R. (1987) *Vocabulary: Applied Linguistic Perspectives*, London: Routledge and Kegan Paul.

Carter, R. (1998) 'Orders of reality: CANCODE, communication and culture', *ELT Journal*, 52: 43–56.

Carter, R. and McCarthy, M. (1995) 'Grammar and the spoken language', *Applied Linguistics*, 16(2): 141–57.

Carter, R.A. and McCarthy, M.J. (1997a) 'Written and spoken vocabulary', in N. Schmitt and M.J. McCarthy (eds) *Vocabulary: Description, Acquisition, Pedagogy*, Cambridge: Cambridge University Press, pp. 20–39.

Carter, R.A. and McCarthy, M.J. (1997b) *Exploring Spoken English*, Cambridge: Cambridge University Press.

Carter, R.A. and McCarthy, M.J. (1999) 'The English get-passive in spoken discourse: description and implications for an interpersonal grammar', *English Language and Linguistics*, 3(1): 41–58.

Carter, R.A. and McCarthy, M.J. (2002) 'From conversation to corpus: a dual analysis of a broadcast political interview', in A. Sánchez Macarro (ed.) *Windows on the World: Media Discourse in English*, Valencia: University of Valencia Press, pp. 15–39.

Carter, R.A. and McCarthy, M.J. (2006) *The Cambridge Grammar of English*, Cambridge: Cambridge University Press.

Chafe, W. (1982) 'Integration and involvement in speaking, writing, and oral literature', in D. Tannen (ed.) *Spoken and Written Language*, Norwood, NJ: Ablex, pp. 35–53.

Chafe, W. (1985) 'Linguistic differences produced by differences between speaking and writing', in D. Olson, N. Torrance and A. Hildyard (eds) *Literacy, Language, and Learning*, Cambridge: Cambridge University Press, pp. 105–23.

Chafe, W. (1992) 'The importance of corpus linguistics to understanding the nature of language', in J. Svartvik (ed.) *Directions in Corpus Linguistics: Proceedings of Nobel Symposium 82, Stockholm, 4–8 August 1991*, Berlin: Mouton de Gruyter, pp. 79–97.

Chang, P. (2002) 'Who's behind the personal pronouns in talk radio? Cartalk: a case study', in A. Sánchez Macarro (ed.) *Windows on the World: Media Discourse in English*, Valencia: University of Valencia Press, pp. 115–52.

Channell, J. (1994) *Vague Language*, Oxford: Oxford University Press.

Charteris-Black, J. (2004) 'Why "an angel rides in the whirlwind and directs the storm": a corpus-based comparative study of metaphor in British and American political discourse', *Language and Computers*, 49(1): 133–50.

Clark, H. and Carlson, T. (1982) 'Hearers and speech acts', *Language*, 58(2): 332–73.

Clayman, S. (1991) 'News interview openings: aspects of sequential organization', in P. Scannell (ed.) *Broadcast Talk*, London: Sage, pp. 48–75.

Clayman, S. (1993) 'Reformulating the question: a device for answering/not answering questions in news interviews and press conferences', *Text*, 13(2): 159–88.

Clayman, S. and Heritage, J. (2002) *The News Interview: Journalists and Public Figures on the Air*, Cambridge: Cambridge University Press.

Coates, J. (1986) *Women, Men and Language: A Sociolinguistic Account of Sex Differences in Language*, London: Longman.

Cook, G. (1989) *Discourse*, Oxford: Oxford University Press.

Cook-Gumpertz, J. and Gumpertz, J. (1976) *Papers on Language and Context*, working papers no. 46, Berkeley: Language Behavior Research Laboratory.

Coperías Aguilar, M.J. and Andreu Besó, J.V. (1999) 'The battle of words: a political and linguistic analysis of the Northern Irish conflict', *Studies in English Language and Linguistics*, 1: 41–56.

Corner, J. (1991) 'The interview as a social encounter', in P. Scannell (ed.) *Broadcast Talk*, London: Sage, pp. 31–47.

Cotterill, J. (2003) *Language in Court: Power and Persuasion in the O. J. Simpson Trial*, Palgrave: Basingstoke.

Coulthard, M. and Ashby, M. (1975) 'Talking with the Doctor, 1', *Journal of Communication*, Summer: 140–7.

Davies, B. and Harré, R. (1990) 'Positioning: the discursive production of selves', *Journal of the Theory of Social Behaviour*, 20: 43–63.

Day, R. (1961) *Television: A Personal Report*, London: Hutchinson.

Dimbleby, J. (1975) *Richard Dimbleby: A Biography*, London: Hodder and Stoughton.

Dines, E. (1980) 'Variation in discourse – and stuff like that', *Language in Society*, 1: 13–31.

Dittman, A.T. and Llewellyn, L.G. (1967) 'The phonemic clause as a unit of speech decoding', *Journal of Personality and Social Psychology*, 6: 341–49.

Drew, P. (1985) 'Analysing the use of language in courtroom interaction', in T.A. Van Dijk (ed.) *Handbook of Discourse Analysis*, vol. 3, *Discourse and Dialogue*, London: Academic Press, pp. 133–47.

Drew, P. (1992) 'Contested evidence in courtroom cross examination: the case of a trial for rape', in P. Drew and J. Heritage (eds) *Talk at Work*, Cambridge: Cambridge University Press, pp. 470–520.

Drew, P. and Chilton, K. (2000) 'Calling just to keep in touch: regular and habitual telephone calls as an environment for small talk', in J. Coupland (ed.) *Small Talk*, London: Longman, pp. 137–62.

Drew, P. and Heritage, J. (1992) *Talk at Work: Interaction in Institutional Settings*, Cambridge: Cambridge University Press.

Driscoll, M. (1994) *Psychology of Learning for Instruction*, Boston: Allyn and Bacon.

Drummond, K. and Hopper, R. (1993a) 'Backchannels revisited: acknowledgement tokens and speakership incipiency', *Research on Language and Social Interaction*, 26(2): 157–77.

Drummond, K. and Hopper, R. (1993b) 'Some uses of *yeah*', *Research on Language and Social Interaction*, 26(2): 203–12.

DuBois, S. (1993) 'Extension particles, etc.', *Language Variation and Change*, 4: 179–203.

Dudley-Evans, T. (ed.) (1987) 'Genre analysis and ESP', *ELR Journal 1*, Birmingham: University of Birmingham English Language Research.

Duncan, S. (1974) 'On the structure of speaker-auditor interaction during speaker turns', *Language in Society*, 2: 161–80.

Duranti, A. (1986) 'The audience as co-author: an introduction', *Text*, 6(3): 239–47.

Eggins, S. (1994) *An Introduction to Systemic Functional Linguistics*, London: Printer.

Eggins, S. and Slade, D. (1997) *Analysing Casual Conversation*, London: Cassell.

Fairclough, N. (1988) 'Discourse representation in media discourse', *Sociolinguistics*, 17: 125–39.

Fairclough, N. (1989) *Language and Power*, London: Longman.

Fairclough, N. (1992) *Discourse and Social Change*, Cambridge: Polity Press.

Fairclough, N. (1995a) *Media Discourse*, London: Arnold.

Fairclough, N. (1995b) *Critical Discourse Analysis*, London: Longman.

Fairclough, N. (2000) *New Labour, New Language*, London: Routledge.

Farr, F. (2002) 'Classroom interrogations – how productive?' *Teacher Trainer*, 16(1): 19–22.

Farr, F. (2003) 'Engaged listenership in spoken academic discourse: the case of student–tutor meetings', *Journal of English for Academic Purposes*, 2(1): 67–85.

Farr, F. and O'Keeffe, A. (2002) '*Would* as a hedging device in an Irish context: an intra-varietal comparison of institutionalised spoken interaction', in R. Reppen, S. Fitzmaurice and D. Biber (eds) *Using Corpora to Explore Linguistic Variation*, Amsterdam: John Benjamins, pp. 25–48.

Farr, F., Murphy, B. and O'Keeffe, A. (2002) 'The Limerick Corpus of Irish English: design, description and application', *Teanga*, 21: 5–29.

Fellegy, A.M. (1995) 'Patterns and functions of minimal response', *American Speech*, 70(2): 186–99.

Fisher, S. and Groce, S. (1990) 'Accounting practices in medicine interviews', *Language in Society*, 19: 225–50.

Foucault, M. (1972) *The Archaeology of Knowledge*, London: Tavistock.

Fraser, B. (1975) 'Hedged performatives', in P. Cole and J.L. Morgan (eds) *Syntax and Semantics*, vol. 3, New York: Academic Press, pp. 187–210.

Fraser, B. (1980) 'Conversational mitigation', *Journal of Pragmatics*, 4: 341–50.

Fraser, B. (1999) 'What are discourse markers?', *Journal of Pragmatics*, 31: 931–52.

Fishman, P.M. (1978) 'Interaction: the work women do', *Social Problems*, 25: 397–406.

Fries, C.C. (1952) *The Structure of English*, New York: Harcourt, Brace.

García Gómez, A. (2000) 'Discourse, politeness and gender roles: an exploratory investigation into British and Spanish talkshow verbal conflict', *Estudios ingleses de la Universidad Complutense*, 8: 97–125.

García Gómez, A. (2002a) 'The semantics of conflict talk: encoding attitude in British and Spanish talkshow conflictual episodes', in L. Iglesias Rábade and S.M. Doval Suárez (eds) *Studies in Contrastive Linguistics*, Santiago: Universidade de Santiago de Compostela Publicacións, pp. 437–44.

García Gómez, A. (2002b) 'A cognitive approach to topic management in verbal duels on American talkshows', *Studies in English Language and Linguistics*, 4: 145–70.

García Gómez, A. (2004) 'Aproximación al habla conflictiva como acción social: estrategias pragmático-discursivas y construcción de identidades sociales', unpublished thesis, University Complutense of Madrid.

García Gómez, A. (2005) 'Appraisal and involvement: analyzing the interpersonal semantics of American talkshow interaction', *Círculo de lingüística aplicada a la comunicación*, 21: 1–17.

Gardner, R. (1998) 'Between speaking and listening, the vocalization of understandings', *Applied Linguistics*, 19: 204–24.

Gardner, R. (2002) *When Listeners Talk: Response Tokens and Listener Stance*, Amsterdam: John Benjamins.

Gardner, R. (2004) 'On delaying the answer: question sequences extended after the question', in R. Gardner and J. Wagner (eds) *Second Language Conversations: Studies of Communication in Everyday Settings*, London: Continuum, pp. 246–66.

Garfinkel, H. and Sacks, H. (1970) 'On formal structures of practical actions', in J.C. McKinney and E.A. Tirakian (eds) *Theoretical Sociology*, New York: Appleton-Century-Crofts, pp. 337–66.

Gavruseva, L. (1995) 'Positioning and framing: constructing interactional asymmetry in employer–employee discourse', *Discourse Processes*, 20: 325–45.

Godard, D. (1977) 'Same setting, diffferent norms: phone call beginnings in France and the United States', *Language in Society*, 6: 209–19.

Goffman, E. (1974) *Frame Analysis*, New York: Harper and Row.

Goffman, E. (1981) *Forms of Talk*, Oxford: Basil Blackwell.

Greatbatch, D. (1986) 'Aspects of topical organization in news interviews: the use of agenda-shifting procedures by interviewees', *Media Culture and Society*, 8: 441–45.

Greatbatch, D. (1988) 'A turn-taking system for British news interviews', *Language in Society*, 17: 401–30.

Gregori-Signes, C. (1998a) 'The overall structure of the American tabloid talkshow', *Studies in English Language and Linguistics*, 0: 73–89.

Gregori-Signes, C. (1998b) 'Telling it all: a genre-based approach to the analysis of the American tabloid talkshow', unpublished thesis, University of Valencia.

Gregori-Signes, C. (1999) 'The use of interventions in media talk: the case of the American tabloid talkshow', *Studies in English Language and Linguistics*, 1: 187–200.

Gregori-Signes, C. (2000a) *A Genre Based Approach to Daytime Talk on Television*, Valencia: Lengua Inglesa University of Valencia.

Gregori-Signes, C. (2000b) 'The tabloid talkshow as a quasi-conversational type of face-to-face interaction', *Pragmatics*, 10(2): 195–213.

Gregori-Signes, C. (2000c) 'Undermining the communicative role of the expert', in M.J. Coperías (ed.) *Challenging Discourses*, Valencia: University of Valencia, pp. 105–14.

Gregori-Signes, C. (2001) 'Opening phases in American tabloid talkshows, in I. de la Cruz, Santamaria, C. Tejedor and C. Valero (eds) *La lingüística aplicada a finales del siglo XX. Ensayos y propuestas*, Alcalá: Servicio de Publicaciones de la Universidad de Alcalá.

Gregori-Signes, C. (2002) 'Heroes and villains: theory-building in tabloid talkshow story-telling', in A. Sánchez Macarro (ed.) *Windows on the World: Media Discourse in English*, Valencia: University of Valencia, pp. 153–75.

Harness Goodwin, H. (1997) 'Byplay: negotiating evaluation in storytelling', in G.R. Guy, C. Feagin, D. Schiffrin and J. Baugh (eds) *Towards a Social Science of Language: Papers in Honour of William Labov*, vol. 2, *Social Interaction and Discourse Structures*, Amsterdam: John Benjamins, pp. 77–102.

Harris, S. (1991) 'Evasive action: how politicians respond to questions in political interviews', in P. Scannell (ed.) *Broadcast Talk*, London: Sage, pp. 76–99.

Hall, J.K. (1995) '(Re)creating our worlds with words: a sociohistorical perspective of face-to-face interaction', *Applied Linguistics*, 16(2): 206–32.

Halliday, M.A.K. (1978) *Language as Social Semiotic*, London: Edward Arnold.

Halliday, M.A.K. and Hasan, R. (1976) *Cohesion in English*, London: Longman.

Halliday, M.A.K. and Hasan, R. (1989) *Language, Context and Text: A Social Semiotic Perspective*, Oxford: Oxford University Press.

Halmari, H. (1993) 'Intercultural business telephone conversations: a case of Finns vs. Anglo-Americans', *Applied Linguistics*, 14(4): 408–30.

Harris, S. (2001) 'Being politically impolite: extending politeness theory to adversarial political discourse', *Discourse and Society*, 12: 451–72.

Heritage, J. (1984) 'A change-of-state token and aspects of its sequential placement', in J. Atkinson and J. Heritage (eds) *Structures of Social Action: Studies in Conversation Analysis*, Cambridge: Cambridge University Press, pp. 229–345.

Heritage, J. (1985) 'Analysing news interviews: aspects of the production of talk for an overhearing audience', in T.A. van Dijk (ed.) *Handbook of Discourse Analysis*, vol. 3, *Discourse and Dialogue*, London: Academic Press, pp. 95–119.

Heritage, J. and Greatbatch, D. (1991) 'On the character of institutional talk: the case of news interviews', in D. Boden and D. Zimmerman (eds) *Talk and Social Structure*, Cambridge: Polity Press, pp. 359–417.

Heritage, J.C. and Roth, A.L. (1995) 'Grammar and institution: questions and questioning in broadcast news interview', *Research on Language and Social Interaction*, 28(1): 1–60.

Heritage, J.C. and Watson, D.R. (1979) 'Formulations as conversational objects', in G. Psathas (ed.) *Everyday Language: Studies in Ethnomethodology*, New York: Irvington Publishers Inc., pp. 123–62.

Herrington, A. (1985) 'Writing in academic settings: a study of the contexts for writing in two college chemical engineering courses', *Research in the Teaching of English*, 19: 331–59.

Hofland, K., Lindebjerg, A. and Thunestvedt, J. (1999) *ICAME Collection of English Language Corpora*, Bergen: The HIT Centre, University of Bergen.

Holmes, J. (1984) 'Hedging your bets and sitting on the fence: some evidence for hedges as support structures', *Te Reo*, 27: 47–62.

Holmes, J. (1988) 'Doubt and certainty in ESL textbooks', *Applied Linguistics*, 9: 21–44.

Hopper, R. (1989) 'Sequential ambiguity in telephone openings: "What are you doin"', *Communication Monographs*, 56(3): 240–52.

Hopper, R. (1992) *Telephone Conversation*, Bloomington, IN: Indiana University.

Hopper, R. (1998) 'Emergent grammar', in M. Tomasello (ed.) *The New Psychology of Language*, Hillsdale, NJ: Lawrence Erlbaum Associates, pp. 155–75.

Hopper, R. and Drummond, K. (1992) 'Accomplishing interpersonal relationship: the telephone openings of strangers and intimates', *Western Journal of Communication*, 56: 185–99.

Hopper, R., Doany, N., Johnson, M. and Drummond, K. (1991) 'Universals and particulars in telephone openings', *Research on Language and Social Interaction*, 24: 369–87.

Horton, D. and Wohl, R.R. (1956) 'Mass communication and para-social interaction: observations on intimacy at a distance', *Psychiatry* 19(3): 215–29; also in G. Gumpert and R. Cathcart (eds) (1979) *Intermedia–Interpersonal Communication in a Media World*, Oxford: Oxford University Press, pp. 185–206.

Hughes, R. (1996) *English in Speech and Writing: Investigating Language and Literature*, London: Routledge and Kegan Paul.

Hughes, R. and McCarthy, M.J. (1998) 'From sentence to discourse: discourse grammar and English language teaching', *TESOL Quarterly*, 32: 263–87.

Hutchby, I. (1991) 'The organisation of talk on talk radio', in P. Scannell (ed.) *Broadcast Talk*, London: Sage, pp. 119–37.

Hutchby, I. (1996a) *Confrontation Talk – Arguments, Asymmetries, and Power on Talk Radio*, Mahwah, NJ: Lawrence Erlbaum Associates.

Hutchby, I. (1996b) 'Power in discourse: the case of arguments on a British talk radio show', *Discourse and Society*, 7(4): 481–97.

Hutchby, I. (1999) 'Frame attunement and footing in the organisation of talk radio openings', *Journal of Sociolinguistics*, 3(1): 41–63.

Hutchby, I. and Wooffitt, R. (1998) *Conversation Analysis – Principles, Practices and Applications*, Cambridge: Polity Press.

Hymes, D. (1972) 'Models of the interaction of language and social life', in J. Gumpertz and D. Hymes (eds) *Directions in Sociolinguistics: The Ethnography of Communication*, New York: Rinehart and Winston inc., pp. 35–71.

Iacobucci, C. (1990) 'Accounts, formulations and goal attainment strategies in service encounters', in K. Tracy and N. Coupland (eds) *Multiple Goals in Discourse*, Clevedon, OH: Multilingual Matters, pp. 85–99.

Ilie, C. (1998) 'Questioning is not asking: the discursive functions of rhetorical questions in American talk shows', *Texas Linguistic Forum*, 39: 122–35.

Illie, C. (1999) 'Question–response argumentation in talk shows', *Journal of Pragmatics*, 31: 975–99.

Ilie, C. (2001) 'Semi-institutional discourse: The case of talk shows', *Journal of Pragmatics* 33(2): 209–54.

Jaworski, A. and Galasiński, D. (2000) 'Vocative address forms and ideological legitimisation in political debates', *Discourse Studies* 2(1): 65–83.

Jefferson, G. (1972) 'Side sequences', in D. Sudnow (ed.) *Studies in Social Interaction*, New York: The Free Press, pp. 294–336.

Jefferson, G. (1973) 'A case of precision timing in ordinary conversation: overlapping tag-positioned address terms in closing sequences', *Semiotica*, 9: 47–96.

Jefferson, G. (1984a) 'Notes of a systematic development of the acknowledgement token "yeah" and "mm mm"', *Papers in Linguistics*, 17(2): 197–216.

Jefferson, G. (1984b) 'On stepwise transition from talk about trouble to appropriately next-positioned matters', in J.M. Atkinson and J. Heritage (eds) *Structures of Social Action: Studies in Conversation Analysis*, Cambridge: Cambridge University Press, pp. 191–222.

Jefferson, G. (1990) 'List construction as a task and resource', in G. Psathas (ed.) *Interaction Competence*, Lanham, MD: University Press of America, pp. 63–92.

Jefferson, G. (1993) 'Caveat speaker: preliminary notes on recipient topic implicature', *Research on Language and Social Interaction*, 26(1): 1–30.

Jordan, R.R. (1989) 'English for Academic Purposes EAP', *Language Teaching*, 22(3): 150–64.

Joseph, J. E. (2004) *Language and Identity*, Basingstoke: Palgrave.

Jucker, A. (1986) *News Interviews: A Pragmalinguistic Analysis*, Amsterdam: John Benjamins.

Kaplan, R. (1966) 'Cultural thought patterns in inter-cultural education', *Language Learning*, 16: 1–20.

Kennedy, G. (1998) *An Introduction to Corpus Linguistics*, London and New York: Longman.

Kettermann, B. (1995) 'Concordancing in English language teaching', *TELL and CALL*, 4: 4–15.

Kristeva, J. (1986) 'Word, dialogue and novel', in T. Moi (ed.) *The Kristeva Reader*, Oxford: Basil Blackwell, pp. 34–61.

Koester, A. (2000) 'Getting things done and getting along in the office', in M. Coulthard, J. Cotterill and F. Rock (eds) *Dialogue Analysis VII: Working with Dialogue. Selected papers from the 7th IADA Conference, Birmingham 1999*, Tübingen: Max Niemeyer Verlag GmbH, pp. 197–207.

Koester, A. (2006) *Investigating Workplace Discourse*, London: Routledge.

Lave, J. and Wenger, E. (1991) *Situated Learning: Legitimate Peripheral Participation*, Cambridge: Cambridge University Press.

LeBaron, C.D. and Jones, S.E. (2002) 'Closing up closings: showing the relevance of the social and material surround to the completion of interaction', *Journal of Communication*, 52: 542–65.

Leech, G. (1999) 'The distribution and function of vocatives in American and British English conversation', in H. Hasselgard and S. Oksefjell (eds) *Out of Corpus*, Amsterdam: Rodopi, pp. 107–18.

Lenk, U. (1998) 'Discourse markers and global coherence in conversation', *Journal of Pragmatics*, 30: 245–57.

Livingston, S.M. and Lunt, P. (1994) *Talk on Television: Audience Participation and Public Debate*, New York: Routledge and Kegan Paul.

Long, M.H. and Sato, C. (1983) 'Classroom foreigner talk discourse: forms and functions of teachers' questions', in H.W. Seliger and M.H. Long (eds) *Classroom Oriented Research in Second Language Acquisition*, Rowley, MA: Newbury House, pp. 268–86.

Lorenzo-Dus, N. (2001) 'Up close and personal: the narrativisation of private experience in media talk', *Studies in English Language and Linguistics*, 3: 125–48.

Lorenzo-Dus, N. (2003) '"Emotional DIY" and proper parenting in Kilroy', in J. Aitchison and D. Lewis (eds) *New Media Discourse*, London: Routledge, pp. 136–45.

Lorenzo-Dus, N. (2005) 'A rapport and impression management approach to public figures' performance of talk', *Journal of Pragmatics*, 37(5): 611–31.

Louw, B. (1993) 'Irony in the text or insincerity in the writer? The diagnostic potential of semantic prosodies', in M. Baker, G. Francis and E. Tognini-Bonelli (eds) *Text and Technology: In Honour of John Sinclair*, Amsterdam: John Benjamins, pp. 157–76.

Macaulay, R.K.S. (1991) *Locating Dialect in Discourse: The Language of Honest Men and Bonnie Lasses in Ayr*, New York: Oxford University Press.

McCarthy, M.J. (1994) 'It, this and that', in M. Coulthard (ed.) *Advances in Written Text Analysis*, London: Routledge and Kegan Paul, pp. 266–75.

McCarthy, M.J. (1998) *Spoken Language and Applied Linguistics*, Cambridge: Cambridge University Press.

McCarthy, M.J. (2002) 'Good listenership made plain: non-minimal response tokens in British and American spoken English', in R. Reppen, S. Fitzmaurice and D. Biber (eds) *Using Corpora to Explore Linguistic Variation*, Amsterdam: John Benjamins, pp. 49–72.

McCarthy, M.J. (2003) 'Talking back: "small" interactional response tokens in everyday conversation', *Research on Language in Social Interaction*, 36(1): 33–63.

McCarthy, M.J. and Carter, R.A. (1994) *Language as Discourse: Perspectives for Language Teaching*, London: Longman.

McCarthy, M.J. and Carter, R.A. (2000) 'Feeding back: non-minimal response tokens in everyday English conversation', in C. Heffer and H. Sauntson (eds) *Words in Context: A Tribute to John Sinclair on His Retirement*, Birmingham: ELR Discourse Monograph no. 18, pp. 263–83.

McCarthy, M. and Carter, R.A. (2002) '*This that and the other*: multi-word clusters in spoken English as visible patterns of interaction', *Teanga*, 21: 30–52.

McCarthy, M. and Handford, M. (2004) '"Invisible to us": a preliminary corpus-based study of spoken business English', in U. Connor and T.A. Upton (eds) *Discourse in the Professions*, Amsterdam: John Benjamins, pp. 167–201.

McCarthy, M. and O'Keeffe, A. (2003) '"What's in a name?" – vocatives in casual conversations and radio phone in calls', in P. Leistyna and C. Meyer (eds) *Corpus Analysis: Language Structure and Language Use*, Amsterdam: Rodopi, pp. 153–85.

Markkanen, R. and Schröder, H. (1997) 'Hedging: a challenge for pragmatics and discourse analysis', in R. Markkanen and H. Schröder (eds) *Hedging and Discourse: Approaches to the Analysis of a Pragmatic Phenomenon in Academic Texts*, Berlin: Walter de Gruyter, pp. 3–18.

Martin, J.R. (1985) 'Process and text: two aspects of human semiosis' in J.D. Benson and W.S. Greaves (eds) *Systemic Perspectives on Discourse*, vol. 1, Norwood: Ablex Publishing Corporation, pp. 248–74.

Martin, J.R. (1996) 'Evaluating disruption', in R. Hasan and G. Williams (eds) *Literary in Society*, London: Addison-Wesley.

Martin, J.R. (2000) 'Beyond Exchange: APPRAISAL Systems in English', in S. Hunston and G. Thompson (eds) *Evaluation in Text*, Oxford: Oxford University Press.

Matoesian, G.M. (1999) 'The grammaticalization of participant roles in the constitution of expert identity', *Language in Society*, 28: 491–521.

Maynard, D.W. (1997) 'The news delivery sequence: bad news and good news in conversational interaction', *Research on Language and Social Interaction*, 30: 93–130.

Maynard, D.W. (2003) *Bad News, Good News: Conversational Order in Everyday Talk and Clinical Settings*, Chicago, IL: University of Chicago Press.

Maynard, D.W. and Heritage, J. (2005) 'Conversation analysis, doctor–patient interaction and medical communication', *Medical Education*, 39(4): 1365–2929.

Maynard, S.K. (1989) *Japanese Conversation: Self-Contextualisation through Structure and Interactional Management, Advances in Discourse Processes*, vol. 35, Norwood, NJ: Ablex.

Maynard, S.K. (1990) 'Conversation management in contrast: listener response in Japanese and American English', *Journal of Pragmatics*, 14(3): 397–412.

Maynard, S.K. (1997) 'Analyzing interactional management in native/non-native English conversation: a case of listener response', *IRAL*, 35(1): 37–60.

Merrit, M. (1976) 'On questions following questions in service encounters', *Language in Society*, 5: 315–57.

Mervis, C.B. and Rosch, E. (1981) 'Categorization of natural objects', *Annual Review of Psychology*, 32: 89–115.

Minaeva, L. (1998) 'From comrades to consumers: interpersonal aspects of the lexicon', in P. Chilton, M. Ilyin and J. Mey (eds) *Political Discourse in Transition in Europe 1989–1991*. Amsterdam: John Benjamins, pp. 87–94.

Montgomery, M. (1986) 'DJ talk', *Media, Culture and Society* 8: 421–40.

Moss, P. and Higgins, C. (1979) 'Radio voices', in G. Gumpert and R. Cathcart (eds) *Intermedia-interpersonal communication in a media world*, Oxford: Oxford University Press, pp. 283–99.

Mott, H. and Petrie, H. (1995) 'Workplace interactions: women's linguistic behaviour', *Journal of Social Psychology*, 14(3): 324–36.

O'Keeffe, A. (2002) 'Exploring indices of national identity in a corpus of radio phone-in data from Irish radio', in A. Sánchez Macarro (ed.) *Windows on the World: Media Discourse in English*, Valencia: University of Valencia Press, pp. 91–113.

O'Keeffe, A. (2003) '"Like the wise virgins and all that jazz" – using a corpus to examine vague language and shared knowledge', in U. Connor and T.A. Upton (eds) *Applied Corpus Linguistics: A Multidimensional Perspective*, Amsterdam: Rodopi, pp. 1–20.

O'Keeffe, A. (2005) '"You've a daughter yourself?" a corpus-based look at question forms in an Irish radio phone-in', in K.P. Schneider and A. Barron (eds) *The Pragmatics of Irish English*, Berlin: Mouton de Gruyter, pp. 339–66.

O'Keeffe, A. and Adolphs, S. (2002) 'Response in British and Irish English: go away!', paper presented at the first IVACS international conference, Limerick, June 2002.

O'Keeffe, A. and Adolphs, S. (in press) 'Using a corpus to look at variational pragmatics: listenership in British and Irish discourse', in K.P. Schneider and A. Barron, (eds) *Variational Pragmatics*, Amsterdam: John Benjamins.

O'Keeffe, A. and Breen, M. (2001) 'At the hands of the Brothers: a corpus-based lexico-grammatical analysis of stance in newspaper reporting of child sexual abuse cases involving the Irish Christian Brothers 1998–2000', unpublished report for the Irish Christian Brothers.

O'Keeffe, A. and Farr, F. (2003) 'Using language corpora in language teacher education: pedagogic, linguistic and cultural insights', *TESOL Quarterly*, 37(3): 389–418.

Overstreet, M. and Yule, G. (1997a) 'On being explicit and stuff in contemporary American English', *Journal of English Linguistics*, 25(3): 250–8.

Overstreet, M. and Yule, G. (1997b) 'Locally contingent categorization in discourse', *Discourse Processes*, 23: 83–97.

Pennycook, A. (1994) 'The politics of pronouns', *ELT Journal*, 48(2): 173–8.

Pérez de Ayala. S. (2001) 'FTAs and Erskine May: conflicting needs? – politeness in question time', *Journal of Pragmatics*, 33: 143–69.

Perrott, E. (1982) *Effective Teaching: A Practical Guide to Improving Your Teaching*, New York: Longman.

Peters, P. (2001) 'Corpus evidence on Australian style and usage', in D. Blair and P. Collins (eds) *English in Australia*, Amsterdam: John Benjamins, pp. 163–78.

Pomerantz, A. (1984) 'Agreeing and disagreeing with assessments: some features of preferred/dispreferred turn shapes', in J. Atkinson and J. Heritage (eds) *Structures of Social Action: Studies in Conversation Analysis*, Cambridge: Cambridge University Press, pp. 57–101.

Powell, M.J. (1985) 'Purposeful vagueness: an evaluative dimension of vague quantifying expressions', *Journal of Linguistics*, 21: 31–50.

Quirk, R., Greenbaum, S., Leech, G. and Svartvik, J. (1985) *A Comprehensive Grammar of the English Language*, London: Longman.

Rama Martínez, M.E. (2003a) *Talk on British Television: The Interactional Organisation of Three Broadcast Genres*, Vigo: Servicio de Publicacións da Universidade de Vigo.

Rama Martínez, M.E. (2003b) 'Accomplishing closings in talk show interviews: a comparison with news interviews', *Discourse Studies*, 5: 283–302.

Renouf, A. (1997) 'Teaching corpus linguistics to teachers of English', in A. Wichmann,

S. Fligelstone, A. McEnery and G. Knowles (eds) *Teaching and Language Corpora*, New York: Longman, pp. 255–66.

Rosch, E. (1978) 'Principles of categorization', in E. Rosch and B. Lloyd (eds) *Cognition and Categorization*, Hillsdale, NJ: Erlbaum, pp. 27–48.

Rosch, E., Mervis, C.B., Gray, W.D., Johnson, D.M. and Boynes-Braem, P. (1976) 'Basic objects in natural categories', *Cognitive Psychology*, 2: 491–502.

Sacks, H. (1992) *Lectures on Conversation*, Oxford: Basil Blackwell.

Sacks, H. (1995) *Lectures on Conversation*, 2nd edition, Oxford: Basil Blackwell.

Sacks H., Schegloff, E.A. and Jefferson, G. (1974) 'A simplest systematics for the organisation of turn-taking for conversation', *Language*, 50(4): 696–735.

Sánchez Macarro, A. (ed.) (2002) *Windows on the World: Media Discourse in English*, Valencia: University of Valencia Press.

Scannell, P. (ed.) (1991) *Broadcast Talk*, London: Sage.

Scannell, P. (1998) 'Media–language–world', in A. Bell and P. Garrett (eds) *Approaches to Media Discourse*, Oxford: Blackwell, pp. 251–67.

Schegloff, E.A. (1968) 'Sequencing in conversational openings', *American Anthropologist*, 70: 1075–95.

Schegloff, E.A. (1972) 'Sequencing in conversational openings', in J. Fishman (ed.) *Advances in the Sociology of Language, II: Selected Studies and Applications*, The Hague: Mouton, pp. 91–125.

Schegloff, E.A. (1979) 'Identification and recognition in telephone conversation openings', in G. Psathas (ed.) *Everyday Language: Studies in Ethnomethodology*, New York: Irvington Publishers, pp. 23–78.

Schegloff, E.A. (1982) 'Discourse as interactional achievement: some uses of 'uh huh' and other things that come between sentences', in D. Tannen (ed.) *Analyzing Discourse. Text and Talk*, Washington: Georgetown University Press, pp. 71–93.

Schegloff, E.A. (1986) 'The routine as achievement', *Human Studies*, 9: 111–52.

Schegloff, E.A. and Sacks, H. (1973) 'Opening up closings', *Semiotica* 8(4): 289–327.

Schegloff, E.A., Jefferson, G. and Sacks, H. (1977) 'The preference for self-correction in the organization of repair in conversation', *Language* 53: 361–82.

Schiffrin, D. (1987) *Discourse Markers*, Cambridge: Cambridge University Press.

Schiffrin, D. (1999) 'Oh as a marker of information management', in A. Jaworski and Coupland, N. (eds) *The Discourse Reader*, London: Routledge and Kegan Paul, pp. 275–88.

Schiffrin, D. (2001) 'Discourse markers: language, meaning, and context', in D. Schiffrin, D. Tannen and H.E. Hamilton (eds) *The Handbook of Discourse Analysis*, Malden, MA: Blackwell, 54–75.

Schwartz, N., Ellsworth, L., Graham, L. and Knight, B. (1998) 'Accessing prior knowledge to remember text: a comparison of advance organizers and maps', *Contemporary Educational Psychology*, 23: 65–89.

Scott, M. (1998) *Wordsmith Tools* (software), Oxford: Oxford University Press.

Sifianou, M. (1989) 'On the telephone again: differences in telephone behaviour: England versus Greece', *Language and Society*, 18(4): 527–44.

Sinclair, J. McH. (1996) 'The search for units of meaning', *Textus*, IX: 75–106.

Sinclair, J. McH. (1997) 'Corpus evidence in language description', in A. Wichmann, S. Fligelstone, T. McEnery and G. Knowles (eds) *Teaching and Language Corpora*, London: Longman, pp. 27–39.

Sinclair, J. McH. and Coulthard, M. (1975) *Towards an Analysis of Discourse: The English Used by Teachers and Pupils*, Oxford: Oxford University Press.

Swales, J.M. (1988) 'Discourse communities, genres and English as an international language', *World Englishes*, 7(2): 211–20.

Swales, J.M. (2002) 'Integrated and fragmented worlds: EAP materials and corpus linguistics', in J. Flowerdew (ed.) *Academic Discourse*, London: Longman, pp. 153–67.

Tang, R. and John, S. (1999) 'The "I" identity: exploring writer identity in student academic writing through the first person pronoun', *English for Specific Purposes*, 18: S23–S39.

Tannen, D. (ed.) (1993) *Framing in Discourse*, Oxford: Oxford University Press.

Tannen, D. and Wallat, C. (1993) 'Interactive frames and knowledge schemas in interaction: examples from a medical examination/interview', in D. Tannen (ed.) *Framing in Discourse*, Oxford: Oxford University Press, pp. 57–76.

ten Have, P. (1986) 'Issues in qualitative data interpretation', paper presented at the International Sociological Association, XIth World Congress of Sociology, New Delhi, August 1986 (http://www.pscw.uva.nl/emca/mica.htm).

Thornborrow, J. (2001a) 'Authenticating talk: building public identities in audience participation broadcasting', *Discourse Studies*, 3(4): 459–79.

Thornborrow, J. (2001b) 'Authenticity, talk and mediated experience', *Discourse Studies*, 3(4): 391–411.

Thornborrow, J. (2001c) 'Questions, control and the organization of talk in calls to a radio phone-in', *Discourse Studies* 3(1): 119–43.

Timberg, B.M. (2002) *Television Talk Show: A History of the TV Talk Show*, Austin, TX: University of Texas Press.

Tognini-Bonelli, E. (2001) *Corpus Linguistics at Work*, Amsterdam: John Benjamins.

Tolson, A. (1985) 'Anecdotal television' *Screen*, 26(2): 18–27.

Tolson, A. (1991) 'Televised chat and the synthetic personality', in P. Scannell (ed.) *Broadcast Talk*, London: Sage, pp. 178–200.

Tottie, G. (1991) 'Conversational style in British and American English: the case of backchannels' in K. Aijmer and B. Altenberg (eds) *English Corpus Linguistics*, London: Longman, pp. 254–71.

Tracy, K. (1997) 'Interactional trouble in emergency service requests: a problem of frames', *Research on Language and Social Interaction*, 30(4): 315–43.

Tracy, K. and Anderson, D.L. (1999) 'Relational positioning strategies in calls to the police: a dilemma', *Discourse Studies*, 1: 201–26.

Tsui, A.B.M. (1992) 'A functional description of questions', in M. Coulthard (ed.) *Advances in Spoken Discourse Analysis*, London: Routledge and Kegan Paul, pp. 89–110.

Tsui, A.B.M. (1994) *English Conversation*, London: Oxford University Press.

van Dijk, T.A. (2001) 'Critical discourse analysis', in D. Schiffrin, D. Tannen and H. Hamilton (eds) *The Handbook of Discourse Analysis*, Oxford: Basil Blackwell, pp. 352–71.

Ventola, E. (1987) *The Structure of Social Interaction: A Systemic Approach to the Semiotics of Service Encounters*, London: Frances Pinter.

Wales, K. (1996) *Personal Pronouns in Present-day English*, Cambridge: Cambridge University Press.

Walsh, S. (2002) 'Construction or obstruction: teacher talk and learner involvement in the EFL classroom', *Language Teaching Research*, 6: 3–23.

Walsh, S. (2006) *Investigating Classroom Discourse*. London: Routledge.

Ward, G. and Birner, B. (1992) 'The semantics and pragmatics of "and everything"', *Journal of Pragmatics*, 19: 205–14.

Wedell, E.G. (1968) *Broadcasting and Public Policy*, London: Michael Joseph.

Weizman, E. (2003) 'News interviews on Israeli television: normative expectations and discourse norms', in S. Stati and M. Bondi (eds) *Dialogue Analysis 2000*, Tübingen: Niemeyer, pp. 383–94.

Whale, J. (1977) *The Politics of the Media*, London: Fontana.

Whalen, M.R. and Zimmerman, D.H. (1987) 'Sequential and institutional context in calls for help', *Social Psychology Quarterly*, 50(2): 172–85.

White, S. (1989) 'Backchannels across cultures: a study of Americans and Japanese', *Language in Society*, 18: 59–76.

Wilson, A. and Zeitlyn, D. (1995) 'The distribution of person-referring expressions in natural conversation', *Research on Language and Social Interaction*, 28(1): 61–92.

Wood, L. and Kroger, R. (1991) 'Politeness and forms of address', *Journal of Language and Social Psychology*, 10(3): 145–68.

Wortham, S.E.F. (1996) 'Mapping participant deictics: a technique for discovering speakers' footing', *Journal of Pragmatics*, 25: 331–48.

Yokota, M. (1994) 'The role of questioning in Japanese political discourse', *Issues in Applied Linguistics*, 5(2): 353–82.

Yngve, V. (1970) 'On getting a word in edgewise', *Papers from the 6th Regional Meeting*, *Chicago Linguistic Society*, Chicago, IL: Chicago Linguistic Society.

Zhang, Q. (1998) 'Fuzziness – vagueness – generality – ambiguity', *Journal of Pragmatics*, 29: 13–31.

Zimmerman, D.H. and West, C. (1975) 'Sex roles, interruptions and silences in conversation', in B. Thorne and N. Henley (eds) *Language and Sex: Differences and Dominance*, Rowley, MA: Newbury, pp. 105–29.

Zwicky, A.M. (1974) 'Hey whatsyourname!', *Chicago Linguistic Society*, 10: 787–801.

Index

Related titles from Routledge

An Introduction to Discourse Analysis: Theory and Method, 2nd edition

James Paul Gee

'If you only read one book on discourse analysis, this is the one to read. Gee shows us that discourse analysis is about a lot more than linguistic study; it's about how to keep from, as he says, "getting physically, socially, culturally, or morally 'bitten' by the world".'

Ron Scollon, *Georgetown University, USA*

James Paul Gee presents here his unique, integrated approach to discourse analysis: the analysis of spoken and written language as it is used to enact social and cultural perspectives and identities.

Assuming no prior knowledge of linguistics, the book presents both a theory of language-in-use, as well as a method of research. This method is made up of 'tools of inquiry' and strategies for using them.

Perspectives from a variety of approaches and disciplines, including applied linguistics, education, psychology, anthropology, and communication, are incorporated to help students and scholars from a range of backgrounds formulate their own views and engage in their own discourse analyses.

ISBN10: 0–415–32860–8 (pbk)
ISBN10: 0–415–32861–6 (hbk)

ISBN13: 978–0–415–32860–9 (pbk)
ISBN13: 978–0–415–32861–6 (hbk)

Available at all good bookshops
For ordering and further information please visit www.routledge.com